Dedicated to the descendants of John Bateson, Henry Abbey of Long Marston, Benjamin Beverley, James Walker, and the Smyth family of Holbeck.

Wortley

John Bateson – Maister Clothier - his four sons -
Matthew and Jane (Hepper) Bateson -Jane is used to avoid confusion – she was Ann – but we will allow a little licence
Jack Bateson
James and Nancy (Lupton) Bateson
Joseph Bateson
                his three surviving daughters,
Elizabeth (Bateson) Lister
Mary (Bateson) Beverley
Sarah Bateson
Matthew Bateson's daughters; Mary, Anne, Nannie and Sarah

Molly an indentured servant at Greenside
Benjamin Beverley- Wool Stapler and Clothier etc.
Samuel Beverley – eldest son of Benjamin Beverley

James Walker and Mary (Musgrave) Walker
William Walker (Merchant)
Grace Walker – unknown relationship to the above

Armley

Old Thomas Lupton - Clothier
John Lupton – son of Old Thomas Lupton
Jeremiah Walker - partner of James Hebdin (Beeston Royd Coals) and son in law of Old Thomas Lupton

Long Marston

Henry Abbey- Brewer of Long Marston Hall – his children - Henry Abbey junior, Phillip Abbey

Benjamin Gott, Merchant and Manufacturer

Reverend James Wood – President of the Methodist Conference 1800 and 1808 - author of "A Dictionary of the Bible"
His son, Robert Wood.

John Smyth of Holbeck– Lord of the Manor of Wortley
His children - John Smyth Junior of Bramham
Lydia Smyth

*

The Reverend J. - an itinerant Methodist Minister

Dan Grady – workhouse orphan

David Parr - attorney

Chapter One

the patriarch

The Maister Clothier of Yorkshire is a particular breed. He owns his loyalty to the guilds and the traditions of the wool cloth industry of days gone by. He adheres to the etiquette of the Cloth Halls, works to maintain it, and abhors both the rise of the factory and the break with past customs regarding selling cloth. He often owns his soul entirely unto the Methodist Society in honour of the distant puritanism of his forefathers and against the interests of the gentry and nobility who own the land and support the Established Church. He makes fine wool cloth and is proud of his reputation. If he is wise, he has now bought land with his profits as an investment against the sometimes volatile cloth marked. He has set his sons up on their own behalf in business to make their own cloth and commits them to life long service in this trade. His daughters, educated and trained in the crafts of spinning, weaving and good book-keeping, will be married to his fellow clothiers and that too, is an investment for the future.; maintaining partnerships and keeping the money in the family…..

His life is ordered in the old way, with a household that includes family, servants, apprentices and sometime journeymen weavers and cloth finishers. In the close knit township communities the mutual dependence of the cloth maker, the miller and the dyers is a way of life. He keeps his looms close by or in his home and those that work for him in their cottages also build their lives around their looms and webs and the rhythms of the shuttle and fulling mills.

Scripture readings and Psalm singing are daily rituals in his old rambling house and all is ordered and efficient and secure.

The Wortley Maister, John Bateson was just such a clothier. He had won his fortune by the working of a water mill back in the years of honey when fortunes were amassed by the lease or ownership of such essential mills. His small and water powered mill had been set upon the Wortley Beck and had scribbled the wool and pounded the weaver's work, and his tenters lined martial on his newly bought land stretching out his felted cloth in stripes across the landscape, to remedy the shrinking in the wet pounding of the fulling stocks. In the old days, the Maister's cloth was sold at his Stand in the Cloth Hall to the Merchants who dyed and finished it but times were changing.

He had wisely invested his profit in land. The scribbling mills would not forever make so great a profit for outlay and the fulling could be done by others with a little capital or an easy gentleman landlord. And then there were the threatening mills, with their engines and their mechanical monstrosities that could speed up so many of the many processes. But land! John Bateson had bought land; he had bought the Lepton fields and the Wood Royds, the Rob Crofts, the Tenter Fields and more besides. And he ever advised his sons to do the same. 'When there's spare', he said, 'lay out in the fields of the Township. In cottage and workshop, barn and meadow. And if there's clay or stone or perhaps coal, well then buy now, and wait. You'll see as good return for these in the end as for cloth, my boys.' And in due course, this happened. But that is not our concern just now.

John Bateson considered himself to be a fair man, a righteous man and a just father to his children. He was not often affectionate nor understanding. He did not advise them nor seek their opinion. But he ruled his family with a rod of iron. Or he thought that he did this. His second wife Anne Robinson agreed with him on every count including the application of the stern discipline he imagined, but only for the sake of a peaceful life.

John Bateson thought it was unwise to be too open and would guard himself; keep his own counsel and make his decisions based on clear principals. In other words, he liked his own way in things. He believed that he exercised good control over himself and that his family and his business partners, could not fool him or get the better of him. His main partners were Old Tom Lupton and Benjamin Beverley.

That Benjamin and Old Tom were considerably more wealthy than John Bateson, suggests that John Bateson was not so canny as he believed himself to be. Or it might be, that the Maister had done more for his children than his partners; that he had - against his better judgement – assisted in the investment in a steam powered engine and had helped to finance his sons Matthew and James in setting up a large and semi integrated woollen mill. In truth he had assissted them reluctantly with a little investment while fending off the consequences of a disastrous mill fire on Water Lane that had come near to ruining his son Jack.

But that was in the past. Now, he had seen his son Jack and his youngest son Joseph in partnership again lease the rebuilt mill - a mainly water powered mill in Water Lane in Holbeck. It was mainly water powered because the landlord has not seen fit to replace the old fire engines. Such improvements would require more capital from all parties concerned. All this business complication may have been something of matter in his moderate wealth when compared to Beverley and Lupton his principal partners.

Be that as it may, John Bateson considered himself a man of iron and his sons and daughters knew him to be as soft as butter from the churn. That he was protected from realisation of this dissonance was fortunate for his ease of mind. That his judgement was flawed in the assessment of his sons' capacities might be imagined by the reader. That his second son Jack was most dear to him, being reticent, plain spoken and entirely avowed and dedicated to the cause of traditional cloth making through the old ways, will be material in our tale. His opinion of his third son James was unfortunate and unrealistic but James was blessed with a talented wife Nancy, that John Bateson correctly perceived and valued highly. Nancy and the Maister's wife between them - managed the Maister well with regard to the unfortunate James - as did Matthew's wife Jane. There were many things that the Maister thought he had in hand, that were arranged carefully by his household and family to ensure his contentment and the general peace within the family and their trade.

Of his first and eldest son Matthew, so strong in the Methodist cause and so reliable, compassionate, diligent and wise, John had complete trust and Matthew was taken for granted without thanks or praise. If he had been told this he would have grinned, shrugged his shoulders and clapped the messenger on the back. It was almost as if Matthew was part of the stones of the house at Greenside, strong and enduring to hold up the House of Bateson. For his heart was a good one, his word was true and he was held in universal respect. Never was his judgement unsound. Except.

Joseph his youngest son had been a great favourite with John Bateson's first wife Hannah and had been overprotected and indulged and John (with his rod of iron) was perhaps rather too tolerant of the boy and made allowances for him because of his weak lungs and as we shall see, expected the his youngest son in his youth to be as good a business man as his brothers had become in their maturity. John Bateson was blessed with four fine sons and without a doubt, had relentless high expectations of them all.

In the blighted rural landscape of Wortley, that Township that rose north over the Beck claimed by Farnley and Holbeck both, extending to the commons of Armley and near to the banks of the Aire in the east, we find the Maister secure in the knowledge that his sons will not let him down and will continue to make good wool cloth and become wealthy men. When he assesses his worth, as he does from time to time, he includes in his evaluation the certainty that those two companies known as M. and J. Bateson, and J. and J. Bateson will thrive and prosper and maintain the reputation of his House and name.

Chapter Two

a noble sense of industry

The ladies and gentlemen of the family, and their guests were now inside the house. Many paned windows were lit with a magnificence of wax that proclaimed wealth and comfort to the county across the gathering dusk. The hunt had been a social success for the Gentleman of the hall, if not for the foxes on his estate - with sport and entertainment across the fields, woodlands and commons followed by an elaborate supper, music, wine and dancing for all his equals and betters.

Jack Bateson peered at the huge mansion commanding the wide lawns that stretched before it and then, shivering a little at a sudden gust of east wind, turned and went under the arch and into the stable yard, where the stable lads still had work to do, hauling water and feed and settling horses worth a small fortune in the extensive stables. His own hack was waiting, saddled and ready. He might not have had an invitation to the great house this evening, but he had rode well today and been spoken of for his courage and sporting prowess. The hunter he had ridden he had borrowed for a favour from a wealthier man and it was to be returned tomorrow

At this moment Jack content. But the air was chill as the night came on and he shoved his arms into his wool great coat and threw over this his dark riding cloak, nodding a farewell to the grooms and the few gentlemen that still fussed around their valuable horses or stood smoking and reliving the glories and disasters of the day, and a few shouted a cheerful farewell. It was a long, dark ride back to his house in Holbeck. He would see how far he could get before the last light faded and then wait at the roadside inn for the moon to come up. With that he should reach home in time to get some sleep before the morning shift began in the mill. That is, if he did not drink so much at the inn that he would need to bed down there for the night. He did not intend to do that. But sometimes, the best laid plans go awry. This was his thinking as he put put his foot in his stirrup and mounted. He felt in his pockets for some coins and bending from the saddle paid the lads. Then he kicked his horse into a trot and set off across the heath to the Doncaster road and the long ride home.

    Yes it had been a good day. Jack liked the rough riding and the danger of the speed and obstacles. He had been in the lead and had not baulked to risk his life once across a sudden ditch and fence, not even in consideration for the horse that he had loaned. Since the death of his young wife, he had been increasingly occupied with physical challenges – running and riding and whole days spent with his dog and his gun along by the brushy river bank or up in the woods of Farnley. Armitage's game keeper and he were old allies. A man of the cloth trade was as good as any gentleman for game - if he had a healthy bank balance. Jack shook his head. He should see about the wool. He would, he told himself, tomorrow. If he got back to his house tonight, he would see to it tomorrow. Or the day after. This week certainly. There was not much stored now in the mill. Perhaps his brothers would lend him some? But he put that thought out of his mind. No need to bother the family. He should have bought more in the spring but he'd chosen not to, thinking that the market price must fall. And then there was coal. Best not worry about what could not be fixed just at this moment. From out of the dark, dark wings swooped low across his path and he reined his horse, startled, the mare unsettled and sidling. Just an owl, he told himself. Over the hedgerow he could see a distant spark of light. That would be the inn. He'd wait up there until the moon rose. Now he saw the lights he realised he was in great need of a drink. He thought of brandy. Yes, he needed some brandy. Maybe a mug or two of ale to follow. He urged his dark mare back along the deep shadowed lane at a rather good pace for the dark rutted lane. But she settled, responded and bravely carried him onwards.

It might have been his emerging sobriety that reminded him of the paper he had signed today as his horse splashed through an unexpectedly deep rut in the road. The brandy had passed freely among the gathered hunters all day. It had seemed a good idea at the time, urged and applauded by men he thought well of. It was a small accommodation considering his standing. There had been talk around him of some special concessions for coal, should he just oblige. Ah yes. These were the men to make friends with! These were the sort that owned the collieries and could strike a deal with a man! And Jack Bateson had his own mill. Well no, not quite. But he had a lease on a very extensive premise on the banks of the Aire. He had his own workshops too and easy labour all around him. He could afford to lend money to the men that would help him and remember his accommodation. Yes by God, he would show Matthew and James how it was done! A man needed to think big nowadays and he was thinking big. And of course, the arrangement was for his own purse, and not the company's. It was a private arrangement between gentlemen.

He had been thinking big, but perhaps Jack should have allowed a little more imagination to colour his decision.. A sober head might have suspected that signed accommodation papers in the farrier's workshop of a great estate was not something a gentleman would request if his affairs were in order. Even his father, a middling sort of man, would have brought an "investor" into his neat office at Greenside and had his attorney with him. Or one of his sons at least. But on the whole, John Bateson did not lend money to gentlemen. On the whole it could be said, that gentlemen had loaned him money and had seen good profit thereby. But while Jack Bateson was a good clothier, he was a man of little imagination. The inn came into view from the darkness and the lights came closer and soon Jack could see the inn sign and the welcome light spilling from the old doorway. He rode with a clatter across a cobbled run of the lane and into the inn yard, sliding agilely from his mount and calling in his deep voice for an ostler and a brandy, and waking the drowsy inn keeper who jumped up startled and angry and then recognised the familiar customer and hurried out to wait upon him.

Chapter Three

Where James Bateson and Mr. Gott meet again...

The heavy and highly polished oak door swung open to reveal the merchant and two other gentlemen seated in the book lined office. The merchant stood to receive his visitor; impeccably dressed as usual, and he smiled thinly, recovering from astonishment and summing up the situation rapidly.

'Ah! Mr. Bateson. I was not expecting you to honour me with a visit this morning. Perhaps your appointment was not recorded by my clerk? No? I am sure that must be the case. Be that as it may, your are here,' Gott allowed himself a barely perceptible sigh, 'and here are other gentlemen who I am sure will be happy for us all to become acquainted. So let me present my company. Mr. Samuel Brown, and his assistant, Mr. Parr. Mr. Brown, Mr. Parr, this is James Bateson of Wortley. He is a rising man in this district. He and his brother have invested in a new mill - in the West'. Benjamin Gott waved his hand slightly in that direction and his gesture was both expansive and dismissive in the same moment. He continued, 'and are, I believe, flourishing through their hard work. An example to us all.' The company exchanged slight bows and studied James carefully, since Gott had given such a good recommendation. Then James, who was of course in error to have taken the liberty of calling informally on the senior merchant, and was caught off his guard, snatched at the nearer gentleman and enthusiastically shook his hand. His victim, a plump and ruddy cheeked man of mature years winced slightly at the firm grasp of his new acquaintance.

James understood Gott's exaggerated compliment. He caught both the genuine respect and the just slightly suggested sarcasm of the moneyed merchant towards the lesser men of the Townships who had dared to make a small copy his integrated enterprise at Park Mills on the River Aire. There had only comparatively recently been, let us say - an incident between the influential merchant and the aspiring but young manufacturer of the Wortley Township, which made such an unannounced morning call uncomfortable to both parties. Difficult even, although they had met frequently at the Cloth Hall or in the streets of Leeds and had exchanged brief, polite and distant courtesies. He understood it, but he could not think how he should receive it.

Matthew Bateson, his brother and senior partner in the firm of M. and J. Bateson and Co. had for some time tactfully arranged that any dealings or meetings with the worthy Leeds Merchant should be his own duty rather than James'. But Matthew now thought the time had come for James to get on with business and forget about past events and had told him to arrange to conduct this matter, expecting the problems to be resolved. Without doubt, Matthew Bateson would have advised that James must fully reconcile himself with Mr. Gott because their House supplied a great deal of cloth to Gott. James did want to put the past behind him but had many misgivings about his ability to do so because some trauma still attached to those past events. To himself he owned that forgetting his social misadventures came with much facility to him but Gott's part in the misery caused to others – that he could not forget so easily.

Matthew would have expected James to make a polite and considerate appointment and James had intended so to do. But had not done so. And had stood outside Gott's house knowing that his brother had entrusted an important matter to him and that he had already made a mess of it. And as was his wont, he had just brazened it out without being able to imagine the reactions there might be to what amounted to bad manners.

James now released the hand of his new and astonished friend as suddenly as he had grasped it and looked directly at Gott for a moment or two. Then James grinned. Benjamin Gott drew in a short breath, raised an eye brow, breathed out, and smiled back. Another less measured man might have given a slight shake of his head. But Gott was a fair man, an intelligent player, and besides, he had always liked James Bateson. In the affairs of business and trade in Leeds, an honest, enthusiastic and transparent Clothier was a good and useful contact. The Bateson House produced excellent cloth. And that James was particularly interested, as he was himself, in the details of water and steam power, was a solid quality in a clothier. And now, had heard Gott, there were scientific investigations in the dyeing processes in hand in Wortley and that was all to the good.

So Gott went on to set the young man at his ease, forgiving the surprise intrusion. "Mr. Brown has travelled down from London. And Mr. Parr too, has returned to our town after some years in the capital.' The gentlemen bowed to each other. Gott continued to lead. 'And so Mr. Bateson. Or rather James,' Gott smiled and this time his eyes did agree with his smile, 'how may I be of assistance to you this morning? Or if the matter should be of a more confidential nature, we could withdraw to another room?'

'No,' said James Bateson decisively. 'I am merely come to present this envelope and I can be of certain faith that you will ensure that it is put into the correct hands.'

James handed Gott an envelope addressed to James Lawton – the agent of Mssrs. Boulton and Watt in the North of England, who was a close confidante of Gott. Gott weighed it in his hand while reading the title.

'Ah. I see. Thank you. Well done then. I am happy to arrange this for you. And now sir, won't you join us in a glass of wine?' Gott indicated a fine chair by the window. James sat down and Gott handed him a glass, as James studied the carving on the chairs, rubbing his hands on them and turning from side to side as he did so in admiration of the skill of the carver....

Mr. Brown, as has been noted, was a stout and also a well dressed man with an apparently genial smile. His assistant, Mr. Parr was emaciated. This is the kindest description that can be given of him. Dressed all in black, he was obviously an attorney or clerk of some kind and James lost interest in the chair and wondered what Gott was about in the matter of investment and trade, looking from one to other of the strangers, uncomfortable still in spite of Gott's forbearance and tolerance towards him.

Parr had a sharp nose, a pock marked face and a complexion that was mottled and sallow. His visage spoke of high living and resultant impaired health. He turned his head towards James, smiling just a little, and he watched the young Clothier in his lingering discomfort, assessing the young man's clothes to devise his circumstances. He had also some thought that he had heard the name before, and that this was somehow significant. Parr looked away and out of the window at the grey drizzle of the day and then smiled again. Oh yes, he remembered now.

The assembled company made miscellaneous small talk and James sipped his glass of wine without tasting it. He felt discomfort again at blundering into some private business meeting and this unease increased further under Parr's gaze. He could not hear the conversation around him for a moment or two and the attorney kept staring at him. He came back to awareness with a start.

Gott had picked up the Intelligencer from a table and read, 'Hear this sirs! "The defeat of the French at the Battle of the Nile has been called a check! If we keep drawing on them at the same rate we shall soon break their bank and leave them nihil". So I read in the Intelligencer and I did delight in the metaphor!'

'Of course you did, Mr. Gott. A certain point for a man of education!' chuckled Brown with sharp eyes, 'what do you think of that Mr. Bateson?' James hesitated unsure of the question. He frowned. 'I find I am not quite sure what you mean, Mr Brown?' Brown raised his eyebrows at Gott and smiled thinly and James blundered on, 'You see, as I understand it, it is ourselves as a nation that may be bankrupted with the drain on the economy of the fleets and the disruptions to trade. To conduct this war has left a burden on the nation as wars must always do. But apart from that, it was a good pun that the editor made and we did discuss it at home and my wife was amused by the very same passage. Otherwise, I don't think there can be any doubt that Mr. Gott is a well educated man. I believe this is common knowledge but, of course, it is a compliment to him that you have honoured him by pointing it out. I don't have all the figures of national expenditure on the war to hand but if you wish I can explain the basic economic costs for all the various nations …..'

'Mr. Bateson. I hear from my friends that you are married to a Lupton girl?' butted in Parr, nodding unnecessarily. James became fixated with the lawyer's teeth which just showed through his lips and he found himself disconcerted at being interrupted and annoyed at hearing Nancy described with seeming familiarity as "a Lupton girl" while still thinking deeply about the cost of war and if he should have mentioned the obvious fact Brown was flattering Gott because they were in business negotiations. He realised that there was a silence and that the others were looking at him oddly and he should now say something and that he should not continue with his thoughts on the economy. Perhaps. Parr smiled and nodded again.

'I am a very fortunate husband,' he said, ruffled and affecting a calm and composure he did not feel. 'My wife is indeed a Lupton "girl" as you so rightly state. We have been married for 5 years and have a fine son and a beautiful daughter. Mr. Gott I hear -'

Parr interrupted. 'I have met the Lupton family. I had the privilege of meeting Mr. Thomas Lupton some years ago in Armley on matters of business. With a previous employer of course.' Parr looked away then looked back directly in James' eye. 'I knew Nancy Lupton.'

James was still interested in the man's teeth. They were yellow stained and chipped. Although he had heard every word the man had said he did not understand why he found Parr so offensive. He gave himself time to think and the merchants lost interest in the exchange and began to discuss the weather, noting the rain has eased off and remarking on the necessity of the soft water for the good of the wool cloth. Parr considered James with a crooked smile that the other gentleman could not see. James shook his head and got to his feet. He could no longer endure the man and needed to escape.

'Mr. Gott, Gentlemen. I have much to do. If you should with to hear the details of my thoughts on the economy I am happy to oblige you another time with my notebook for accurate figures by mutual arrangement. It has been a great pleasure to meet you sirs. But I must leave you to your business and be about mine. If you will excuse me. It has been a pleasure to meet you. Mr. Brown, I hope we may meet again. So good of you to see me at such short notice. I must away….'

James walked backwards to the door as he spoke. Parr still watched him with that broad smile exposing his teeth and for some odd reason, James had the feeling that he would like to punch the man very hard in the face. He clenched his fists and with an effort, made a small bow and departed.

'My word Mr. Gott! Is this your Yorkshire man of business sir? He's very young and extremely abrupt. Has too much to do has he? That was downright rude I think. He has left your wine in the glass and missed the opportunity of making contacts and influencing people who could have been of service to him. Extraordinary behaviour! What a bore!'

'Yes. I fear this is true. He is sometimes a little odd. Yet even that was somewhat out of character in our friend. However, he is a talented young man and well, let me say, I think very highly of his abilities in the Trade. But perhaps we have also been fortunate. Our young friend has certain enthusiasms on which is he ever happy to share his finesse and I think this might have, on balance, been as much prolonged as his attention today was brief. If you see my equation.' Brown and Parr shook their heads. 'So, Mr. Brown, I toast your good health, and let us turn to our own affairs then. Mr. Parr will you be so kind as to continue with your details for the enterprise.'

A sudden shower of rain fell on Leeds and went on it's way down the Aire Valley. The late afternoon sun returned and made the stout cobbles of the lanes of Leeds shine. James had hurried his way through Leeds troubled and confused, made a call at Beverley's workshops and by late afternoon went for his good horse Stocking in the stable yard of the Old George Inn. He set off at a careful trot but as he reached Kirkgate, he glimpsed Benjamin Gott, Samuel Brown and Parr as they walked together. The merchants had stopped and were deep in conversation and so Parr was attending and waiting on them, standing to one side. Thus Parr faced James and recognised him and even from a distance the expression on his thin face and the slight nod of his head gave James annoyance. More than annoyance. Something he could not put into words. And he knew he should not do what he intended to do. He could hear Nancy's voice. 'What did you do? You rode into Benjamin Gott and other gentlemen. How could you do that! Of all things. It was very impolite. Worse than impolite. Extremely rude and boorish behaviour. You'll be arrested and put in the stocks. Your father will fry you with his glare……. ….What possessed you to do such a thing…...' And more admonishments to that effect.

 The gutter in the road was carrying its load of muck, soil and water as the rain of the day had run off from the stone roads and gathered in spate down the middle of the thoroughfare. James spurred his horse on and taking the centre of the lane, rode through the filth of the drain at small speed, causing a small explosion of foul fluid which fortunately caught only Parr as James sped past.

 'What the? Damn you sir! Look where you're going. Jesus Christ!' Parr swayed between anger and distress at the state of his clothes and outrage at the riding of the miscreant. He watched James ride away and ground his teeth.

  Benjamin Gott observed this coolly. He also watched James Bateson canter off, considering the incident and what it might mean. Parr took out a handkerchief and made ineffectual attempts to wipe down his coat and breeches, cursing under his breath and with his face like thunder. Gott turned to one side and said quietly, 'Mr. Brown. I must just mention to you, that in this particular matter, I prefer to use my own attorney at law. I trust you will understand. I am sure your Mr. Parr is an excellent man. But for local matters it will be more expeditious to myself to deal directly with those who are concerned and who are nearby. Letters going back and forth and so on waste valuable time as I am sure you must agree.'

Samuel Brown studied Gott for a moment with shrewd eyes and weighed his meanings. 'Yes. Of course sir. I bow to your experience of Yorkshire trade. Whatever is most agreeable to you will suit me just as well as anything else.'

Chapter Four

the amusements of Leeds

'You're a fool man. What were you saying to that young man at Gott's? This will cost me dear and we had everything arranged. Gott is going to get the better of this now and I hold you personally responsible. Get yourself back to London on the next coach. I'll not be paying for your keep in Leeds for no gain. Get out of my sight.' Samuel Brown's erstwhile amiable face was now purple with rage. He took up the nearest object, an innocent ale jug and threw it into the fireplace with a relieving smash.

Parr scowled, clapped his hat on his head and took himself and his grubby attire away to the coaching inn. Yet still, he took the chance of another night in Leeds, laying out what little he had of coin for a room at the inn. He had lost his fee for the lucrative dealings of Brown but there was a good chance that he would make amends to his finances by the end of the evening. There were always opportunities at the cards or dice, or even cock fights or dog matches, to while away the Autumn evening. In his better waistcoat and second best coat of brown wool, Parr set out in the twilight into the dark lanes and courts, following a familiar path to a dirty tavern by the river. Shouts came from nearby; groans and curses and the noise of men enjoying some sport crescendoed then subsided. Securing a glass of brandy and hot water from his host he wandered out into the court yard to find exactly what he sought.

The favourite was a scarred and evil looking bird with lengthy claws and just the one eye. It was the survivor of six such sporting nights in the back ways and alleys of Leeds town and was thus the champion for the moment, known by the name of the Marston Mauler. The proud keeper of this infamous warrior was a young gentleman from the village of Long Marston. From a bucolic background and upbringing, Henry Abbey had learned much about the potential and handling of the game cockerel and with a mind sharp for business he calculated the risks and possibilities of this bird winning yet another bout. There was enough already in his pocket to stand a loss should the cockerel finally succumb and so he calculated rapidly as he crouched in the circle of spectators that had come now together to watch this next match. He was a realist. It might win just once more. And then he would make a killing. He was a risk taker and the chances of success and failure gave him a thrill. He grinned and waited, listening to the wagers and nodding at times to those bets he agreed to take without taking his eyes from the new opponent. Men pushed and shoved and money changed hands and changed hands again. The cockerel in the wicker cage was a first time sparrer. It was big and meaty; a strong and young fighter; but it was the bird's first fight. Jack Bateson, a miller and Clothier from an outer Township stood with his arms folded and nodded agreeably at Henry. 'S good 'un!' he shouted cheerfully at his rival.

 Parr approached behind Abbey and he bent and whispered in his ear. The boy looked round briefly and he nodded and turned back to the ring, still smiling, although the wager represented an amount that would annoy him to lose. But sport was sport. What was the fun if there was no risk, no excitement, no rush of fear and blood in the joy of the moment? The crowd stilled; a hush descended. Bateson and Abbey opened the cages almost, but not quite, simultaneously. The young cock was first out and it took the old warrior on with vicious enmity, attacking with its claws and by blind chance taking out the champion's remaining eye. The old cockerel attacked sightlessly and sank its own talons into any part of its enemy that it could reach. The young challenger was hurt and bled but renewed the attack as the wounded champion whirled hopelessly searching for its foe. The rest of the battle was messy and brief.

When the dying cockerel had been removed and as the ring was being swept and covered with a scattering of straw and sand, Jack Bateson came to Henry Abbey and shook his hand. 'Thy fighter is done laddie,' he stated with his usual perception, and he smiled and nodded and went to collect his winnings.

Parr approached the loser. 'Come outside Sir, if you please,' said the lad pleasantly enough in the circumstances. 'We'll settle this in private I think!' Parr smiled and relaxed. He had done well.

Parr now had funds to satisfy his appetite for brandy and for other entertainments that he craved. He left Henry Abbey shrugging and shaking his head and gave the inn keeper a tossed coin. He wrapped himself in his dark cloak before leaving the brightness of the smokey, tallow lit interior and ventured out and down, away towards the river and the other attractions of the district. The evening had been productive and it was compensation enough for his master's reprimand and the disgrace of what he hoped was a temporary dismissal.

He wanted only the final reward and amusement. Such evenings of success always left him with a hunger. The necessary object was soon found.

The girl waited on the corner of a lane, her pretty young face peeping out from a dark wool shawl. As she saw the man approach, she let the woven protection drop, and stood, allowing herself to smile at the potential customer. She rehearsed in her mind all the things that she had been told she might say to any interested client. He did not need much patter. He made her come near to the light of the lanthorn that hung from the warehouse frontage. This was the best yet. Here was a young innocent and lovely girl with the emphasis on young.

He paid the object of his need, pushing coppers into her bodice and thrusting her away into the dirt of the ground.

Things had worked out well tonight. He had had the last laugh after all. He watched her depart.

The girl half ran half stumbled away, struggling to breathe and half stunned. On the wet dirt lane she lost her footing and fell. She glanced back but he did not follow her. He was still smiling. Leaning on the warehouse wall and smiling. Hauling herself up she fled once more. She had been on the streets for some months. But this was the worst. The worst. She had been told that some men were like this. She had not believed the other whores when they had told her, not completely. It was not so much his violent roughness, his blows, his hand around her throat until she had panicked and choked that had been the worst thing. It was that he had laughed when she screamed with pain. That he had gripped her throat again and harder as he finished with her.

Terror took her now.

Chapter Five

In which James is made aware of an impending problem

James had soon brought Stocking under control as he encountered the Leeds Bridge where a cantering horse would certainly have caused consternation and alarm. He rode across the bridge with care, successfully navigating the brewer's drays and the carts brimming with corves of coal, the porters and the peddlars and the pack ponies; and he set off down towards the heart of Holbeck. In doing do he passed the old mill on Water Lane which was the main premises of "J. and J. Bateson". The mill had been largely rebuilt since the fire that had nearly brought ruin on them all, but the engines had not been replaced with the more efficient modern inventions and it was something that played on James' mind. He had the calculations in his notebook and had talked to Lister and Murray about it but Jack had told him to mind his own business. Which James had done, not from pique but because he often took messages very literally. So he had let the matter drop then, but uneasy now because of the day's events, he wondered if he should talk to his wife Nancy about the engines. She would know what to do. And he could put other problems out of his thoughts.

The scribbling and fulling mill was secured with strong barred gates and there was ever a trusted watchman stationed there. Holbeck was a busy industrial area, the site of many scribbling and fulling mills; of Marshall's famous flax mill and the engineering foundry of Fenton, Murray and Wood. There were potteries, brick kilns, foundries and tanneries and a multitude of smoking chimneys. But the times were hard and the Townships had seen their fair share of disaffection and unrest and the gates of Jack's mill was always well guarded and James noted this with satisfaction although something was amiss and he slowed to think what it was. He noticed that a new chimney was rising, probably for the pottery and wondered if he should make a detour and get a closer look.....

'Hoi! Bateson! Hold on there man, wait up.' James gently brought Stocking to a halt and turned in his saddle to see his friend James Walker on foot some distance behind him. Seeing his fellow Clothier from Wortley, he dismounted and waited.

'You rode right past me. What's on your mind then? Thinking of Mistress Bateson's supper I'll wager. No? Best thing you ever did, friend, taking on that woman to do your cooking. No disrespect of course, to your good wife.'

The Clothier's shook hands over this and James asked, 'So what are you about Walker? Looking for cloth from Holbeck I take it? Or just wandering around lost?'

'Well since you bring the matter to the front, I'm looking for your brother Jack or at second best, that little snapper Joe. Jack's not at home according to his man, and not expected back this night. So where has he got to, that's my query?. Because he's got quite an order from me for my next consignment and if he don't get himself together, he'll miss the date for the barges and I'll lose a big sale. I'll be on him for compensation.'

James shrugged and made a face at Walker. 'Nothing like a few threats to ease the road, eh? But come, where are you bound? If you're coming home we can walk together and you can tell me all about it and then we can see how best we may support your fledgling trade agreements. You do know, don't you, by the way, that if my father were to discover that Jack and Joe have arrangements with you, without the benefit of the Cloth Hall, he would be in something of a lather?'

'Yes to both. I'm on my way back - so we shall make our way together as good Clothiers should. And you can work out for me how the Batesons are going to make good this abysmal lack of business fidelity. And how to spin it past the Maister.'

'I was thinking of that too. About fidelity, acumen perhaps I mean. Not so much how to pull the wool over my father's eyes. Get your wife and mine to do that - but how Maister Walker has not a horse to bring him to the town. You prefer the exercise I take it?'

'Oh damn you Bateson. Alright. You are perceptive today I see. The horses are up at Farnley for pasture. Budget constrains sometimes and hay's risen high. And my bay is lame, damn her. But I do need your help – that is, if your Jack can't honour his agreements. I'll be put in a sore way if this deal flounders. That's honest of me, isn't it.'

James nodded and feigned surprise. 'Yes. You are making a fresh start. That's good and I highly commend you for it – you have seen the Light. If this continues you can be assured that I will personally arrange for the very next itinerant Methodist Minister that comes our way, to be lodged with yourself and your family. Mrs. Walker is half converted, or so Matthew's wife told me. It will be good for your business too – no more worrying about those Leeds Merchants – you can still go to Mill Hill but they'll talk to you about matters of doctrine, science as well as trade. Go on, you know you want …..

But Walker had thumped James hard and then was able to commence a more directed conversation about the necessity of fulfilling a promise of cloth for the next venture of himself and his partners which was an export via the ports to the Americas. The cloth had been promised today and was to be shipped down the Aire tomorrow. 'How much?' asked James frowning. 'Thirty pieces Bateson,' said Walker darkly. 'Oh', said James appalled. 'I had better come over with you then tomorrow morning?' 'Yes,' replied Walker, 'I think you better had. Although if your brothers don't have it ready and waiting at first light then it will be too late.' They were passing Marshall's noisy mill by then and James looked back over his shoulder towards Water Lane. He realised now what had troubled him about his brother's mill. The windows of the weaving lofts had been darkened and the hum of machinery was absent, notwithstanding the background of the other manufacturing noises of the area. And he wondered that Jack was absent from his house and premises when there was so much work to be done and an outstanding and major order unfulfilled and the mill quiet. 'I'm going to leave you Walker and ride on home. We're going to need to sort this out tonight….' Walker nodded grimly. James called out, 'but you'll owe me!'

Chapter Six

Nancy takes notice

At the Weaving House in Wortley James ate hungrily while his wife Nancy watched him and smiled, baby Hannah on her knee. Thomas their son and was dividing his attention between his father and climbing under the table. This was their little family and never a day passed but James gave thanks to the Lord for this family and more especially for the birth of his son.

It should be explained that this was an uncommon gratitude that had its roots in past distress. James was not a superstitious man. Indeed, he was an educated man of science. Alas, some time ago, James had had an unfortunate encounter with a woman of vision, whose prophetic interference had unsettled his world. He had believed for a space of time that he would die if he did not have a son and the death of their first son John had seemed to fulfil the curse of the witch. But that was then and things were settled now and going well. Still, the protection marks of the carpenters that had been scribed into the roof beams of his house, these daily gave him cause for thought and remembrance of such times. One day he would build a better house without such reminders. That would be the best thing. Such was the nature of his scientific and enlightened thoughts, briefly passing through his mind as ever they did when he was stressed - ,as he was this evening as he chewed his meat.

'Have you finished man? Or are we to wait all night for the plates? The water will be cold in the scullery.'

'You want me to choke on my meat? Shame on you Nancy Bateson. What would you do then, should such a misfortune occur?'

Nancy stood and with the baby on one hip, she began to clear away the dishes. 'I'd marry again sir. How many looms have we? And the half of a scribbling and fulling mill. There would be a queue and that's for certain. Or I could just thump you on the back. So what does Walker want and why?'

James followed her to the scullery door and leaning there told her how Walker was frustrated for the sake of the cloth that Jack had promised and which would miss the consignment for export. Nancy stopped wiping at the plates and turned. Her face was serious now.

'Oh you should have told me this when you came in, instead of gobbling your supper! This is terrible. That's twice now I've heard that Jack is letting his business down. Here, hold the baby while take off my apron. Shout Betsy to do these pots for me will you? She's just gone down to shut the chickens up.'

James took baby Hannah, found Betsy and returned to the parlour, sitting on the floor before the hearth and the bright fire while Thomas and the baby played on the floor with him before they could be taken up to their beds.

Nancy came and perched herself on the edge of the old fireside chair, her face lit by the dancing flames and James waited to hear what she would say about Walker's cloth. Her hands laid still in her lap, she watched the flames leap and her brow was furrowed.

'We'll find it for Walker. I know I know I know. But if Jack perhaps does not have it then there is no other option. You need to go back tonight and find either Jack or Joe but we must organise ourselves urgenlty because if they don't have it then we must supply the missing orders. Tonight. We can't wait until the morning and then find their warehouse empty! I'll go and speak to Matthew.'

'What about our orders, and our income? Can we stand, what, four weeks delay? We'll lose trust if we can't meet our own order from Hull.'

'Yes I know. Some of our other customers must wait a week - and that will have to serve. And Walker will be making me cloth for a few weeks. There's a strange turn of events! I don't know that Walker cloth is so much the worse than what our weavers are making. They are all of the same school after all. You go and find out what's up with Jack and Joe and leave Greenside to me. Do you understand?' James nodded but did not.

'This will have to go round your father and needs discretion. He won't like it and we will have to borrow some of his stock. But he is not to think that it is down to you because he'll be angry and won't co operate. So I will talk to Matthew – and Jane and Mrs. Bateson too and they can keep your father out of the way while we sort this out.'

'I should be worried about Jack and Joe then? I was going to talk to you about their engines and the coal'

'Yes, you should James. Be worried I mean. Don't bring engines into it now. We will talk about that later. But we can first help over this problem and then we'll find out what else needs to be done.'

'We don't know what Walker has orders for, what colours….'

'In the circumstances I think Walker will take what he can get. And to be fair, and I do hate to say this, your coloured cloth is by far the better range and quality than Jacks. Yours and Matthew's I mean. Yours, mine, and Matthew's I should say.'

'Oh really. And here was me thinking that you were just our book keeper and stock manager. So now you know about dyeing cloth Mrs. Bateson? I am very impressed. And not a stain of it on your hands at all. Very impressed.'

'I just click my fingers and hey presto, indigo! But think of it like this James. Walker will owe us and we never know when we might need to call in the favour.'

'Even such an innocent lamb as myself knows that the Walkers will never be in a position to lend us money, Mrs. Bateson. I do wonder how they survive. So how they can repay such a rescue as we are planning for them, I cannot fathom. But I am sure you have it worked out. Along with that particular blue dye that has so pleased you that you have a new skirt I notice…..'

'Weavers and spinners and croppers and burlers. Power. Coal. They have. We need. There are two great forces involved in the success of a manufacturing enterprise boy. One is debt and the other is capacity. You know this really. If we can, we get our stock balanced by Jack on the double. But otherwise James Walker will owe us a lot of money instead of Jack and Joe and they'll have to be grateful too. And if it should happen that he does not have money, we will take a payment in cloth, capacity or coal even.' By now Nancy had moved from her perch on the fireside chair and had joined James on the wooden settle. He kissed her. 'I would agree with you wife, about capacity. However, debt is something that I am anxious to avoid.'

Nancy murmured sweetly in his ear. 'Not what you owe, what others owe you. What luck I keep the books for you miller. Just you keep your eye on the dye vats and let me do the rest. Get yourself off now and down to Holbeck. And wrap up warm.'

As James returned to Holbeck, Nancy tucked up their little ones and then walked briskly up to Greenside to bring the difficulty to Matthew, who agreed with her that they must assist Walker in lieu of the defaulted cloth without waiting to see what James would find at Holbeck. There were hurried and quiet instructions and as Matthew's wife Jane sent in her children Mary and Anne to sing to their grandfather, and Mistress Bateson kept watch by the back door, cloth was hefted onto shoulders and carried to waiting wagons a safe distance from Greenside where is could be taken to Walker's mill to be sent into Leeds for the morning. James had found Jack at home in Water Lane and had been promised rapid compensation and it seemed that all would be well and the Maister would perhaps never need to be troubled about the matter. Still James cautioned Jack that come morning there would be a more thorough discussion with both himself and Matthew about business in general and Jack growled angrily at his younger brother but accepted that it must be so.

And so were William and James Walker able to send out this order across the Atlantic. I regret to tell you, that the cloth might have been sent to Liverpool and from there to Ireland, to be a cargo that avoided the duties and complications that might otherwise have impeded its progress. Certainly this became a means of trading Wortley cloth betwixt the Walkers and George Coggill - their agent in the United States, as the annals will testify.

James did confess his earlier misdoings of the road to Nancy that night, as they lay together in their ancient bed with the hangings drawn close against the cold of the night. Nancy spoke her judgement.

'Surely that is no crime. I believe that whenever one is able, that it is only right to splash an attorney at law. A puddle will do if that is the only water source available. Forget about it. Now if it had been Benjamin Gott that you had soiled! That would be a different matter. But attorneys deserve what they get.' With such absolution James did not consider it necessary to reveal that he had arrived rudely at Gott's without appointment, or to mention his new acquaintances of the morning. Which was perhaps, just as well. She lay safely in the arms of her strong, young and kind hearted husband and the nightmares of her youth were a things of the past.

Chapter Seven

In Halifax

Sarah Bateson, youngest daughter of the Maister John Bateson, sister of James Bateson, and promised bride of John Lupton, had been resident in Halifax for some two years or more. After the death of her mother Hannah, she had grieved so, and foundered so, that it was expedient that she should remove to another place and to be in a situation in the world which allowed some useful application of her abilities. And some beneficial occupation of her mind. Her foundering had been in no little part due to difficulties over the marital arrangements that had been made with her father's partner Old Tom Lupton. How could she know if she truly loved John Lupton when she had so little experience of the world? How could he know if he loved her when he spent so much time idling and socialising with other eligible young women? She had come this far into the bleak moorlands of the Pennine towns in order to gain more experience of the world and also to serve God. Here might she resolve her dilemma and contribute in Mission to the work of the Methodist Society.

These experiences included the education of the little children at the Methodist schoolroom, Sundays spent in meetings and services and evenings of sewing and gossip with the families of the Clothiers and the other middle sort of society in the district. Additionally, there arose benefit to her health of wild walks in the wind and rain, which tested her boots and her endurance and that of any friend or servant that accompanied her.

Those that know about such things will tell us that absence makes the heart grow fonder and perhaps she did think of John

Lupton with fondness and regret. She did remember her home in Wortley and the love of her married sisters Mary Beverley and Elizabeth Lister. There were even some situations that made her recall her brothers too. Her eldest brother Matthew she missed a great deal. Jack a little less so. Joseph she missed because she had no one to taunt. James she thought of at times, but could manage very well without. Sight of a weaver of spinner would begin such thoughts and the fine prospects of the chimneys and mills of Halifax focussed these more clearly. Letters home were the result of such reminders and those that bothered to reply, mainly her sisters and her brothers' wives, were awaited with impatience and scanned with a hunger for gossip and reassurance.

Certainly her days were not fully filled with prayer and labour in the vineyard. There were opportunities to meet with other young people and there were a number of fine upright Methodist cloth workers who were pleased to be able to see such a fine young lady from such a famous family and her dower was as interesting to these as her pretty face and pleasant form. Sarah was of course, quite aware of all this and held herself proudly and with distance so that those that admired her might be of the most determined kind. She had had her fill of dilatory admiration and inconsistent courting. She would be wooed with respect; with fire and passion as nearly equal requirements; but single minded commitment was what she would recommend to win her heart and hand. So she told herself anyway and as she did so she would put her hand unconsciously upon her breast where she would habitually keep the sporadic missives of her now contrite swain. John Lupton was not remarked upon for his devotion to work of any kind, certainly not that which made physical demands of him. But as for Sarah, the absence of a loved one made adjustments to his affections and he did find that he could write love letters which surpassed his personal wooing by considerable measurement. This was because he was able to present his admiration and regard for her without interruption and scepticism from the object of his desires. From Sarah.

On one particularly inclement Autumn night, a traveller sought shelter in the huddled farmhouse where Sarah had found herself lodged. The kitchen door banged wildly as the stranger came stumbling, bedraggled and wild, through the threshold and into the bright room, bringing a scurry of snowflakes with them that were soon melting on the flag stone floor. In his arms he carried a heavy bundle swathed in tarpaulin.

'Why man, thou art frozen. And the hour so late! Thou hast best come in, whoever thou art – this night's a foul place and that's no lie. Come in, come in.' Mrs Humbold fussed the wretch out of some of his soaked wrappers and brought the contents – a young man, to the fire, and sat him down. His bundle proved a leather bag, that he began to unwrap and the contents of which he laid with care upon the floor beside him

Sarah had been sat quietly by the fire with her desk on her lap, she had been writing a letter to Nancy Bateson. Mrs. Humbold continued, busy about the kitchen, hanging the wet cloak on a peg and putting more logs on the fire.

'Oh dear. What a wild night. How does it happen that tha' art out so late sir? Did tha lose tha way?'

The young man was now struggling with his boots and thanking his rescuers, heaving at his footwear and simultaneously apologising for the state of his attire in the clean, bright parlour. Having won the fight with the crusted boots, he set them neatly onto the hearth stone and then stood with a grin. 'Mistress Humbold. Friends! A thousand apologies for this sudden intrusion into your stronghold. Allow me to introduce myself. I am the Reverend J., and I understood that I could be sheltered here because you are friends and this a godly house of the district. Indeed, I have in my pocket -' and here he halted in his impromptu speech and reached inside his waistcoat, searching from side to side and at length producing a soggy piece of paper that was impossible to unfold, so much water had it absorbed. He shook it out but it was not to be salvaged and so looked around him sheepishly but without real penitence.

'Did Reverend Wood not write to you? Well, this is difficult indeed. But I trust to your mercy friends. I do indeed. This is no night for man or beast to be abroad.' He put his hand together in attitude of prayer but smiled charmingly as he did so. 'And I pray you will allow shelter to this pilgrim, this night at least, so that I may find my lodgings in Sowerby I think, when the sun is risen and the way is clear before me.' He flapped the remains of his letter of introduction regretfully. 'I hope my books have fared better than this sad rag! Little else have I in the world and so precious are they to such as I.'

Sarah had remained seated as the young man had declaimed all this in a strong, clear and commanding voice – a pulpit voice if ever she had heard one – and she watched the Minister of God as he made himself his case for shelter, waiting for his pronouncements to end that she might introduce herself. Her eye glanced at the satchel beside him. It looked a weighty burden.

It might be now added, that the Reverend J. was a very young but very well made gentleman. His accent was from another county, very fine and clear. His voice was surprisingly deep given his lack of years, his build was athletic and he was possessed of regular features, eyes that were dark and bright, and his hair was also dark and just presently, wildly disordered.

Mistress Humbold, once she understood that this was a new itinerant Minister of the Society come among them, became flustered and red in the face so great was her burden of duty to the Methodist cause. Or, so well did the young man look stood tall and dark by her hearth. We cannot know which of these motives caused her to be so put out. She set about with alacrity, to find something for the gentleman to take for his supper. Some medicinal wine? Ale? A blanket? Cheese? She began to stoke and prod the fire to encourage the flame and the Reverend J. took the poker from her, turned her gently away and saw to the fire with his own strong hands. And then he turned and smiled at Sarah. 'And who have we here?' asked the Minister, with a smile that would have melted the ice on the Hardcastle Crags

So it was, that one Mr. J. had arrived, newly ordained in the Methodist Ministry, in the district of Halifax.

Chapter Eight

Of the old house at Greenside.

The Maister, John Bateson who we know well now, was wont to count his blessings in his daily prayers, where his household gathered in the early light, family, servants and journeymen, sat as they could on settle and stool and some of them hoping for brief readings of the good book. He was as yet, innocent of family plottings and the dangers to one of the family business branches.

Not least among these blessings were his grand children and those children born to his eldest son Matthew were his chief joy because they lived in one side of the old house at Greenside and they had ever been woven into his life since the days of their births.

His eldest granddaughter was a fine girl, sensible, dutiful and cheerful too. Mary Bateson was by far the most serious of the four girls and this attribute suited her grandfather very well. Now she was twelve years old and she and her next sister Anne (a rather more independent character) were often to be found in their grandfather's study at the back of the house where they would come to do their lessons, to sit and sew, or to entertain their grandfather with their childish games and play. It may be that the lessons were most often the occupation of Mary and the childish games were those of Anne. Their younger sisters, Nanny and Sarah were boisterous, mischievous and noisy, and as yet their grandfather did not allow them to make inroads into his private preserve. He did however see them often and he would habitually watch them at play from the safety of the low window.

'Grandpa! This is wrong. You have made a mistake. This column here. Look.' Mary hung over her grandfather's ledger and studied his figures and he pushed his spectacles further up his nose to attend to the place where her small finger pointed. 'Alas my child, you are right. My eyes fail me. Come sit by me now and check the rest of the column.' John Bateson moved over on his cushioned chair and let Mary sit snugly next to him, she kicking her shoes on the spars of the seat and he patient as never was known by his own children, with the energy and enthusiasm of a favourite child. Anne got up from her stool and came to peer at the problem. 'Now Anne, here is some other work that needs checking too. You bring your stool to me and do your duty as your sister does!' John Bateson nodded at Anne and looked severe. She laughed explosively. 'Grandpa! We're not all as daft as Mary! What a thought is that, to encourage a child of ten to see to your accounts! A child not even allowed in the Grammar School! Ha! I'm off up the road to tell Uncle James that I'm to do your books now. See what he'll say to that! Indeed!' Anne hurriedly gathered up her books and sewing basket and ran from the room in mock horror. John Bateson called after her. 'Little rogue. To tell tales on me to the family fool! Indeed! And if he sets you on to weaving it's your own foolish fault child. Mark me if you don't have to weave on the looms for a day for your impertinence to an old man!'

But he laughed all the same. And Mary stayed with him, helping him with his figures and conscious of her own responsible behaviour in comparison with her sister's naughty independence of mind and impertinence to the patriarch.

And while this mathematical experience was Mary's lot, James and Matthew had begun at first light to make urgent enquiries with J. and J. Bateson and were anticipating pressing discussions with the Walkers later in the day. John Bateson at the moment, was not aware of any clouds on his horizon. Had he gone out and down to the warehouses where his cloth was stored for the Cloth Halls along with that made by M. and J. Bateson and that of a few other associated Clothiers – the Heppers and the Lupton brothers – he would have been chilled to find it half empty and have set off a hue and cry about the village. As it was, Molly, his general house servant watched him walk out late morning and set off down the lane towards Town End, no doubt to look at the Beck and the mills upon it.

'It's alright Mistress. He's gone down that a way. He'll not be in the warehouse today.' Mistress Bateson breathed out slowly.

'Oh dear Lord! I thought he was going to do a sudden stock check!'

'Why would he? He leaves it to Master Matthew, doesn't he?'

'Yes. Well there's a blessing! Pray that the boys can sort it out between them. And look, I have this.' The old woman produced from her pockets her key chain and on it was the large key that held the padlock on the warehouse.

'That's a good idea,' commented Molly, folding her stout arms and nodding her white cap, her lips clamped in approval. 'Will I make dumplings for the Maister's dinner?'
'Aye my dear. Dumplings it is.'

Chapter Nine

Nancy takes even more notice

The day was unduly cold even for November, the sky dark and the wind biting and cold from the north. Nancy had dwelt upon the dangers of the financial situation now they were dependent on the activity of J. and J. Bateson or indeed, the solvency of the House of Walker. With an anxious mind she decided upon a visit into Leeds to settle her own mind and to dispel her fears. Well, near to Leeds in fact. James was at work in the mill by the Beck on this day, again excited by some measurements of the dye process and would in all probability not come back to the house until the supper was on the table if then. Therefore she had many hours in which to safely carry out her plan.

James and Matthew had already been to call on their brother Jack some days ago, riding through the grey dawn in a frost limed landscape down the back lanes to Holbeck. They had been reassured that Jack and Joe would within days replace the cloth that had gone out to Walker; there would be cloth for the Cloth Market and then more to fill the warehouse. Jack had convinced them that a delay with raw fleece and coal had occurred in the early autumn and that all was now well; that the weaving shop in Holbeck was to be fully occupied, no mind to the cost of candles - making good the temporary shortfall in production and that there was nothing to worry about. He had even volunteered to make some financial compensation to them for their contribution to Walker. He gave them his word that he and Joseph would be able to increase production in the coming weeks and months even. He had offered them wine to seal the agreement and they had shaken hands together as brother traders should.

'But why?' asked James, genuinely puzzled. 'Why did you not come to us and let us know you had a big order that you could not meet? I can't understand that. We would have taken it from you and if it had been commissioned in good time, then we would have had no difficulties in placing orders either on our own behalf or with our associates. I really can't see the problem.' Matthew shook his head at James. Jack scowling, said nothing. Matthew explained to keep the peace. 'He has told us already James.'

'Several times,' growled Jack. Matthew held his hand up to calm them. 'Jack was too proud to ask James. He tells us that Walker knew about it and that Walker should have gone to other houses. Walker didn't do that for his own reasons not least that he don't always pay in a timely manner. So that is that. Its was a mistake and Jack,' he looked now at his brother, humped in a chair and staring at the bare table, who nodded without looking up, 'Jack will not be so foolish again. It was a bad mistake. But it is now managed and amends will be made.' They took their leave then, but James was still trying, without much success, to imagine himself in a similar situation to Jack and failing to ask Matthew for help and he stared at Jack as he departed. Jack just glared at him and nodded.

'I'll go talk to Walker. You go back and if father should ask for anything, then bid him wait until I return. But it should be alright. I'll see you tonight after supper James.' Matthew had parted from his brother at Walkers Mill, leaving James to return on foot to their own mill a mile further along the Beck.

But Jack had left immediately they had departed and had taken himself out to Cottingley, a village south of Holbeck to occupy himself with a gun and a dog and any wild creature unlucky enough to stand across his path. He had delayed only to send a message to his young brother Joe which read

> Get hold of as much fleece as tha can from anywhere tha can get it and go talk to Brown or Duce for slubbings if there's spare get that in as well. Think there's some at Norths? Leave off with the coal for now and fetch in the wool instead. Tha'll have to pay over for it but we need to be working or there'll be the devil to pay. Then get back to the mill. I'll see thee tomorrow.
> Jack
> And go and get Williams to pay his bill. We need that now and he can't have more time. Not with Matthew hopping about on us.

   Which left poor Joe with impossible tasks. As the junior partner in the company and not privvy to the meeting with his brothers he had now to buy in materials at the worst possible time. Even before Jack's scrawled instructions were placed in his hand in the back room of the Old George, he had been refused wool by two staplers that they commonly did business with. 'Waiting on it laddie,' had said one of these, kindly. 'Waiting on Hull and it's froze.' And then with more compassion, 'tell thee what Master Joe, soon as I get any it'll be thine, straight off and no delay and with just 5 percent for profit. Shake my hand on that young man.' And Joe had shaken hands but it did not help right at this moment. He read Jack's note and began to cough.

'What's up Master Joe? Not ailing?'

'No, no,' said Joe struggling to breathe, 'just my chest as usual. Does tha know who's got wool I can get?' The clothiers shook their heads. One Morley man leant across the table with a smile, 'Try your kin Joe. They'll help out, I know they will. And old Beverley has a lot of stock they say and so get thy Matthew to help out. Yes?' Joe stared miserably and said nothing and the others waited, not unsympathetic to his plight. At last, since he could do nothing else, Joe said, 'We can't ask them. That's all. But if tha hears of anyone that's selling send them to me. I'd better go. Don't forget if you hear of any – or slubbings?' The clothiers nodded and then shook their heads at his departing back.

'No good'll come of this!'

'Jack's done for. Shame about the young 'un though.'

'Aye. Knew it were no good. Should have invested in the Autumn. Too late now. Unless Matthew helps them?'

'He would aye, but Jack's too proud and that's a fact.'

'Aye. But pride don't get wool in. And what will be the price now in this hard frost? The barges say that the water's to freeze. There'll be nothing this side of the spring, mark my words.'

'He had it bought though, didn't he? In Hull. Went to Hull and shook on two cargoes but then they backworded. So I heard anyway.'

'That's as might be. But that won't get the cloth made, will it?'

Joe had given up in the end and fretted himself hurriedly back to Water Lane. They should tell Matthew they had no wool or very little and Matthew would help them out. He was sure of it. But Jack was so stubborn. Well, if Jack thinks there's wool to be bought, let him go buy it. Joe had had enough of it. When he reached the mill the workers were idling and Joe, now distraught, tried to organise things but the cold had done it's work and he was forced to retreat to the mill house, just managing to beckon the Overlooker to follow.

'Tha's in a mess Master Joe. When's wool coming?'

'Tomorrow. I've appealed for help.'

'To thy kin? About time too.' Joe shook his head and coughed some more. 'No, not yet. One more day and then maybe. But don't say anything to Master Jack about that will you?' The overlooker sighed loudly and stomped back out of house to the mill yard where he gathered men round him and Joe could see them all, discussing his failure, glancing up at the house from time to time and probably, deciding to seek work elsewhere.

Jack out at Cottingley with his dog, his gun and a thumping head walked morosely over the fields, wrapped in hopeless thoughts and cursing himself for a fool. He had bought a little time today and Matthew trusted him. Such thoughts did not make him feel any better. The ground was hard with frost and the ways were ridged, pitted and hard to walk but he made his way back to the town and did manage to make a few deals for slubbings which would see them through for a week or so. It was the best he could do and he knew he had been robbed. Then he took Joe and they walked over to Batley and then Dewsbury to see if matters were better over there and so were again absent from the struggling mill when Nancy made her reconnaissance

The confidence even of Matthew, was not enough for Nancy Bateson. Jack was not her brother, and she owed nothing to young Joe. She had oversight of all the accounts and ledgers for M. and J. Bateson. It was her home, her dower, that was mortgaged to fund the new mill in Wortley and the new Boulton and Watt steam engine. She had sympathy for Jack who had lost his new wife so soon after their marriage. But that did not mean that she would make allowances for him. He was a good cloth maker, that she knew - but the running of a mill required more than the knowledge of the weaving trade and Jack had foundered badly once already. He was also a very stubborn man. She did not believe that Jack had the business sense of the other Batesons. Her misgivings had been shared with her sister in law, Elizabeth Lister and her husband William Lister – a mason and iron founder of Bramley and of Holbeck. And Elizabeth, who loved her younger brother James Bateson very well because of her early responsibility for him, had counselled her to do what was needed to monitor the situation and to ensure her own position was not compromised.

'Our Matthew and our James, your James I mean, they should not have to carry Jack and Joe if they are not prospering as they should. If they cannot work independently, then their company must close, pay where they can and then they can work for you and all will be safe. William agrees with this. He also mentioned that their engines are not up to modern standards and that this too, is something that must be dealt with in the near future and that as you know, is a tremendous burden on credit and from what I hear that can't happen now. Father must get used to the idea, that Jack is not so smart as he thinks he is. Get James to go back and oversee the mill on Water Lane and make sure that everything is right. He has some ideas about the fire engines I believe and should take a closer look and if it is possible to retain the mill he'll say so. Matthew is sometimes too trusting of others.' Nancy had nodded and determined to do that. Well, perhaps she would do that but first she would take a look and make up her own mind on matters.

So on this cold grey morning, she wrapped her shawl over her bonnet and her cloak over all that - because of the frost that had arrived overnight and that glittered on the brambles and the hedgerows along the Holmfield Lane. She took with her John Bateson's house servant, a perceptive woman. Molly had been an Indentured servant at Greenside for longer than she herself could remember and the Batesons were as a family to her and she followed Nancy, with her stout boots on, red in the face and quickly out of breath.
'What art tha about Mrs. Nancy? What am I doing a paying visits to the mills? I hear that Walker's have sent up some cloth for the warehouse and the Maister don't know about it, but that's going on alright, I'm sure. There's nowt discovered or the Maister would be on his feet and making a dance. And he's a quiet as a lamb. Long may it continue!'
'I don't know m'dear. I just think that we should keep a close eye on all, so as to be safe in business. Master Matthew said all would be well. But my husband did say something again about duck. About Jack getting us some ducks for the table when he gets back. So where is Jack? That would be well enough but I don't know how he would be finding ducks on the River Aire. A man that has ducks in his larder has been out and about with his dog. Who has time for that in the Trade? We have the word of Master Jack that he will be working night and day for us. I thought I might see that that is so. Duck indeed!'

'Aww, Mrs Nancy!. Duck's a change from pigeon this time of the year. I'd like a duck or two for the spit.' Molly licked her lips.

'Duck! That's not for us right now. More like porridge and peas. It's not the time for hunting, that I do know. Come along now, keep up.' This made Molly pensive and she thought much about roasted duck as she struggled to stay abreast of Nancy.

Together they paced the lane that led towards Armley, passing Benjamin Beverley's Beech Grove and his workshops at the crossroad where the lane led north to Armley and then turning, they headed to Holbeck out along the Wortley Lane to Mill Green. The site of Will Turner's terrible accident. Along this road, the air grew heavier with the smoke of the many chimneys of the mills that jostled for place near to the amenable wharves of the south bank of the Aire River and Navigation. Dark clouds hung like a pall over the district and then drifted over the town of Leeds. Although they were accustomed to the many unpleasant odours of the cloth trade in their own village and in Armley, in Holbeck the air was foul and the Hol Beck and the River Aire were noisome with ordure and chemical contaminations. The tannery at Holbeck added its own particular aroma to the revolting mix.

Mr. Sowry stood in his apron in the mill yard supervising the lading of a cart, doffed his hat to her by his workshops. Nancy and Molly stopped by Marshall's new flax mill to wonder at the size and noise of the great many floored edifice but at length they came to Water Lane near the bridge and Nancy looked around her with a keen and perceptive eye. There was bustle in the lane with carts and wagons laden with raw materials, with ale, with coal and with sacks of potatoes and cabbages making their way in and out of Leeds. Labourers and traders carried their goods and tools but not so many were abroad as usual for the weather was severe and unrelenting.

'It's a nice quiet spot this Molly! I think we'll best pay a call here?' Nancy put her ear to the mill gate and then inclined her head. Molly nodded with pursed lips. She too had noted that the mill was idle. This was Nancy's worst fear realised and that the whole district must be aware of it was a thought that hit her hard, like an icy blow. She just prayed that the weaving lofts were busy.

Nancy banged with her fist on the timbers and after quite some delay, during which Nancy and Molly exchanged significant looks, they heard the bars being drawn on the inside and one side of the barrier creaked open a crack. A gnarled, unshaven face peered up at them through the opening. 'We's not taking on. No weavers needed. Off with ye.'

'Good day to you too, my man. And is it spectacles you need? I am Mrs. James Bateson and I have come to speak a word to your master.'

'He ain't 'ere. Try at t'house. But he ain't there neither I'll be bound. Nancy put her foot in the gap and pushed on the wide planked door. 'My good man, let me explain. I have just a small favour to ask of you. Do let me in to see what is here. I never get to look at a mill! Do we Molly? And myself, I am a Clothier's wife and I always would like to see what goes on inside a good mill.' Nancy smiled now, quite persuasively and said anything that came into her head. As she prattled she got herself by small degrees more surely through the gate and Molly deftly followed close behind her so that the gatekeeper could not close upon them without injuring them. Nancy continued to dissemble. 'I have so wanted to be in this mill. Maister Jack has told me so much about it, and all about his workers too. So well he speaks of you all. Paragons he tells me…..' The watchman looked doubtful and puzzled but gave way before Nancy's pressure and the two investigators found themselves within the mill yard. 'Now,' whispered Nancy.

As no doubt arranged, Molly took upon herself to have something of a fit of the vapours and with good dramatic effect began to swoon. Nancy rose to the occasions and with convincing alarm in her voice called upon the workers now gathered in the nearest doorway to provide water. And a chair, she added as an afterthought. Whilst these items were sought and such found of good enough quality for a decent woman and her canny maid, Nancy took herself a survey of the yard and the mill and workshops, turning upon her heels as Molly became increasingly incapacitated revealing a hitherto unknown aptitude for the dramatic arts. Amid the commotion and without leave Nancy headed for the steps that led up to what she assumed was the weaving shop and she mounted these before the distracted workers were aware of her foray. She had not got far across the threshold of the darker chamber when she was hailed by a shout from within the shadows. 'Oi! What is this? Tha's no business in here! Oh. Mistress. I beg pardon, but this is not a suitable place for a lady to come on social calls. Go back the way tha's come or I'll not answer for the consequences.' Now Nancy's eyes had quickly accustomed to the gloomy interior of the loom shop and she took in what was before her. A man had stood from the comfort of his chair and a mug of ale was in his hand. He peered at her as she stood outlined in the doorway and if he could have seen the fire in her eyes he would have retreated then and there.

There were ten looms in the workshop but only two had webs to them and there were three other men besides the overlooker, apparently the remaining weavers, who were sat on their stools around a card table. These looked up with alarm and muttered among themselves.

    Nancy put her head on one side, narrowed her eyes further and put her hands on her hips. She said nothing and was forbidding in her silence. Then, with firm step and assertive gaze she strode along the workshop, noting everything, taking a look at the looms and the set of the gears and slays. Touching the pegs where the waiting new spun weft would be hung and looking very closely at the two pieces of cloth that were in progress, assessing the sizing and gauging the tension and the quality of the spun wool, shadowed now by the protesting weaver. She turned suddenly round and confronted him.

    'Well?' she said.

    'Well! Mistress? Who….? What the devil art thou doing?' The overlooker stumbled over his words in dismay then took courage by swigging a draught from his pewter mug. He wiped his mouth on his sleeve. 'Yes. What the devil does tha mean, barging in here like this? This aint for thee – unless tha's a weaver or summat like that. And we aint takin' on no way. Anyways -' he tailed off, suddenly realising that whoever had come calling was not either a weaver or a friend, that the woman was not intimidated by his raised voice and that he was possibly making things a lot worse for himself. He gazed forlornly at the bottom of his tankard, his bravery gone with the ale.

    'I can weave a good cloth, never you fear, my good man. But there's nothing of that ilk being done today, is there? Now you will come with me - and you and I will have a little chat. I am Mrs. Bateson. Mrs. James Bateson and I think there is some explaining to do here and additionally, the devil as you have reminded me, to pay. We are promised ten lengths by the end of the week, thirty in all in a short time, and it would appear that this commitment will not be met. If I were you, I would now be very, very worried. Come.'

Nancy led the now abject man down the stone steps and into the cold, bright yard where he stood with his hat in his hands, turning it round and round and studying his feet as if these could provide him with some answers for this inquisitor.

It would have been within Nancy's capacity to take over the workshops and even to command the mill workers to continue with whatever they were employed to do, but she was in a state of shock at the reality of the situation. Also, the lack of raw materials would have prevented such a course of action. Molly, having made a speedy recovery from her recent indisposition, looked with a penetrating stare at each worker in turn and they in their turn, looked at the cobbles, or the walls, or the sky and shuffled their feet. 'Cold today?' began a young man, hopefully. 'Sh!' said Molly with feeling and sudden authority.

'Tomorrow,' said Nancy, in clear voice, looking first left and then right, 'tomorrow, you will all report for work at 6 am sharp. You will be either given work here or in Wortley - if the wool is not sufficient in this mill or other material lacking. And if should be that there is not work for all, then some of you, will be finding other masters. Who is in charge?'

A man shouldered through the small crowd of now angry but also shame faced workers. A stooped man who non the less tried to stand tall before the intruder. ' Warren. John Warren Mistress. I'm, I'm the manager now.' He looked about him, at the small crowd of workers and the tumbled state of the stone yard and realised that the situation was indefensible. 'Mr. Crowther's gone. I was the overlooker, and begging your pardon M'am, I'll be going at the end of the week.' Some of the crowd began to mutter then. Nancy peered at him narrowly.

'Take me around the whole works Mr. Warren, if you please.' Nancy made for herself a thorough inspection of the entire complex and reached many conclusions. One of these conclusions was that there was no coal at all in the stores and that the mill had been running on water power only for some time. One pair of the fulling stocks needed urgent repair. There were five willeying machines and seven scribbling machines that looked well oiled and clean. 'This is your work then Mr. Warren? You're a millwright then?' 'Aye Mistress. The machines are all good. They'll fetch a good - ' He stopped and Nancy glanced at him shocked. Then she shrugged. The vast warehouse behind the scribbling mill was strewn with empty barrels and baskets and echoed to their footsteps. It was dark and moisture ran down the walls and Nancy shivered and hurried back through the machine rooms and stopped then suddenly to examine the skeps untidily stacked near the great doors.. There was no raw fleece. Warren offered hesitantly, 'We finished Mistress, about a week ago.' Nancy nodded at him, her face blank. 'Master Jack, he said Master Joe would be arranging for the stuff. I laid off half the workers after Mr. Crowther left, though it were hard to do it. I was going to let the rest go on Friday.'

'Oh God,' said Nancy. 'Your master is in trouble and you know that. Why didn't you come to us with this. You know that his brothers would help him!' The manager bowed his head at this and mumbled. 'Thought it would come right. Been right afore now and things been worse. The man's in a mess, right enough, and the little master too. Thought they'd make it right. Didn't want to see 'em go down.'

'Well they're down now! You must know that the rent has to be paid, if the yard is working or not? Wages for the men too. There's families will go hungry man! Those you've laid off will have to find other places soon enough or go hungry and look at the weather coming in! We would have taken them on over our way and seen them given something, if only from the Poor Rate to tide them over. And given your master some good advice. Now what?' Nancy sighed and turning slowly thought quickly but could see no way that this would mend. Warren waited agitated and fearful beside her until she spoke again, this time kindly. 'See that all are here in the morning. It will be Master Matthew or Master James that comes to sort this out. Of course you were right to be discreet and I should not have accused you – a faithful worker you've been, of that there is proof. I am sorry but it is hard to take this in. Tomorrow things may improve. Good day.'

   Nancy departed, holding Molly's arm for comfort and Molly, her face grim looked up at Nancy's face with sorrow. That feeling of just indignation which had warmed them both at first now drained away as they thought of the reality of the situation. 'We'll go over the fields Molly. You've got your boots on and the ground is hard today. I can't face walking back through Mill Green or past Mr. Beverley's.' Molly nodded. They took the footpaths across the fields then and reached Wortley coming up the rising ground from the valley. Molly held her tongue. She could see her companion was laden with cares and although she wanted to question her, probe and be assured that all could be salved, she knew better than to interrupt Nancy's thoughts. As they helped each other over the last stile, Nancy gave her one small smile. Molly nodded, pursed her lips and shrugged.

   Despite the bright autumn sun the day grew colder as they walked and the clear skies spoke of harder frosts on the morrow. In sheltered crannies, the frost of the morning remained, giving a hint of the cold, cruel winter that was to come.

'Wilt thou go to the Maister Mistress?' asked Molly as they neared Nan Tan House.

'No, no. You hold your tongue for now my love, and I'll get the other masters to know this first. There's more to this than we two can know just now. Don't say owt until the menfolk have it digested. If there's grief it will do in the morrow just as well as this evening. Do you make sure that John Bateson has a good supper tonight though.'

'Twill break his heart Mistress Nancy. Jack's his favourite tha knows don't thee? Always was. Something about his namesake maybe for all that. But he's always soft on Jack when the others get short shrift for nowt.' The others in this case being James, which Nancy well understood.

'I know. But I doubt it will break his heart. His bank balance maybe.'

'What about thy faither? I mean Mr. Lupton. He's not going to like this is he? I mean, begging thy pardon Mrs.Nancy, but there's going to be some to do about such a -' Molly was not a gentle servant. She was as hard as she had needed to be with such a master as she had had and with such responsibilities as had been hers, but the tears came now., rolling unheeded down her wrinkled apple cheeks. Perhaps the thought of Old Tom Lupton in a storm of rage had been more than she could endure. Nancy put her arms round Molly.

'What will be, will be. We'll mend where we can and then if the worst comes, well, um, well we can both take to the loom, can we not?'

Molly choked on her tears. 'Oh Lord Mistress. I never knowed how to weave. Sure an' I'll have to be a spinner!'

'Come then. Let's be brave. Here, wipe your face and go in cheerful or the game will be up. Heads up Molly.'

Chapter Ten

Little Mary recommends forgiveness.

'I with I could do something. Help somehow. I have heard our Grandfather's voice and he sounds very – very quiet and so is angry. Why cannot we go in and offer ale and biscuits. I am sure it would help. Tea. Tea will help and there are enough cups, aren't there Molly? Why don't you put the kettle on?'

'Shush child. This is for the men to deal with. We stay out of the way unless someone calls for summat. There's nowt to be done that will mend what's broke just now. Tha's to find thyself something to occupy thee. But mind, not piano practice. There's no need to make matters worse. Here, read this,' and Molly fetched the Bible from the shelf and thrust it unceremoniously into Mary's hands.

'Yes Mary,' said Anne pertly. Read something soothing from God's Word. Turn to the back. Apocalypse. That's today.' She stuck her tongue out at Molly. 'Womenfolk cannot be part of any important matters. Molly is right as ever she was. Only Nancy and our mother are allowed in there. Oh. Now I understand. Molly, you mean children are not to know what's up? That was what you meant, was it not?' Anne was by far the more perceptive child. Molly reached out to box her ears, but Anne was already out of reach and away out of the kitchen door and into the garth where she could no longer hear the muffled but tantalizing voices of the family conference and trial. This was her way of dealing with the anxieties of the day and the distress of the adults in her life, to be outside in the frosty air - for as long as her poor chest allowed anyway. But the sisters had also younger siblings and one of these, Nanny, had found herself a more comfortable and convenient place in which she might in some way monitor the meeting. She was upstairs in a lodging room above the great parlour, laid on the floorboards, peering through the gaps and listening to what was being said by the menfolk (and some of the womenfolk) of the family. If it was not for the care of her baby sister Sarah, it would have been a good spying place. But Sarah was bored and began to sing to amuse herself. Reluctantly Nanny pulled her roughly away from the best spyhole. 'You pest child,' she hissed. 'Stop singing. There's all sorts being said down here. Oh get out you minx. Sh, sh, sh.' Nanny grabbed Sarah's pudgy hand and dragged her away down the far stairs while looking regretfully back at her spy hole in the floor. They were intercepted by Mistress Bateson - who smiled and then remembered herself and tutted at the pair of spies as they retreated down the hallway to the kitchen.

At the scrubbed table the girls were given milk and bread and quizzed by Molly and Mistress Bateson who were unable to contain their fears and their need for information in spite of the dubious and illicit source of such knowledge.

'So what's happening then Miss?'

'Uncle James says he going to thrash Uncle Jack! He did, I swear it!'

'Now then miss. That's enough I'm sure. Swear it indeed. What kind of talk is that from a child! What else did he say?'

'That I'd like to see,' remarked Molly to the scullery door.

A sudden clatter outside made them start, exchange frightened looks and run to peer into the dusk, where a dark horse was being met by the stable boy with his lantern. Molly and the mistress of Greenside watched a cloaked figure dismount and hand his horse over and looked at each other, nerves jangling and hearts thudding as they waited for further disaster. But as Molly flung open the kitchen door she recognised the wide smile and sharp features of James Wood in his sodden cloak, and battered tricorn hat. 'Oh Reverent Wood, Reverent sir! Come in, come in. Oh I am so glad to see thee. Get in now out of the frost and come here by the fire. Oh, I am so glad thou art come!' James Wood was hauled unceremoniously by agitated Molly into the warm hallway.

'Why Molly? What's amiss? Surely it's not like you to be in a fuss? Mistress Bateson, greetings and God's blessing on this house. Girls, how are ye? Is the Maister Home?' Then the women folk avoided his eyes and the little girls sat motionless and he realised that something was amiss. The Minister's face changed and he looked about him at the kitchen - bright as usual, the fire glowing and the supper in the pots in the old range in the hearth – but as well as the reserved reception of the womenfolk, his arrival had not been noted by others who would by now usually have come to greet him and his heart missed a beat.. Mistress Bateson came to take his cloak from him, shaking it and hanging it by the door - asking of his journey but with a face that told of her strain. He took her hand and when she looked up, he gave her a piercing look. 'What's this my dear? Tell me – what is wrong?' She broke down then and he put his arms about her. At last she composed herself, and Molly brought her a cloth for her face while the children whispered to themselves in the background. Wood waited, his old face creased with concern, until his friend could manage to speak.

'Oh Lord, Mr. Wood! Indeed thou art welcome this dark night - but the men have, have business that presses - it might be some time before the Maister can greet thee. They are all here and Mr. Lupton too. Come warm thyself and take some ale. It's as Molly says. Thou art come timely to this house today.'

'Not Old Mr. Lupton sir, the young one that's to have our Sarah', put in Molly quickly and received a relieved smile.

When the Minister had been told all that the women could decently tell him of the pressing issues that had brought all the family together this day, he thought himself better to wait for the hour when the meeting was done. 'Well my dear friends. I will have to wait to be received then but I will stay tonight, if it is possible? And assist as I can. In the mean time, I will about the village and make a few calls on our people. And who is to say but then I might be entertained with much gossip, which you must understand, is the reason why I am come! I'll soon find out all the best tattle or I'm not the man I think I am.' He was rewarded with slight smiles. He took Mrs. Bateson's hands in his. 'Rest ye calm Ann and put thy trust in the hands of the Lord. I will return as soon as I have wrought all the best news from your neighbours and if I can get supper three times then I will indeed - praise the Lord. But that does not mean, dear friends, that I do not expect to have my reward in this house and if that stew pot is empty – ' he advanced and sniffed meaningfully, 'well, why should I come again to be so abused?' This brought at last laughter to Molly and her mistress.

James Wood, Methodist Minister, went abroad again, into the cold and dimming light, to walk now about Wortley and to minister to his faithful flock and even to his unfaithful flock. But his brow was furrowed as he pulled his cloak about him and trudged across the cobbled lane for he loved John Bateson well and his sons and daughters also. He was also very tired, cold and wet and took shelter just two doors down from Greenside where he knew there was fire and a kettle and there would be hot tea and a warm welcome. He stretched his stiff legs before the fire and listened to the chatter of the neighbouring house and defended himself against questions which he could not answer as to the congregation of the cloth makers at Greenside, while he fretted inwardly over what had caused such unsettling dismay to the family and what this boded for his good friend John Bateson. At least it was merely business that had made his friends so low – but there must be a very serious set back to cause such long faces under that roof.

Jack Bateson was under examination beneath the lodging room floor and within the great parlour at Greenside, sullen and subdued – along with Joe, white faced and trembling. Jack had little to say - only that he had already told Matthew and James last week, Friday he thought, that they had no wool and that coal was dear. They knew, he asserted, that things were going to be hard and should not bear down with such force on a man, for a few days lapse of labour. He and Joe had been forced to seek wool down south and that was justifiable absence. Matthew shook his head at this. Joe shivered again, uncontrollably.

Matthew replied, 'but Jack, when we came to see about the, the matter last week, we had not seen your accounts and the picture we have now is changed. The books have told us the hard facts. We should have sat with you last week and we should have audited properly. You have only delayed the storm not averted it! I'm sorry about it. But you are in serious debt and one of your main creditors at the moment is myself and James.' Jack stared at his boots and there was a general pause.

James played with a pencil and paper, doodling in the margin of his note book, and caught his father's frigid stare and stopped. 'Well,' began James with a frown, into the silence, 'you always said I was the fool for thinking of going into milling. Not that you meant that our father is a fool,' meandered James now momentarily uncertain if he had offended his father, who indeed had worked a water mill. But when there was no spoken response he went on, 'But you told us, told Matthew and me when we thought to bring in the steam, that you would stay with cloth making because that is what you were good at. Are good at. So it would seem now, that you should have believed your own words.'

'What are you burbling about boy? Just speak when you have something to say that is of relevance.' The Maister was cold but Jack was on his feet, red in the face and breathing hard. 'Are you – are you, of all people, calling me, a fool? I'll not be called such a thing by you - you would not be where you are today if it was not for Matthew's protection! You've already threatened me and I'll not hold my arm if you begin again.'

'That will do Jack,' growled the Maister. 'Sit down! No threat and no insults. This must be discussed rationally. James, mind your tongue.'

Matthew said nothing but he clamped his mouth and looked down and then over at Nancy who gave him tight smile. And James missing all this but noticing that Joe was trying to smother a cough, ploughed on, avoiding his father's eyes and fixing his gaze on that notebook before him. 'I did some thinking about that mill and -'. John Bateson let out a groan, 'and I don't think it can make enough profit without the engines being replaced. That being so -'

'Do be quiet!' said John Bateson raising his voice just a little. Matthew held up his hands and made a placating gesture. 'Listen please, sir. I think James has been giving it a lot of thought in his own way. Let us hear him out. Go on James.'

'Well if the engines were replaced with modern - and the bills for coals reduced - then in five years -'

'Five years!' said John Bateson. 'I should live that long!' James looked now across to the head of the table where his father sat with his grey hair and wondered how his father's age was of matter. But he continued, 'Yes five years and then the mill would be in profit again. However, with the price of coal rising each week, it would seem, then there is not now at this time, and has not been any time in the last two years when Water Lane could have made enough profit to pay Atkinson's rents and other outlay and do more than break even, never mind a reasonable profit. And while these rents were reduced before – I have to mention this -' James looked across at his wife and she nodded at him and smiled to encourage him.

'Before your wife died Jack, then you made some little profit. But I've done a full analysis and the mill can't go on. And I am sorry I threatened to hit you. It was because Nancy was upset you see that? But I should have done something about this before because I was fully aware the engines were bad and were eating coal. Jack, you were right to fall back on your wheel but then your capacity was reduced and the rent did not reflect that reduction. You should have let go many more of the workers at just that point. We have to balance everything in a mill and take a longer view, than the length of a piece of cloth. Because that can be measured with a rule of any other physical kind, even a tenter frame, if it's marked out properly. Waterproof paint as well so as not to be rubbed off.'

'James?' said Matthew quietly. 'You have forgotten what you were talking about. What conclusions have you come to about the mill in Water Lane?'

'Oh. Just that we should have intervened before this time, well I should. Well I should have taken action sooner but then I have been preoccupied with the dyes you see? So Jack and Joe have to - will have to – what we've seen the books I mean –

probably. They're going to be insolvent and have to settle as bankrupts.'

'Well thank you then James,' said John Bateson curtly. 'As if this was not what we already knew this morning. It's nearly supper time and that is as far as you have got.'

Matthew's wife spoke up then. 'Now father sir. That's not fair. James has explained it well and we can now see it was inevitable. So that is some comfort I suppose.'

'Not to me,' said Jack darkly. 'He is saying he could have come and blathered at me and saved us all from ruin. All he's doing is saying " I told you so".'

'Yes,' said Joe, 'glad to defend Jack (and himself). 'And with a long wind as well. If he knows everything, then he can tell us what to do next, I would suppose.' Nancy rested her chin on her hand and sighed. James took Joe's comment quite literally.

'Yes. You need to declare insolvency, unless one of two things happens. Matthew and I have discussed this already and I know that Nancy agrees. And Jane. The first is that father and his partners lend you an unknown and large amount of funds so that you can pay all your creditors and avoid formal bankruptcy. Then you will both have to come back into his employ and labour in the village. The second is that you can find another company to take on the remainder of the lease, and your workers and so on, looms and machinery, who can fund a new engine, or new engines I should have said, and then you have to work for them as managers or labourers for hire – or come back into employ with us.' Jack was purple and Joe watched his brother in alarm. But James concentrating on balancing his pencil on his thumb went on oblivious. 'But those things are unlikely at the present time and if you are insolvent, you have to become bankrupt and come back to the village....'

'You little bastard,' spat Jack. 'You have nothing to say but that we are done for and must work for you. I would throw myself in the river before that ever happened.'

John Bateson, shocked at his son's venom and bewildered at James' revelation that the whole matter had been spoken of between every significant member of the House, except himself, began to breath heavily and unjustly glared at his third son.

'Wait, wait,' begged Matthew, now on his feet, 'Just sit down Jack. Don't use such words before our wives please. And hear him out. We must all sit down. I know where he is going with this. Just wait. Get to the point, do James, do try to focus. Or shall I finish?'

'That might take less time and at least have a point, Matthew,' remarked John Bateson without feeling.

James, puzzled and hurt, shook his head at Jack, glanced briefly at his father and met a cold stare, and raised his hands to Joe so much as to say, look I am reasonable - but Joe looked away. He looked at Matthew who nodded. So he did carry on, as they had agreed, because coming from James, the idea would be challenged and all the various solutions properly considered by those involved.

'And after the matter is finalised, then Joe will be able to begin in business and re found the company making cloth here. Which is to say,' he said quickly in case his brothers were angry at this final suggestion, misjudging completely the effect of his words, 'that you Jack can do what you are best at and Joe can continue his training and manage the accounts and any contracts or investments. I'm sorry if that upsets you,' he added at the end, reading his brothers' faces quite wrong. Matthew added, 'and for that Jack? Joe? We will be able to give you support and some funding. We cannot just now relieve you and to be honest, and James is too kind to say it, we would be foolish to do so. We certainly cannot take over the mill and provide the investment it needs to be profitable. But in a smaller venture then we can assist and indeed, I am certain that Beverley and some others would be interested too. But that is for the future and the coming months are going to be very difficult.'

Joe took one deep breath and his breathing eased but Jack appealed one last time to his father, who shook his old head at his favourite son though it hurt his heart to do so.

Nancy saw the time was ripe to bring up one other point. 'Matthew, have you told the Maister about the debt to Jeremiah? Can we find a way to moderate that? It seems a pity that we cannot ease things with negotiations.'

'You can try Nancy if you like. Try to speak to your father perhaps and then maybe Jeremiah will wait. But I understand he is under pressures of his own. I firmly insist that all the local traders and the people we work among must have their bills paid before the crisis comes. But if we could hold off the coal bill that might give us more time.'

John Bateson said, 'John Lupton? You have sat silent this day. You've come in the place of your father. What would he think if he was asked to plead for more time from Jeremiah Walker?'

John Lupton blanched. 'No sir. I would not ask that. If I told you that his response to an invitation tonight was ill natured, it would be something less than accurate. Not I for that work. Maybe my sister Nancy. But I would not like to do such a thing. And I know that Jeremiah is not a free man here. Hebdin's widow wants her portion and settlement. If Hebdin were still here it might be different. But I know for certain that Jeremiah is fast calling in all his debts and there will be a few that struggle to pay them.' He nodded vaguely at Jack. 'So unless my sister can work some magic, I think there is no likelihood of mercy on this.'

'You don't think,' enquired Matthew's wife softly, 'that here if ever there was, is a chance for you to show your loyalty to the House of Bateson? Is there not something to be gained, for you?'

John Lupton sucked his lips and frowned. It was true. He had much to gain with Sarah Bateson's hand not won, and much to lose. But still he shook his head in realistic understanding of his father's words to him before he had come to this urgent meeting. 'See that no more money is wasted on that scoundrel; I hear he's been about the county like a gentleman riding with hounds when he should have minded his looms. Once on the brink of disaster is enough. John Bateson needs to be man enough to see the boy go down. And my boy, if ever you think to idle and be profligate, don't come to me for loans and leeway. Phsaw! Bateson's a fool and he can be a fool by himself,' - had been his father's angry pronouncements on the matter. 'Tell you what,' had said Old Tom Lupton up at the Heights, 'let him earn his living with sports, for that's what he likes to do. And tell John Bateson I said so.' And John Lupton had left his father, confused and anxious - for if the Batesons had decided to bail out son Jack, his own portion would be sore at risk. Would he take Sarah without a dowry? He had argued it all the way down the hillside and across the fields. And in the end, to his credit, he had decided, that he would.

'If only Mistress Jane! If only my father listened to me,' pleaded John Lupton, his mind again on Sarah. ' You could try Nancy? He might take note of you if you put it the right way.

He might lend a little if he was won round?' Nancy's eyes grew wide at this. John Lupton added hurriedly, ' I mean -'

'Pshaw,' said Nancy, cutting him short. 'And I know exactly what he will say. But I will go and try to bring him round. Trade is as good on debt as on credit. It's the way the world is. There is nothing wrong with debt. It's a useful commodity.'

John Lupton shook his head and looked askance at his sister Nancy.

'Debts?' said Jack, coming back into the conversation after digesting what James had said. 'Yes. And so what will happen then, with the Walkers?'

Matthew had shot him a warning glance but it was too late. John Bateson's eyes widened and he turned his head stiffly to James. James shifted uncomfortably in his hard seat. The Maister continued to regard him with eyes of ice. Then he said, 'Is there something about the Walkers in this - other than Jeremiah's coal? Might the Walkers of Wortley have been involved - more mining and spare coal - and waiting for payment for fuel? Do please explain. James. I had not realised that our friends had added coal deliveries to their business,' said the Maister with dangerous calm and composure.

James looked at Matthew and then at Nancy but both had been taken short by the sudden and disastrous revelation, and then he shook his head slightly as it seemed he would have to answer. He had begun before Matthew could stop him.

'Sir. There has been a small, er, well, quite a large amount of help needed by James Walker and Co. William Walker of course too,' he added hoping to mitigate this admission. (His father did not despise William Walker as he did James Walker). 'It has nothing to do the coal from Walker's estate. It was just some cloth we have lent to him….'

'Cloth! He's lending our cloth! My how generous we are at this time of trial! Do continue to explain boy. This is surely most interesting. As if I have not heard enough folly for one day. Now we are in league with an agency that does not honour the Cloth Hall. Heavens forfend I should live to see this day!'

James found he could not find anything else to say. A long silence ensued. John Bateson stood abruptly and pushed away his armed chair. Matthew, signing the others to remain, followed him out of the great parlour where there were further disagreeable revelations in store for the Maister.

Compassionate Mary found her grandfather later. He was sat by a sputtering wood fire in his study alongside his friend the Reverend James Wood, with grim face and random vengeful thoughts. She ran to him and put her arms round his shoulders but he did not bend to her and sat as upright and unyielding as ever.

'Grandpa, don't be sad. There is no problem that cannot be lessened, not be made right by our prayers and Our Lord's care. Is that not right, Reverend Wood?' Wood nodded and smiled. John Bateson said tiredly, 'Go to bed little one. These are not things for you to ponder. Let those of us who carry the burden deal with the load. Go! Little one, go away now.'

But Mary persisted. 'Grandpa, you are vexed with Uncle Jack and Uncle Joe, aren't you? Don't be angry with them. Think that you must but just forgive them. That is the way, is it not Reverend Wood? And then all can be right and you will feel happy again.'

'Aye, Little Wisdom. But leave your Grandpa now. He has much to think about and he needs some peaceful time to himself just now. Off you go my love. Say your prayers. Sleep well.' Wood remained with his old friend some while, quietly sat in prayer and John Bateson studied the wainscot until a late hour.

Chapter Eleven

A reason to be thankful

Not the least of the purposes of the Reverend James Wood's visitation was news of Sarah Bateson, sometime intended of John Lupton, who, as we have seen, was enjoying the raw weather and blighted moors around Halifax and tending to the education of the children of the poor. John Lupton having only very recently come to realise that he would marry her even if she came without a lump sum, was at his mill on the Beck today, watching the carters loading spun wool from his office window, leaning on the wall with hands in his pockets. Now his mind was decided, he was impatient and restless and wondered if Sarah would be able to travel home for Christmas. Or would she have found other company over the hills and choose to remain? Now he was filled with doubt and paced the room, feeling wretched. Should he saddle his horse and make for Halifax and bring her home? What would she say to such a romantic gesture? He would wait a day and keep an eye out on the weather. Perhaps tomorrow or if the weather cleared a little. But by then, who knows, it might too late! He settled moodily by the window and watched the activity in the mill yard once more, sighing occasionally.

As an itinerant, as were all the shepherds of the Methodist flock at this time, James Wood was often in Halifax, or Manchester and other parts of the realm, preaching, raising funds, and encouraging the continued growth of the Society. He was a leading light of the Methodist Conference, and he was an important and significant influence on the Methodist movement - both with his preaching and his writings. That Leeds had been the centre of much controversy over the principles of Methodism was certain and that Wood had been sent now to the area was due in no part to this debate. Alexander Kilham and his adherents advocated much that was useful but the debate had become bitter and division and discord had occurred. Wood was a peaceful and just leader and his role was to unite and to arbitrate a troubled and numerous community. But his pastoral duties were many and it was some days after the crisis family meeting that he found space to visit Wortley again and at this time John Bateson was sufficiently recovered to have interests apart from Jack's failure. Sarah had not managed to return home and John Lupton had not absolutely decided upon any kind of plan to rescue her.

'And what news of my daughter then sir? I trust she is well and happy. She is expected home for the Christmas Season but with this vile weather it might be that she should not travel. It might not be wise.'

'She is well indeed, or was so, when last I saw her. The packs will keep coming unless snow falls. Do not give up hope yet friend. Those of us that come over do not flinch because of a little ice! Or howling winds……..I do wish to mention her to you though. We have a somewhat interesting new Minister in Halifax….'

'Have you indeed! And what does such an interesting new Minister have to do with my Sarah? For example, is he young and handsome and is this to cause a further rift between myself and Mr. Lupton?'

'He is I think, a very fine young man. That he is a very good scholar and speaker I do know but of Sarah's heart I cannot say so much. That is beyond my ken. However, old friend, my advice would be for John Lupton to make sure he is here at Christmas and that he attends to Sarah should she be able to make the journey. She is a woman well worth waiting upon. I can hardly begin to relate how her service in Halifax is valued. Something I think, of her father's good sense and practical abilities, have passed to her as her inheritance. But I believe her legacy might be more than such and therefore any followers she may acquire would be well to regard her with respect – yet might more worldly ambitions recommend her to some. And then her good missions to others in a particular case.' He added almost to himself, 'and in her person I have seen her blossom whilst she has been far from home.'

'You think she might have formed, be forming another attachment? Or that she is likely to be put under pressure?'

'I cannot speak for your daughter. But the young man I have mentioned, and a stalwart young man he is, he has asked me much about her and about her background and if there is any attachment forming in all this, I must think it is perhaps from this quarter that any danger, if danger is even the correct term, interest I suppose might be the better word. If such interest must arise.'

'Humph,' said John Bateson. 'You had better call on the Luptons at the Heights then. It'll be best for you to have a word with John. He'll not want interference from me. But you have licence to guide in such pastoral matters. And who's not to say that a nice family Minister might not be something agreeable. Keep you out of my hall sir! Eating me out of house and home and always with your hat out for money!'

Wood laughed. 'Yes and so would a Minister in your own family bosom not be a continuing and unavoidable drain on the purse! Ha!'

'Ah. I had not thought of that,' lied John Bateson. 'But of course, that is right, now you mention it. And Matthew has already committed more than he should to the new chapel in these compromised times. The Lord does well by the Batesons.

Perhaps we need a miller more than we need a Minister. And John Lupton has made a good beginning for all he has the wheel and not the engine. I begin to think he will succeed in the milling trade in the end. I am moderately impressed with him. We'll give him one last chance then I think.'

'I would not interfere though John. I think between these two young people they must resolve their own path. It has I know, always been a delicate matter. Your daughter may remain in Halifax and then it is up to Mr. Lupton to decide for himself how to proceed. He might need to have a little more determination.' John Bateson nodded and pursed his lips.

Chapter Twelve

The workhouse kitchen

The night had grown colder, killing cold and a light snow began to fall. Supper had been eaten and cleared;prayers said and the household had begun to settle for the night. Matthew and his father were sat in the small parlour where there was some comfort from a coal fire.

Then there was a banging on the great oak street door. Matthew looked at his father in alarm. Good news did not come late in the evening with such battering. His father nodded expressionless and Matthew stood to answer the door. They were not gentlefolk who would leave such disturbing domestic matters to their servants. Such an urgent knock meant bad news.

But Molly had already answered the door and was ushering a dark figure dusted with snow into the warmth of the hallway – a figure that half carried, half dragged a filthy ragged bundle with him.

'Oh dearest Lord. Oh my, oh my Friend North! What art thou doing out in this and so far from home. Get in and get into the kitchen ...' Benjamin North, wool stapler, staggered on to the stone flagged hall floor and as he did so, he half dropped, half lowered his bundle onto the stones and he stood and looked at Matthew, clearly exhausted. Matthew gaped and then rushed forward. He squatted and bent over the bundle and moving aside the dirty rags that enfolded it, he saw a face. A gaunt thin face with eyes closed and a visage as white as the snow flakes that were swiftly melting away. Benjamin North stood heaving for breath by the door, his face rigid with anger and distress. Matthew looked briefly up at the Quaker, then nodded to himself. 'Molly! Quick! Get some hot water, some hot gruel. Fetch blankets!' He said this turning his head to his father who had come up behind him. For once John Bateson was not cool and inscrutable. His face showed his alarm and he nodded and called to his wife. 'Ann, come quick. Come quick my love. Fetch out some blankets. Oh dear God. What have we here?'

Gathering up the wretched bundle in his strong arms, his big hands holding the child gently, Matthew made his way, turning sideways to come through the kitchen door and with quick strides he reached the rug before the range fire. With infinite care he laid the child down before the glow and began to undo the ragged clothes. Then he held the small pale face between his great work roughened hands. 'Come on now bairn,' he said softly. 'Come on. Thou'rt safe now. Tis friends tha's found this dreadful night. Come on Molly. Get the warming pan too. Oh Lord. What times we live in. What times.' Matthew's eyes filled with water. He turned his head to hide this and took a deep breath.

Molly came and knelt beside him, her arms full of wool and she pushed Matthew away so she could tend to the child. She removed the rest of what served for clothing on the wraith. The child lay now almost naked on the heart rug but the stone flags had absorbed the heat from the day's fire and radiated that warmth into the pale limbs of a boy. She looked at the small figure as it lay pale before her, for some seconds. Then remembering herself she sprang back into action. She laid the blankets on him with gentle hands.. 'Pass me the warming pan,' she commanded roughly, and Matthew reached for it as it glowed now in the open over door. 'Some of ye buggers go fetch some bricks and we'll heat them an 'all.' While she bossed the household so, she carefully moved the brass warming pan around the blankets, careful to keep it moving but sure of her purpose. When the bricks were warmed she touched those brought near her, checked their warmth was mild, and then she placed them round the unconscious boy. Matthew stood nearby willing the child to come round and cursing the elements and those who had brought a child to such a pass on such a night as this.

Benjamin North too, had been brought into the kitchen to be revived and he was sat in the wooden armchair by the hearth, watching the household as they worked. He nodded occasionally. John Bateson stood beside the chair his hand on North's shoulder. He said quietly:

'Well my friend. What is this you have brought us this day?' North looked up at the old Clothier.

'Wait till I tell you Friend John. Oh, here's a sorry tale to be certain.'

'You have done right I think to seek help with us – I am one of the parish officers, but you must have passed many a house coming down? I trust you have not come from Silver Royd to Greenside on this foul night and with such a - such a charge.' John Bateson narrowed his eyes a fraction.

'My Friend - no. I was coming home from up Armley and in this way coming you understand. But when I came to Moorside I saw Smyth's man with this, with this poor waif. So I asked him what he was a- doing, dragging an urchin around and the child hardly able to stand. And he did curse me. He said he had been to thy workhouse. Yes, here in Wortley. And that he had hammered on the door and no light being on and no answer being made he was away back up the hill to leave his – his   - I've seen many things over the years John, but this I will never forget. And the anger of the man for the child and to me too! And he himself wrapped in his cloak and a shawl and with his boots too, against the cold of the night! What inhumanity friend. The world is changing. And he passing every house with lights on and a fire in the hearth!' North shook his head now and bent it to his chest.

John Bateson went to his dresser and set to work making a pot of tea for North. And as he collected the tin of leaves, the pot mugs and found the sugar he spoke to his friend's bowed head. Molly continued to tend the body on his rag rug before the fire and Peter, Matthew's man came through the doorway with an arm full of dry logs for the fire. Mrs. Bateson flustered and on her knees by the child, looked at Molly with stark consternation.

She said to North, 'Well now, thou knows't we have no one in yon workhouse. As does that man of Smyth's. A nasty piece he is! And thou knows't we do not intend to house the destitute in that place. The last wardens we had in were rogues and the parish made a declaration. Those in urgent need must go to the nearest of our brethren or thine.'

'Aye. I knowst that. But I thought I could make it here and that this house would have the fires that could save this unfortunate soul. The lights of thy house were clear and many were abed already for the cold night, the windows barred and all dark within.'

'For pity's sake. For that fool to take this poor soul up again to Armley and so many houses would have taken him in. I am not often vexed my Friend. But I am now.' John Bateson was indeed very angry. His face did not change but his fingers gripped the edge of his kitchen table. He was startled when his wife came and took over the tea things.'Sit down man. I'll do this. You'll break the cups you're that fierce.'

The workhouse in Wortley had been difficult to staff. If the outcome of community care was that the poor soul in need was nursed back to life but then transferred to the Leeds Workhouse was not an issue.

John Bateson shook himself and found an old stool and placed it carefully beside North's chair. He put his hand upon North's arm and said with kindness.'You must sleep here the night my Friend. Now, no protests. Tomorrow in the light you can get home. But you are done for now and in need of shelter yourself I know. You must accept our hospitality tonight. Ann will make up a bed for you.' Mrs. Bateson looked up and nodded firmly. 'And we'll go away into my parlour when you're warmed. You might be able to give some of your wisdom to current difficulties.' Benjamin North looked up and nodded. He looked at the group around the cold body and then sighed. 'Aye then my dears. I'll be here the night and pray for this little soul out of the storm. God bless you John Bateson.'

Behind the old men, a group had gathered now and were peering through the doorway at the drama with wide eyes. The children pushed to get a better view and.Jane Bateson came from behind and yanked little Sarah and Nanny away, bidding them get back to their beds and mind their own business.

A moan was heard, coming from the child. Mary squeezed through into the kitchen and stood with her hands resting on North's chair. He turned to her and put an old gnarled hand on one of hers and smiled. She whispered in his ear. 'Will he die Friend North? Die here. I mean in our kitchen? On the rug?'

'The Lord gives and the Lord takes away Mary Bateson. It will be as the Lord wills it.'

John Bateson said 'not if Molly can help it it would seem.'

The pale child half opened his eyes. Molly put her pudgy arm beneath the boy's shoulders and raised him slightly and carefully. 'There there me darling. What's tha called? See, here thou art all safe and warm an 'all. Where does tha come from little mite.' The child again tried to open his eyes. Molly bent her ear close to his mouth and listened., Then with some triumph she turned to Matthew. 'His name is Dan. I think so anyway. He said that - didn't he sir, tha heard it didn't tha? She announced to the gathered family and their servants. 'His name is Dan. Daniel probably – and he says he's from Burree.'

One of the stable boys had got a good position looking through the legs of the folk in the doorway. He gasped and his eye were huge. 'It's French,' he cried. 'He's a Frenchie!'

There was a wave of consternation with shaking of heads and astonished faces. Mutters of spies and invasion foreigners in their midst.

Benjamin North stood with his tea mug held firmly in his hand and he turned to those in the doorway. 'Bury,' he boomed. 'Bury. In Lankyshire. Boy's come over the hills, he has. From Bury.'

John Bateson said, 'If this is - an invasion of the French I think we have little to fear then! Now get off the lot of you and see to your own business So many idle hands in this house.' Reluctantly the household dispersed.

When James Wood arrived back at Greenside the house was still awake. Molly was on guard over a small body lain by the kitchen hearth. Benjamin North was closeted with John Bateson who had welcomed the solace of a man of North's faith and good standing for the plight of Jack weighed heavily on him.

Reverend Wood took off his snow dusted cloak and hat in the hallway then peered through into the kitchen. 'My God, Molly, who is this. A child? What is happening in this house tonight?'

'It's alright sir. It's been a bad night. Can't get much worse is the truth of it. But look! A little boy come out of the storm.

Poor babe. Poor babe.' Molly caressed the child's head, and the limp dark hair.. Wood came and bent to look at the patient. Molly plaintive, 'He won't die, doest tha think sir? Not here on my floor,' she pleaded looking at her pastor in the eye as if such a thing would be very unreasonable.

Molly the indentured servant had served here for so many years. She had remained unmarried but she was not oblivious to her maternal instincts. These had been met, all had thought, by John Bateson's children and grandchildren. Yet here, on this dark and bitter night, had come a child with no parent, no carer. A child naked on her kitchen hearth with no other to protect him save herself. So it seemed to her. Through the long night she nursed the foundling. When colour returned to his skin she warmed some water and bathed him gently. As the child lay stripped and naked on the hearth rug she had known love that she had never felt before. His thin pale body was born to her, that night in the kitchen at Greenside. When a fever came during the next day, Molly sent the daily girl running for the physician who came immediately to such a prosperous household and Molly answered the door and hustled the doctor into the kitchen. She watched closely at the man's arm, to make sure that the doctor did do no harm, tucking back into place the wool blanket and smoothing the dark hair.

'Well now.' said the physician, after examining the patient. 'He has a fever for sure. And is malnourished certainly.'

'So what can I do?' begged Molly fervently.

'Keep him warm. Make broth. Beef broth. Or chicken. Yes, chicken broth. Bread soaked in milk. The fever will leave him or he will leave this world. Perhaps that would be a mercy.' When Molly cried out at this he moderated his words. 'But be sure my dear, good sustenance will avail. Feed him up. Yes, I think good food will serve here.'

'Oh thanks to thee sir…....I will, God help me. I will see he gets what he needs.' The doctor hesitated in the hallway. 'Is your mistress within,' he asked carefully, unsure of his fee. 'She is sir, she is. But she's well, thanking thee, and no need of thy help! Thanks to thee for coming doctor. Well. Goodbye then.' The physician had no choice but to take his hat which Molly held out to him and to turn and leave. As he trudged home across the frozen lane he was puzzled at to when his bill might be settled.

   Molly had lost no time. She threw her shawl round her shoulders and braved the frost rimmed stones of the yard as she set off in search of a chicken for her broth with her knife in hand.

As the boy recovered his wits and could answer the questions that she, Molly, had asked of him, it transpired that he was the only surviving child of an Irish woman. His mother had lost her husband and her other children in Lancashire. She had vowed that her last surviving child would not die enslaved in the cotton mills of Salford. With little in her purse and less on her back, she had brought herself and her son across the mountains with the pack ponies that carried much of the wool trade across the hills from one county to another. But she had caught a fever and had succumbed somewhere west of Bradford. The pack horse men had brought the child to Leeds but left him in Armley, thinking that the child might be taken into shelter in the workhouses. But his mother's advice had echoed in his head. 'Run from the workhouse Danny. Run away if you can. Get thyself into the wool trade darling. Listen to me. Never think of cotton. Get into the wool trade. I may not live much longer. Promise me my love. Leeds. Get into a factory in Leeds.' His mother had then sunk low and struggled for breath. 'Leeds,' she said and it was her last word before she died.

'Was – was thy, thy mother, was she a Papist?' asked Molly with consternation and excitement. 'Was she?'

'Yes Molly. Me ma was Catholic. I ain't gonna deny her now tha knows. Indeed no. Bless me ma, Molly. Do bless her. She gave her life for me on that journey over the hills. Me, I'm Papist too. '

'Oh!' murmured Molly, more entranced than ever. 'Oh, that is – interesting.' She had nearly said 'exciting' but that didn't seem decent. She thrust a bowl into the Dan's hands and commanded, 'here, eat this. It's rabbit pie.'

Chapter Thirteen

Old Tom

On a bitterly cold day in the dark of December, when the country was so frozen that trade was at a standstill, for the convoys could not sale under Naval escort to Brussels and the other trading ports of Europe, due to the great frost in the harbours, Nancy set off from the Weaving House at Wortley Town End, walking first towards Jubbergate and then climbing by the dry stone walls of the fields over the frost hard paths of the Township. She took with her a manservant laden with a basket that he slung over his back in which were cheeses and a half ham from the village. 'He still won't help James' she had told her husband. 'It don't matter how much cheese you send him. He'll have had wind of the Walker affair and he'll have made his made up about Jack before today.'

'Well do what you can. You're not his favourite child for nothing are you? And just think, if he's adamant about Jack failing, then at least the cheese will see that he has sleepless nights! The old bugger.' Nancy eyed James balefully. 'Now now,' she scolded. 'You'll be old one day yourself and should have a little more sympathy to a poor old man. Should but won't of course. Not enough imagination.'

'Get off with you woman,' he said fastening her cloak for her, wrapping her shawl over her hat, and then stealing a kiss from her laughing mouth.

Nancy took off her outer wrappings in the hallway as her step mother came rushing from the back kitchen with a beaming smile. They embraced and Nancy, still shivering opened the door and went into her father.

'Come to see an old man, are you? About time too. And not brought me grandchildren I see. So what do you want then Mrs Bateson. Dear Lord, you've got cold hands!' Nancy bent to give her old father a kiss on his ruddy, stubbled cheek. She smiled as she pulled his neck cloth straight and patted him on the head. Taking a seat by the fire and arranging her fine wool skirt around her, she reached out her cold hands to the inadequate warmth of the log fire.

Her step mother spoke. 'Now Father, now then. How could Nancy bring the children out on such a day as this? She's right to come alone. And you'll be glad when you see what James Bateson has sent up from his larder.'

'Sent us summat. Gifts is it? He'll be wanting something I'll be bound.' He chuckled and then his face darkened as a thought crossed his mind. He took his stick and banged it on the floor. 'Is that hussy Sarah home yet Nancy? Is she? And if she is, you go down and tell our John,' he waved his stick in the general direction of Wortley, 'time they twos were getting it sorted out.' His tone changed abruptly. He leant forward and said with a hiss, 'it's about that idle bugger Jack, ain't it? It's been all about the place – didn't you say woman, he's been living like a lord and not minding his shop.' Old Tom looked at his wife accusingly.

'Woman? Mind your manners old man.' Tom tutted.

'So daughter. Are you come to borrow money. Again.' He leant back and glared at Nancy.

Nancy made herself more comfortable in her chair, now stretching out her boots before the fire and she turned to Mrs. Lupton. 'John's doing well there Mother. That mill he has, is going at a pace and all the place doing nicely with his labours. Plenty of work for all the town.' She looked at her father who grunted. 'And James is very happy with it all. He says that the wheel and the flow are very nicely tuned. He thinks he did a good job with all that.'

Mrs. Lupton was not always sharp but she caught on. 'Yes Nancy. And those children of yours. Such lovely strong children. And James such a good husband.'

'Matthew's getting on with the new chapel you know. Oh, and Reverend Wood has been to us. Do you know, they're talking of a Sunday School too.'

'Are they now? Well the Lord is good to us all then m'dear.' Mrs. Lupton kept up the defence.

Old Tom chipped in. 'Word comes up the Batesons are getting an infirmary going. In their kitchen I hear. Saints aren't they.' He rolled his eyes.

Mrs. Lupton said, 'Now then father. It's always kind are the Bateson family. And honest. Or John Bateson would not have been our partner all these years past, would he now?' Then she turned to Nancy a little frown on her brow. 'But the carrier told us that there's a child there that's a Frenchie? I can't think there's a truth in that, is there?'

'No Mother. It's a little boy from Lancashire. Came over the hills with his mother and she died before they reached Yorkshire. It's a very sorry tale. But Molly is besotted with him. She won't take him out of the kitchen at all. He's on the mend now after being near frozen to death. Chicken broth he has three times a day.' Old Tom listened to this exchange. He leant forward to poke his wife with his stick and he said in a mock whisper, 'Tis a Papist woman. They Batesons got themselves an Irish orphan and a Papist he is.' Mrs. Lupton's mouth dropped open and then she stood and unable to comprehend such a dreadful thing, she raised her apron to her eyes and rushed from the room, praying to the Lord to preserve her from such dangers as these.

Old Tom laughed heartily now. 'So what is it that you are sent to ask for girl? Money? You think I'll put any money into Jack's mill? Think again. He's been feckless. He's been seen at cock fights and at boxing bouts. He's been up at Gildersome with his horses and then there's been dogs too. If he thought as much of his mill as he did of the hunting then things would not have got into this mess. And it is a mess.' Nancy made to interrupt her father but he gestured her to wait. 'I've not finished lass. And by far the best thing is for the old man to let the boy founder. Because he's not the smartest item. Oh, he does well at the cloth stand but apart from that. Gormless. John Bateson's never seen it. He's been blind. Partiality, that's what this is about. And I tell you the best of them. The best of them is Matthew. Now him I'll work with anytime. Apart from the nonsense with the Walkers, yes, I've heard about that too! Just be quiet now, and I'll finish when I've said what I have to say, and you get back and tell them Batesons as much of it as you'll think they'll like to hear. Jack Bateson won't get any leeway on the coal bills. And he'll get no more coal from Jeremiah. Can't be done, because Hebdin's wife is on the offensive. So any credit has to be from Matthew and your husband. Tell them to get a good deal up for Royds or Thwaites eve and press Smyth on it too. Because that's one gentleman who has no head for business and just wants cash. And if Jack goes bankrupt then it's the lesson he needs to learn.' Old Tom finished and put his hands on the head of his stick.

Nancy stayed put, looking at her father with her head to one side. Then she sighed. 'Well. One thing Father, I know where things stand now.' Old Tom nodded sagely. 'So I'll be off to talk to Mother in the kitchen, while you can find yourself a better frame of mind.'

'I can find me s'en a better frame of mind, but I won't be changing it.' He nodded again. Then relaxing slightly he added, 'but that man of yours girl, he's not turned out so bad, neither.'

'Oh you old rogue!' said Nancy as she went to sooth her step mothers fears of papistry in the kitchen and returning only when dinner was ready to be served in the small parlour.

Now Nancy stayed with her father. She read to him and arranged cushions for his back and his gout ridden leg and she scolded him as he loved to be scolded and entertained him as he loved to be entertained with gossip and with her insights of the world. That the frost would prevent any communication with Hamburg was a blow to the cloth trade. That the war with Revolutionary France was to be renewed and intensified was also a worry and a fear. 'Look father, what it says here, in the Intelligencer.' Nancy spread the paper on the parlour table. 'Dronfield School is to be recommended as a safe haven for the sons of gentlemen, being safely removed from the dangers of the coast -'

'Ha ha. So. Admirable advertisement! Safe indeed. As if Dronfield is a bulwark against attack. Ha! There's always profit from war. Here's to many uniforms my dear. Let your daft husband look to that and may his blue dyes continue. Get him to look into his reds.' Old Tom Lupton rubbed his hands together and Nancy tutted at his avarice.

Chapter Fourteen

Halifax Mission

    The new Minister that had come to the districts of Halifax on a wild night had made a profound impression on the Methodist communities of the valleys and the hills. This profundity was a mixture of admiration, consternation, confusion and fear. His sermons were conducted in the open air and when, as sometimes happened, he was urged to desist or to relocate his person, by the parish constables or perhaps, a rightful and hard pressed employer of the impromptu congregation, then he would would shine his ubiquitous smile and with grace, move obligingly on to whatever place he came upon next in his daily journeys. Cottage nor hall was safe from his ministrations. Chapel and school room was blessed with regular and voluble visitations. In his ministry he was enthusiastic, good natured, long suffering and brash. In many ways, Sarah Bateson was reminded of her brother James. But perhaps an inability to sense when he had outstayed his welcome and that some of his listeners had glazed eyes, was a more useful asset to a preacher than to a Clothier.

  Be that as it may, the little moorland chapels were full now and where an affluent, middling sort of family with a farm or barn were adherents, then he would with gladness conduct meetings and services for them also, being apparently inexhaustible in his desire to sustain, convert and bring salvation.

    This Sunday Sarah had come to the chapel with Mrs. Humbold and she watched with delight as Mr. J. led Worship. In his simple black cloth he stood to lead his flock and his bass voice rang out the hymns and the psalms. The verses of his chosen text were given extra power by his deep, melodious voice, and his loud and persuasive declamation.

And by his handsome features.

A young woman crammed next to Sarah in the packed chapel nudged her in the ribs. And sighed. Sarah had already joined her voice with the family in prayer at first light. She had been once already along the lane to the Chapel. This was the second gathering of the short late autumn day. Her mind wandered.

Reverend J. had been to call on Mrs. Humbold more often than was strictly necessary for the spiritual well being of the already God fearing household. Only this Saturday had he arrived very early in the morning to save their souls, perhaps believing the he had not completely succeeded only a few days since. Striding the hills of the moorlands gave a man an appetite and Mrs. Humbold had a good store of hams and cheeses. But this might not have been the main attraction to the farmstead.

'Why Miss Bateson!' exclaimed the visitor as he entered without knocking on the door, throwing off his cloak and hat and making for the fire side with purposeful stride. 'I hope I have the honour of seeing you well this morning?'

'Oh! Here you are again Mr. J. Please sit down. Would you care for some tea?' enquired Sarah with a resigned air.

'I would! I would indeed - and thank you kindly. And I hope I have not interrupted any important work. What are you writing there, if I may be so bold? It does my heart good,' and he emphasized heart, 'to see a young woman that is so diligent, so industrious and accomplished, so completely considerate of the feelings of others.

'It's just a letter home. I write at least once a week -as a good daughter should.'

'Good. Yes, you are good. I have seldom met with such a dutiful young woman. Such service you do for the Lord in bringing the Word of Salvation to the little ones! God be Praised! And where we would be without such as you. The women of the Connection are the second power -'

'Yes just so.'

'And after tea is drunk, we can pray together. Would you like that Miss Bateson. Or may I call you,' he hesitated to good effect, 'may I call you Sarah?'

'Call me what you like sir. My name is Sarah and I'm not one for ceremony. As I could have hoped you already knew.'

'Ah, Sarah. What a beautiful name. A biblical name. Is it perchance a family name also?' Sarah gave a perfunctory nod. 'Ah what good fortune you have had to be born to such a faithful family. Yes, the old names are the best. Mary and Sarah and Martha.' Sarah said under her breath with her eyes on her half written page, 'Jezebel, Eve, Delilah.' Mr. J.'s face fell for a moment then he gave a hearty laugh. 'Oh ha ha ha, Miss -, I mean Sarah. But I have heard so much good from the Reverend Wood, a man I do esteem most highly I might tell you, of this family of yours. I understand your brother is a staunch pillar of support in your village-'

'Township. It's a township.'

'Township. Yes of course. You must forgive me. In your Township - and your father too, a great source of financial provision for the mission of the movement. Why, I count myself most fortunate, most fortunate, to have met even such a small branch of this family such as yourself -'

'Small?' queried Sarah.

'Dainty. Delicate. A flower of a branch of the true and enlightened faith. And so strong in the faith herself. A true worker in the vineyard. I am minded of -'

'I am minded that the kettle has boiled. Please sit down Mr. J. You are making me dizzy.' Mr. J. had been from his seat and had been engaged in pacing the flagged floor in the relentless zeal of his social call. He took his seat and nodded agreeably at Sarah as she made the necessary arrangements for the brewing of a pot of tea. His eyes followed her as she moved about the kitchen preparing the milk and the cups, but he was unable to bridle his tongue for such a length of time.

'How gracefully you move about the home. Sarah. How the true heart does show itself in the outer form! Why I do delight in watching you perform these domestic duties! Wait! Wait even now I begin to feel a purpose in this moment. I believe that I can make a sermon -'

'Sugar?' enquired Sarah.

'Oh. Er yes. Two sugars if you please. Now, where was I -'

'Somewhere between Halifax and Sowerby I suppose.' interjected Sarah quickly.

He laughed with delight. 'Oh you jest with me. Sarah. Oh how sharp are your wits and this I love to say. Sarah, this is such a fine name. I do delight in -'

'Cake?'

'Cake. Yes, indeed, I would like a slice of fruit cake if that might be possible. Indeed I have not eaten, nor drunk this day and my fast has not been broken. I was at prayer by first light and so I did not perchance feel the need for more earthly sustenance -' Sarah did then sigh, quite loudly and with feeling.

'- but no matter, now I am sustained and feel that God has led my feet across the slough, to a good place. So is the light of my faith rewarded although I am a sinner and my soul is dark as foul night. But should I seek to hold a true heart, then it may flourish with heaven's grace and with humble love and constant communion with the Lord.'

The was a brief silence as the Reverend J. demolished as slice of Mrs. Humbold's fruit cake.

Sarah watched him as his even, white teeth bit into the yielding sustenance and she thought of the respect, fire, passion and constancy that were the requirements of her hand and love. She contemplated in this brief interlude; the impact of bringing a fiery Methodist Minister home to Wortley. So good was the cake that she had time to carelessly imagine the handsome children, dark haired and bright eyed. Adonis- like children. He was a very handsome man. She was considering the consequences of letting loose such enthusiastic evangelism on her obsessive Uncle James and she realistically imagined a conversation between them. Which made her laugh out loud.

'Sarah! You are so happy. What joy to hear your sweet and innocent laughter. You cannot know how this works on me. What thoughts are in my mind.'

Sarah, having been wooed with inconsistent ardour for some time by feckless John Lupton, immediately was on her guard and her feet. She thought that she did know what thoughts were in his mind. A child raised in the country way knows all that needs to be known about such matters. She was an intelligent and perceptive follower of Christ and so she made plans for escape to the hallway or the outer door, should such a thing become unfortunately imperative but left the final decision until she should know which of the ways would be blocked to her.

'Is it time for prayer then Reverend J? Let's get it over with then, I mean - please begin.'

But he stood and approached her and began to fall to his knees. Sarah was good Methodist. She fell to her knees also and bowed her head and joined her hands. Their heads touched, she had misjudged her position in her haste to ensure prayer was the next event of the day. But she did not look up. She remained in attitude of religious duty with mainly downcast eyes. A swift and cunning peep assured her that the minister had closed his bright, dark eyes. And she was keenly aware of his proximity, his manly essences which were pleasant enough, bearing in mind his exertions over the moorland. I think that even at this point that the Reverend J. might have won his cause. In this situation, she was I fear, sorely tempted to at least the indiscretion of a minor sin but that she suspected that would be taken as token of admiration and surrender.

There were then prayers and Sarah endured these as best she might. His person and immediacy proved a great distraction and her mind was momentarily confused. When the time came to say Amen she mechanically repeated the final word, hardly aware of herself now. And the Reverend J. seized the moment and took her hand in his and then pressed it firmly to indicate his regard for her.

'Sarah. Lovely Sarah. Please -' Reverend J. faltered. All credit to Sarah that her sudden frank gaze and expression had daunted him. But he made a rapid recovery.

'I have such respect and admiration for you that I must beg your pardon for what I am about to suggest. I find that my regard for you is great, vast, unmanageable. I feel for you such respect that I am hard pressed to put it into words that convey the sincerity of my feelings. That I am truly impressed by your person and your abilities. I know that I am as nothing to you and that our acquaintance has been but all too brief - but even then would I plead my cause. If you could just give some consideration of my plea. Could give me some hope to think that my dreams might be answered and that our paths in this weary world could be aligned. I dare not say it! But yes, I must. My heart will burst if I do not speak out my honest intentions. I would become - your husband - if this should be possible. Be acceptable. Give me leave to speak to your father! A most respectful -'

Sarah stood and yanked her hand from his. She had not been born to such a family as hers without being able to see the absurdity of their present postures.

'Dear friend. Please stop. I am promised to another. This must not be said and I may not listen to it. I have a betrothed sweetheart already and you must not say any more.' She nodded firmly and took several steps away from her voluble would be suitor.

The rejected gentleman stood and with melancholy visage also stepped back and took his seat in the fireside chair with a thump motion that suggested accurately the heaviness of his tender heart. But then he gathered his strength, rose, smiled and said, 'Ah, I know this is what you must say. It is the demur that must be given by the honest maid! I have been too forward I think. You have been so good to hear my overtures and so I take my leave and abandon you to your labours. I trust in the Lord!'

From this difficult and somewhat embarrassing interview Sarah was relieved by the arrival of Mrs. Humbold who was accustomed to the young minister inhabiting her humble farm kitchen and she proceeded to make him welcome with the hams and the cheeses that were also dear to his heart. He also was rescued from his need to leave and so Sarah did as any young woman in her situation would do; made some excuse and hid in her lodging rooms above, only to be called down by her hostess who had been urged pragmatically to so so.

The man of God was intelligent and occasionally perceptive. He took his leave with passionate humility and also took the liberty of again taking Sarah's hand and applying affectionate pressure to it. All this gave Sarah a great deal to occupy her thoughts. She stayed a while and watched form the low windows as the dark figure strode away across the moors. Then she fetched her writing desk from her chamber and took up her quill pen and she wrote with a mixture of confused feelings.

Dearest John,
I will be returning home for Christmas as you may already know and as is planned. I am well and I trust that you are also. It has been very cold here and I fear that the journey may be difficult. If I am delayed by inclement weather I will write again so that you may keep me in your thoughts.
Make sure to be at home then and I trust we will meet at my father's house in the New Year. We have much to talk about.

Your most loving betrothed,
Sarah Bateson.

Chapter Fifteen

A homecoming.

It was the custom in these rural parts of Yorkshire for a Yule Log to be found which was then brought into the house and burned in the old inglenooks of the county yeomanry. Oak was best, but Ash also burnt with good flame and heat. At Greenside the ash log was brought into the Out Kitchen and used there, rather than in the house proper, since there were so many little children that would come to bring Christmas Greetings to their grandfather.

The good things that had been laid by during the harvest were there in plenty; there were the ales, the pies and the preserved meat. The mill cow allowed that butter was in abundance and fresh bread was baked more than once that week.

At the old house at Greenside though, there was a sombre air which cast a cloud on the celebrations. This mainly emanated from Maister John Bateson. He sat morosely dwelling on the stupidity of his favourite son and the betrayal of his eldest son in the matter of the Walker cloth. Of James's part in all this he thought little good but such was what he expected of the boy. At least the fool had a competent guardian in his wife Nancy Lupton. And, as John Bateson could admit in better times, was the father of his true male heir.

John Bateson had amassed much wealth when he began with scribbling and fulling by the Beck. but much of it had already been allocated to his children; in his daughters' marriage dower and in his sons' business enterprises. Only his youngest, Sarah, would need further provision and if this should go to John Lupton, as her betrothed husband, then it would as good as find its way into the pockets of Old Tom Lupton and that made John Bateson sour because he knew now that Tom Lupton thought ill of his son Jack.

However he was spared by natural paternal bias, the fact that he would have done exactly the same to James. And also if Thomas Lupton junior or any other of that family had foundered in business a second time then he too he would have been left to suffer the consequences. But John Bateson was troubled. In his waking he would argue that he should now pay Jeremiah Walker and the other major creditors of his second son, but by the end of the long day, as the light faded and the revelry of the children wore him down, he would harden his heart and renew his resolution that Jack must take the consequences of his actions, be they what they may. His son Joseph was much in his eye now, for if there was insolvency then of course, Joseph would have to be the one that took over the accounts and business deals. Joseph would be the one to start up in business and support Jack. There was hope in this. An ideal of Master Joe grew in his mind.

The grand children however, had much joy in the season. There were daily prayers and other more secular ceremonies with the lighting of the new flame, the singing of carols, and such treats and delights as might be had in the better households of the Principal Inhabitants of Wortley. Mince pies and gingerbread, frumenty and fruit cake were shared and gorged upon and the family were not solemn as John Bateson believed they should be. And this too made him sour.

'Leave the little ones be, old man,' said his wife Ann Bateson firmly. 'It's not they who have made the losses. Let them be happy and get your boots on! We'll make our calls today and I won't hear no, no I won't John Bateson. There's folk suffering more than you with your pride. Foolish pride.'

She plonked his boots beside him with little ceremony. 'I'll not have people say we did not take ourselves abroad in the Christmas Season and do our duty. And if you think to miss the Service at the Chapel tomorrow – think again!' She scolded him to the door, put his stick smartly in his hand, and wrapping his cloak about his shoulders she propelled him out of the door and away across the frozen ground to partake of the social activities that were required. And as they walked she continued to berate him and those abroad in the bitter night air smiled to see the old man so harangued and so capably led.

Sarah Bateson arrived just after Christmas having been snowed up at the time she had planned her journey home. Even in the brief interval between the storms, the road was treacherous, sheeted with black ice and full of danger. But the pack ponies were ever passing through the old lanes and paths and it was by such a route that Sarah made her way home, on a steady, calm mare. She was accompanied by a clothier and his wares and so reached Birstall by late afternoon where the caravan reached its destination. She called upon her friends in that district to provide a loan pony, see to her horse and a manservant who was to accompany her through the woods of Farnley and down the causeway to the twinkling, welcoming lights of the houses and cottages of Wortley Township. It was to her a joyful sight but she was weary and shaken from such a long and cold ride.

'Father! Ann! Oh dear, such a long ride. My hands are frozen and I can't feel my fingers. I am spent, quite done.' She had enough strength left to her to embrace the family, one by one as they came to the thresh hold at the disturbance of her arrival.

'Dear child, come in now and get set by the fire. Move away Mary and Anne. Nanny! Stop that. How long have you ridden and what weather have you seen on top of those moors?'

'We did not think to see you come at all. Even the ships cannot get out of Hull and yet by some miracle you have made it across from Halifax. Lord deliver us from both!' Matthew greeted his sister with an embrace and a kiss and the family gathered around her, anxious for all the news of Halifax and sharing the warmth of the family again together.

Of course, Jack was missing from most clan gatherings. He had met with his family at the Chapel one morning and had been sober which was something of a relief. He had remained at his lonely house in Holbeck, beside the mill, and was resolved without reason, to try and make what attempts he could to restore his mill and his trade.

But John Lupton, son of Old Tom and affianced lover of Sarah Bateson had been much within the old house at Greenside. Sarah had greeted him next day with sincere warmth and kindness and although the household had taken care that they should only meet within company, or perhaps because of this, the couple had so far exchanged only good natured conversation and pleasant remarks. But this evening they had a little space to themselves within the great parlour.

'Sarah, I'm rite glad to see thee!'

'Aye John. And it is good to be back home. And to see thee of course. Tell me, how does it go at the mill? My brothers have told me already, that the orders are going well and that thy brothers have increased their production. This is good isn't it?'

'What do you mean Sarah. Can I hope I mean?' John Lupton sat beside her and spoke in a low voice that was only for her ears.

'Perhaps. I am giving it my best thought. Maybe. If tha should meet me by the Beck tomorrow. That is if it is not snowing. Or raining. If the weather is suitable I will be there in the morning. Of all this tha may be quite certain.' John Lupton became confused.

'Of the weather? He said. But of thy coming down to meet me? Will tha come or no?'

Sarah smiled. 'I'll come if tha will John.' He put his mouth close to her ear. 'What time?' he whispered hopefully.

'Let me see. After breakfast. Thou art always better after tha's got a full belly. Or no, wait. After lunch is perhaps best. Best make double sure you can think straight. But if it is cold I might not come....breakfast, lunch, dinner maybe? And the weather?'

'Oh Sarah! Please don't. Don't tease me.'

'Tha's getting smart with tha years John Lupton. If we wait tha may yet come to have grown some matter between these two great jugs that adorn thy face so well.'

John Lupton reached a hand to his ears and then seeing Sarah's sly smile, put his hands back to his lap sheepishly.

Seeing some of this and knowing something of the couple, Matthew's wife smiled and distracted the company by calling for music so that those by the fireside this evening might not mark the pair as they renewed their courting.

The day dawned fine. Weak sunshine lit the ice bound lane and a hoar frost gave adornment to the stones and bare branched trees. Chipping the ice from the lattice, Sarah peered from the window at the weather and decided that she would be able to meet with John Lupton. If he fails to come, she thought to herself, that will decide matters. This is his moment and he must rise to the occasion. Although she dressed with haste in the cold of her chamber she chose a becoming mantle and skirt for her intention and arranged her hair with care for her intended. Molly was in the small kitchen inside the house

'Tha's looking nice today Miss Sarah. That's a nice bodice. Is it new?'

'What this? No it's not new!. It's not very new anyway. I made it last summer and I have worn it lots. But thanks to thee anyway,' she said a little crossly.

' Alright, don't snap. I was just admiring thy dressmaking. But it's not like tha's any calls to make today, is it? Nothing special planned I'll reckon. Just thought tha might lend a hand at the bakin' that's all!'

Little Anne was there, drinking milk and eating her bread and butter companionably with Molly. She sniggered. Sarah blushed. A sudden commotion in the stable yard distracted Molly and Little Anne from their quarry and took them scurrying to the doorway. A strange gentleman had clattered in on quite a good horse and was dismounting there with energy. John Bateson had heard the hooves and came from his study to investigate and so was in the hall passage when the stranger was met at the door by Molly. He was obviously a clergyman and so she opened the door wide and greeted him with a civil tongue. 'Morning sir to thee. Is it church business then?' and then with a astonished expression remained like a statue with her hand outstretched for the young man's hat and cloak.

'Good morning, Yes and no. I have called to pay my respects to the family. I am a friend of Miss Bateson. From Halifax - and am come to Leeds as my duties have led me here. Although the journey has been as trial of endurance, with much of it on foot until I came to Pudsey and was there brought to the town by carrier's care. A Blessing on the good man for I was nigh well half perished with the frost and the rigours of the road....'

Molly had permitted the man to enter and he began to take off his outer cloak as he continued his introduction. 'Is Miss Bateson at home today. Yes? Please give her my greetings and say that Reverend J. has called. Thank you so much. And God bless you my dear' Molly stood astounded holding his hat and cloak as the minister took possession of the hallway, lost for words and daunted by the confident demeanour of the tall, dark stranger, and by his claim to have called on her Miss Sarah.

Sarah had heard some of this from the kitchen and she peered around the door frame, and was spotted before she could escape.

'Oh Miss Bateson! How fortunate this is that I have been able to travel the roads – and without mishap too – and have found you. What blessings abound in this day! Sarah, how are you? I trust I find you well. Christmas greetings to you. Where are your family? Come, you must introduce me to them all. I have heard so much about them -' Sarah found herself shaken vigorously by the hand. All her thoughts of John Lupton had vanished and she allowed herself to be brought from the kitchen and pulled towards the visitor who had taken charge of her person with his usual enthusiasm. She recovered herself and said faintly but with a hint of urgency in the direction of her father who remained in the shadows of the hallway, 'Mr. J. how, how pleasant to see you? Let me introduce you to my father. Father. Father! This is the Reverend J. He is stationed in Halifax. Oh my goodness.'

John Bateson studied his daughter with narrowed eyes and just the hint of small smile. Then turning to the young minister, he said, 'Come in sir. Our house is open to you as a minister of the faith. Come into the parlour here where it is warm so that we can become acquainted. Perhaps there is some assistance that is needed.' John Bateson said, under his breath, 'as if often the case.' But he turned and looked back at Sarah. 'Sarah?' he enquired with raised eyebrow. Molly meanwhile remained transfixed in the hallway. The gentlemen had entered the parlour and Sarah hesitated before following them. 'Oh my God,' muttered Molly, 'what a handsome fellow.' And then she looked at Sarah with a mixture of consternation, admiration and shock. Sarah frowning, shook her head and followed slowly in a state of some distress.

The minister was some time engaged with John Bateson and Sarah and was joined then by Jane Bateson, by her children (all four of them) and at last, by the mistress of the house, Mrs. Bateson. The four granddaughters hung on the backs of the chairs and Anne was especially bold and once or twice left her step grandma's chair to take a closer look at the new young Reverend. They were soon under his spell. As the minutes ticked by Sarah became increasingly confused and wretched. John Lupton would be making his way to their assignation and she could not leave to meet him! But fortunately for her, John Bateson managed to find a space in the proceedings to halt the monologue of their guest and he stood, quite abruptly, and said to the hero, 'Well sir and glad we are to meet you.' He held up a hand to silence his prey. 'But we are known here for our hospitality to our men of God, and so -' He again indicated that he would not be interrupted. 'My daughter Sarah will take you around the place now that you may know about the village and the people here, because, I am sure, you must want to know much more about Wortley and our activities. Sarah! Take your "friend" for a walk. You must excuse me. I have much in hand.' And at this point John Bateson dismissed his present household with a slight wave of his hand and walked rapidly out of the room.

Sarah's heart sank. With some trepidation she also left, to equip herself to walk out as her father had directed. Some minutes later she led her friend across the lane and towards the Chapel which was far from the Beck and from her now abandoned John Lupton. The minister walked at her side and made several attempts to take her arm which Sarah with alacrity resisted. It was enough that the villagers would see her walking with a strange young men, even though he was dressed in his clerical black and she though that her father had been especially capricious in forcing such a situation, without he laid public claim to her person.

'Sarah. I have so longed to be here and to see you. How I have missed your lovely person and is it not fortunate, convenient, yay, almost predestined, this meeting of ours today? Imagine my joy when I was asked to come to Leeds and preach here! I have been to Call Lane and I must tell you, although you may think me immodest, still these are things that you should know, I was received with great acclaim and the collection was remarkable. I know this will delight you. And now I am come and we can talk again.' He continued without drawing breath and Sarah walked beside him at as distant a space as courtesy would allow. She nodded her head at regular intervals and did not provide much in the way of information about the activities of the district, nor enquire as to the theme of his wonderful sermon, which was wise of her. It was necessary to steer him though, as far from the cottage doorways and the workshops as she could, taking unnecessary detours, because of the carrying quality of his voice and the content of his conversation. In her head she studied how long could decently be given to such a local introduction and she made a plan to travel in a circle and to arrive back at Greenside before her escort was aware of such a ruse. Began to fear her resolution and constancy in the face of such a barrage of compliment and ardent attention. She led him up towards the lane that led past the Bell Chapel intending to guide him swiftly back to Town End.

By the chapel was a hedge row of thorn and beech that offered shelter and seclusion and taking the lead, Reverend J. set out into the church yard and into the privacy of the burial ground. Never before had she hated this twisted dark barrier with such passion and she followed reluctantly up the stone path. She gritted her teeth. Here, away from prying eyes he grasped her by the hand and made further protestations of his affection and regard for her which caused her much distress and confusion and a slight nagging realisation that if she remained she would succumb and because of this her patience snapped.

'Sir. Mr. J. Please stop. I have given you an answer already and that must stand.'

'But it is well known my dear, that all respectable young women will not immediately succumb to the entreaties of their admirers, if I may make so bold. I have taught myself this that I may not prostrate myself with despair. And it might be that whilst you are with your own folk and comfortable, that you will more easily understand how our joining together will be the most suitable arrangement in all the world. Give me hope my dear, oh my dearest Sarah……..'

Sarah now snatched both her hands and concealed them within her cloak. She looked at the frozen sward and listened as her friend continued with his mighty and flowing addresses. And her way became clear. She turned on her heel swiftly and walked out from the churchyard setting off without a glance behind her as fast as she could with the frost on the trods in the direction of her home. Mr. J. had no option but to follow in her wake and cease his addresses and so thus did the pair return to the old house. Sarah lost no time in unwrapping herself and pragmatically, with no qualms of conscience, declared to Mr. J. that she had a headache and would therefore retire to her chamber. The Reverend expressed concern of an extensive kind and was still explaining his solicitude for her welfare as her feet disappeared up the stairway. Molly had not fully recovered her powers of speech in the presence of the young minister but she did manage to manoevre the guest into the great parlour. She shook her head at the floorboards above and with a tut, went back to her labours by the oven and the care of her little Irish orphan.

    John Bateson was thus forced from his retreat in his study to be polite to their visitor. He was also obliged to make a donation to whatever cause had brought Sarah's friend to Leeds. When Molly was thoughtful in bringing in some bread and some cheese and a jug of ale, John Bateson scowled for her benefit and was forced to endure further assaults on his ears to which he responded with dour silence as the young man alternately declaimed and refreshed himself. As soon as the meal was finished John Bateons wasted no time. 'Come come sir. You must be on your way. Indeed you must. We are all converted here -' Then, with relief at the thought, 'I will send a boy with you down to Beech Grove. Tell Mr. Beverley, if he be home, that I have sent you. He has a deep pocket by the way. Yes, yes. Well now. Goodbye.' They were in the yard outside by this point and John Bateson was shepherding the young man along, nodding to the stable lad. 'Take our friend to Beech Grove young Sam, there's a good boy. Take him the quickest way.' Winking, John Bateson hurried to his house door and shut it firmly behind him. Sarah heard this from the sanctuary of her room and thought it safe then, to recover from her malady.

'Is he gone?' she said softly from the shelter of the stairs.

'Oh Miss Sarah. What a fine man!' cried Molly coming from the kitchen. 'I never seen such a good looking minister. Oh Miss Sarah, what is happening to thee Yes. He's gone. But where art thou……?'

Sarah had grabbed her cloak and bonnet and still donning these she sped from the house, down the Town End Road and the lane that led to the Lupton's Mill past Jubbergate. She hammered on the gates and on being permitted to enter, she ran across the yard and up the out- steps to the Mill office and there found John Lupton. John Lupton had been disappointed yet again and was sulkily reading his newspaper to console himself for this. His feet were on his desk so he was unable to stand quickly and his his mouth dropped open as Sarah burst into his space.

'John. John I am so sorry that I did not come this morning. 'Quick, quick, stand up. We're going to be married next month. And you can kiss me now. Right now. Get on with it. What do you say man? Is this not what you have dreamed off? Are you not happy. Shall we be wed?' John Lupton folded his paper carefully and gave this some thought. Sarah had put her hands upon his shoulders and she shook him while she continued with startling conviction to propose but prevented him from rising by her force upon him.

'There has been much between us, but this should all be forgotten now. Come, I am willing to make amends to you and will strive to be a dutiful wife.' John Lupton looked over his shoulders at her fingers to see if she was in earnest. They were not crossed. He stared hard at his desk.

'When I see how hard you are working here and how the mill is so busy I know that I can trust you to provide for me. Those things are not the most important but still it is best to consider them. I have been much abroad the county and John, don't you let this make you conceited, I have found no one that I like so much as you. Let's let bygones by bygones and start afresh. What do you say John? Let"s be married as soon as we can. It's not as if we don't know all about each other. I don't believe you meant to fail me, not in your heart of hearts. And that you are still true to me is clear. Do you love me John? Shall we be wed.'

Sarah had worked herself into almost a frenzy and had not yet regained her breath from her rapid journey and was still leaning, breathing hard down John Lupton's neck. She pushed herself away from him and sat suddenly on a stool by the desk looking sharply at him; her heart thumping and with a very serious frown on her face. He had taken his feet from his desk now and managed to stand.

'Oh, alright then,' he replied.

'Well Sarah, where have you been? This has been a day for surprises I think. Do please join me in my study and tell me all about this remarkable Minister. I can scarce control my curiosity.' John Bateson spoke evenly. Sarah laid her hat on the old oak chest in the hall and still taking off her cloak followed her father down the dark corridor to the door of his room. A candle in the wall sconce cast leaping shadows as she passed and John Bateson noted that his daughter was flushed and agitated.

'Oh father! Thank you for taking care of that – that…..'

'Upright minister of the church?' Sarah gave a small smile. 'Yes exactly.' She perched on the stool beside her father at his desk and spread her skirts about her. 'But you must understand I gave him no encouragement. I did not ask him here. You believe me don't you?' she asked anxiously.

'My child, you have never yet lied to me and I would not expect it from you. But it would be hard to be as a stone to such a one if he came wooing. A very forceful character. And, shall we say, a fine man too. But you have been cautious and have stayed firmly on your recommended and chosen path. I commend you for your perception and fidelity. So how are your cheeks so warm? Have you been enjoying the solitude of a walk to Farnley perhaps.' Sarah put her hands either side of her face and then smiled again. Her father went on, his face without expression,

'Perhaps by the Beck?'

'Oh. Yes. Do you know everything that goes on in this house sir?'

'My dearest Sarah, I know *nothing* of what goes on this house. I believe all of you, young and old, conspire against me. I am the mock of the town. Why, why do you say that?'

'Well, you will be the first to know this father, indeed you will. John Lupton and I, we have agreed to wed and as soon as possible.' John Bateson turned and took a piece of paper from a sheaf on his desk and reached for his pen. 'I'll just write to that young man that came today….. just in case, you know…..' Sarah's eyes grew large and bright and she leapt to her feet and took up the quill, holding it away from her father's grasp.

' And this is the thanks you give me for telling you what is to happen! You just tease me!'

'Well yes, of course. But in the circumstances my dear, with so many postponements we have to hold our breath just a little.' Sarah protested again and her father took her hand in his. 'But I am happy for you, for the both of you. John Lupton is a good man. Oh, I know he has his faults, but so do we all. But that minister. Well! So handsome!'

He turned and peered into the shadowed hallway. 'And talking of flaws, there's a tread on the flags – come in James. We are going to have a wedding.'

'That was quite quick father. Witty almost. I see you are in good form tonight. And whose wedding are we to have?' Sarah still on her feet, grabbed his arms and shook him.

'Mine booby. Who else? Has John been to tell you already! He has hasn't he? See father, you are not the first to know!'

'Aye child. Didn't I tell you it was always the way in this family?'

James protested his innocence. 'No indeed, I have not seen John Lupton. But then again, there was a boy ran up the street giving messages to people and I think it was one of Lupton's He didn't come near me though! Only think Sarah, it will save you having to announce the event. Yes, now I think of it, that was Lupton's boy that came up all excited and jibbering.'

'Stop it. You did know didn't you?'

'Fool. Always the clown James. Just give your sister a kiss and tell her she will be happy.'

'Dear Sarah, you will be happy. Nancy sends her good wishes too and will come up as soon as she has finished bringing in my shirts and handkerchiefs from the washing line. That's just to remind you of the onerous domestic duties of married life.' Sarah frowned at him. 'Is that your jest James or did Nancy tell you to say that?'

'Ah I see you think that other duties will fall upon you? For example, telling your John what to say?'

'We began today. He has had his instructions and knows what to expect.' John Bateson sighed. 'Go away both of you with your rubbish. What is the world coming too? In my day wives were obedient to their husbands. Things are turned upside down-' but he was interrupted by the arrival of his own wife, with hot tea and toast, who squeezed into the room and began to fuss and scold him and delight in undermining his assertions. 'Take your tea sir and then you must go out for your constitutional. We wives have much to organise now dear. Come out you two – James go home. We want to talk to Sarah about important things in the kitchen. John, you need to be back from your walk when Mr. Lupton comes along to speak to you. Dear me, there's so much to do.'

On this evening, there were rehearsals in the Bell Chapel for the forthcoming Oratorio – and by the time Sarah had seated herself there to join in with the choir as she had in past days, she had been congratulated by all that she met as she came down the lane. John Lupton had come to talk to her father and of course, was given permission to proceed with what had been a long standing arrangement. Tomorrow more practical organisation would begin and Sarah, exasperated at John's precipitous informal announcement of their marriage across the whole world. was in truth within her heart of hearts content that he should have been a fool for her sake. If she had known that only a few days before this, he had in truth arranged to ride to Halifax for her sake and only been deterred by news of her arrival that same day, her happiness would have been complete.

Chapter Sixteen

The Apprentice

The announcement of Sarah and John's final agreement gave John Bateson great satisfaction. Now that her fortune was to be available to his partner Old Tom Lupton he knew that things were as they should be in the district. Old Tom had resented Sarah's fickleness and cursed his own son's delays. But now Sarah was leaving Greenside for her own establishment and security he allowed himself that he might look outside the family for additional investment and perhaps expand his interests. Only Joseph remained unmarried. But the boy was young and there were many pressures on him just now. Still, if there were a suitable match, just at this critical time, then the financial situation could be balanced. However, no sound solution came readily to mind. To consider a young woman, or any woman, as a "sound solution" was a practical and unremarkable thought. This was how it was done, in former times, when woman were dependent on the plans of their fathers and brothers and had few rights of their own. The clothier was not unkind to think in this way. His daughters had found happiness within the cloth trade of the district. They had been well cared for, thought John Bateson. They would be provided for, and their children, should they be left widowed with a family to raise alone. But in addition to all the current dispositions and as a safeguard, other finance might be brought into the business. John had not planned to train any apprentices outside the immediate family but the situation with Jack and Joseph decreed that he should think of it, and endeavour to find further financial backing. There was much to consider.

Jack had many interviews with his father in the New Year and at one of these his father mentioned that he was considering taking on apprentice – not a weaver, but a Clothier and that should this be arranged, then some provision might be made towards averting Jack's ever looming financial crisis. Jack was able to assist his father. He had made friends in the circle of sportsmen that had diverted him from trade and was able to recommend a family as a sure financial prospect, a family from near York. In Long Marston lived a wealthy farmer who had some interest in brewing which was profitable and this gentleman was now looking for an opening into the cloth trade for his sons.

'All of which reminds me Jack', said John Bateson resignedly. 'My wife and her ally Molly are keeping a stray boy in the kitchen and it's time we moved him on. You had better wish me luck.'

'Aw,' said Jack, 'little Dan. Boy's small. Git him into weaving shed, they'll no mind for thy sake.'

'I think they'll mither son. By all acounts he's gone 13 and I don't think they'll have it.'

'Lie then,' replied Jack and he stood and pushed back his chair. John Bateson remained in his seat deciding if to risk his mortal soul was worth his preservation from marital discord and Molly's wrath. He came to two conclusions. That the weavers were not the masters in his House and that the Lord was be sympathetic to a little manipulation of the truth. Certainly the boy could easily by taken for ten. Yes, this could be done.

He broached the matter with his wife first. 'The boy in the kitchen -' His wife sat up straighter in her chair and made a face at her husband that daunted him a little

'Well then, John Bateson, what of the boy- in- the -kitchen. He's not strong enough to go to Leeds yet. And it would be a braver man than you are that would tell Molly she's to send the mite to the workhouse.'

'Yes of course, Mrs. Bateson. But Ann dear, he cannot live in the kitchen. Of course he can't. Nor can he bide in Molly's room. So he must go outside above the stables or we must find another place for him.'

'What about with the apprentices. There's another room up there we could easy get fixed up and there's a bed an'all.'

'I am afraid that room will be for my new apprentice. If the lad from Long Marston comes then we will have to put him there. As you did agree I think, in principle.'

Mrs. Bateson made some short, sharp stitches in the linen fabric that was draped upon her knee, giving vent to her agitation and thinking quickly what to say.

'But the boy can be apprenticed too?' she said hopefully. 'He's no but a little 'un.'

'Yes, and he'd best keep quiet about how old he is. So get Molly to talk to Nancy about it.' Ann Bateson nodded and this was to admit she had been given the bad news to carry.

A week later, Molly rose stiffly before the sun had risen, and wiped the ice from inside the tiny window of her chamber in the attics. She blew her nose. Then she dressed quickly and on tiptoe she reached up to the old carved box in which she kept anything she valued which was concealed in the darkness of the roof timbers. She brought it and laid it upon her mattress. She looked about her before opening the lid. Taking something from within she put it down the front of her bodice and then carefully replaced the box on the beam. In the kitchen Molly checked on the child asleep on the small rough bed by the settle and she let him sleep on as she put kindling on the hearth and poked up the glowing embers under the ash. A flame sprung into the dry twigs and she nursed this until the fire was hot enough to boil water and make breakfast for the household while Dan watched her, smiling as she bustled about. 'Good morrow Molly,' he said, sitting up and stretching. 'Brrr. It's another cold one, isn't it?'

'Don't tha move now Dan. Wait until the fire gets on, does tha hear me? Tha's to stay there now child and Molly'll make thy breakfast. She turned away to hide the tear in her eye. By the time others from the household arrived for their breakfast Dan was up and dressed in his hand me down clothes and ready for anything the world would throw at him. Mary came in today, and sat beside him at the long table and Nanny came and sat on the other side. He smiled from one to the other as they chatted and ate his porridge with his spoon. Molly leant over the table to refill his bowl. Mary smiled at Dan. Now he was sat beside her you could tell that there was little difference in their ages. For in fact, Dan was a year older than Mary. Even in two weeks he had filled out and looked more his age than when he had arrived half dead in the snow. 'Are you ever full?' she asked him with a grin.

'Not full yet Miss Mary! But Molly's doing her best. And grateful I am, to be sure.' Nanny laughed at this and echoed, 'to be sure.' Mary frowned at her. But Dan just laughed. 'Sure 'tis only me way now Miss Nanny. But if I stay here -' he hesitated slightly, 'if I was to stay here one moment longer, 'tis reet grand will be me speaking way.' Which made even Nanny amused. Molly blew her nose again.

'You got a cold Molly?' asked Nanny but without sympathy.

'Sh', said Mary meaningfully.

'Now girls, go find Miss Anne and get thy selves wrapped up for school. Tha'll miss the cart and have to walk if tha stays here burbling by t'fire. Come along the both of thee. And Dan, tha needs to help me clear these dishes'.

Mary turned back and hesitated in the doorway. 'Molly, don't forget he's to practice his writing today. I showed him a lot last night. Give him a moment to do some writing please.'

Molly nodded without turning and went to fetch some clean cloths to polish and dry the dishes.

When all the table was clear and all the things put back on the shelves she took a deep breath. She had taken responsibility for Dan and she owed it to the boy to break the news to him. 'Well,' she said as last, 'we've to go up to the Weaving House now. Tha's to put thy things in that bag. Yes yes,' she added, 'take thy book and thy pencil – but mind now, tha can come back whenever thou art allowed. Miss Mary won't leave tha be, now she's taken it into her head that tha's iducuble like.'

Dan watched Molly bluster and his own fears at being removed to another place were replaced by his pity for her attempt to hide her red eyes. She handed him a sack and he sat on his truckle bed and from underneath he brought out a notebook and paper that Mary had given him - and a book that Matthew had given him on hearing that Dan could read and a few other items that the family and their servants had provided.

When he was finished he stood and smiled at Molly. 'Well, there we are! Let's go then Molly!' At this cheerfulness Molly could not restrain the tears that ran down her ruddy cheeks. So she grabbed him by the ear but lightly and led him out of the kitchen, which indignity he endured for her sake. 'Ouch ouch,' he said comically. 'But Molly should I not thank thy Master and Mistress. But for them I would not be standing here today, even with my ear in thy grip and as for thee, oh Molly!' And he put his arms around her and held her tight. 'No no, thou art not going so far away. Tha'll be back the night and I know tha will.

And Dan?' she dropped her voice, 'I'll keep some supper for thee too. Make sure as tha come in here then, alright boy?' Dan nodded happily at this. Relief flooded his soul. He was not to be taken to the workhouse then as his mother had feared. He was to be near and to be cared for and how that was, he did not know.

It was not far to the weaving house and Nancy knew that Molly and Dan were on their way. She came to the house door and brought them into her parlour, seated herself and regarded Molly and Dan with a broad smile. The panelled walls of the more modern house kept in the heat of a glowing coal fire and two children were playing before it.

'So welcome to our apprentice then Dan.' Dan stared in disbelief. Molly was now in control of herself. 'Hear that Dan? Tha's to be a weaver. What dost that think of that then? A proper weaver and work to be had and not even in a factory but here in the country and making the finest broad cloth in the land. By lad, thy mother would have been proud of thee today!' She gave his ear another tweak although it looked to Nancy as if Molly had to reach quite high up to do this and it would not be much longer the boy would stand it. He looked at the floor and then at Nancy and grinned. 'I don't know what to say to thee both. Sure an I don't. Seems to me I might just be the most fortunate boy in the world!'

'Well then, let's get you sorted out Dan. You've to sleep above the stable mind, but it's warm enough, with the stove. So thanks Molly. You'll be wanting to get back I know.'

Molly twisted the ends of her shawl and looked sideways. 'If I could have one word with thee Mrs. Nancy. Just a quick 'un. Like in the kitchen tha knows.' To Dan she added levelly, 'something about cooking.'

Molly closed the kitchen door behind them and then taking the package from her bosom she thrust it into Nancy's hand. 'What's this Molly?' asked Nancy puzzled and unwrapping it. Five gold guineas laid in her hand. Nancy frowned and smiled at the same time and swiftly grabbed Molly's hand and put the coin back in it. She closed Molly's hand about these and gave her a hard stare.

'Take it, take it,' pleaded Molly. 'It's all I got, but I'm so taken with him. He's such a good boy. Tha won't have a better Mrs. Nancy. He'll be the best of all tha dost employ, he will too.'

'Molly I would not doubt you for the world, but we won't take your money for him. What are you thinking! He'll be well treated in this house I can assure you. And you'll see him too, see him every day. Don't be so daft and get off with you. Really now!' And then Molly broke down completely and Nancy held her tight. 'There there there. You big silly. Blow your nose and get up home. You'll be in bother with the Maister else!' And then Molly left, comforted but still distressed and walked quickly back to Greenside
.

Matthew was sent to Long Marston to proceed with arrangements for the new apprentice and to settle the terms of the investment. When all was satisfactorily concluded he returned to Wortley accompanied by a young man by the name of Phillip Abbey who was therefore destined to become a Clothier and a merchant in wool cloth. A lodging room had been prepared for the new gentleman and had been furnished with a feather mattress and with a private wash basin, personal bucket, and other such refinements. The household came out to greet Phillip, to examine him with curiosity, direct questions and teasing from the granddaughters and by theses means to make him feel welcome in his new home.

The boy was fourteen years old, too old to apprentice as a weaver or other artisan, but a good age to begin in a merchant's role. He was tall enough for his years, slender and he had a cheerful, open face with intelligent eyes. He had come from a large family, albeit without a mother, and he took straight away to the little girls who crowded round him. Matthew's daughters were delighted to have a new friend and he was soon made at home. They explained to him, that he would soon become used to the smells of the cloth industry that overlaid the normal odours of farm yards and livestock.

He was lodged on John Bateson's side of the old house but Matthew's family lived conjoined and the doors to both abodes were always open. The work of this domestic and industrial hub was constant and well organised but they had not had such an apprentice before and so was Phillip left to his own occupations for the first day.

'Master Abbey, might I just ask if tha has emptied thy bucket yet?'

'My bucket Molly? Oh, in my room. Yes, I, er, well I hope it's alright. I did tip it out yesterday.'

Molly made a puzzled face. 'Where? Not in the lane I hope, or the yard! Tha knows what to do with it doesn't tha? Not born in a barn were ye?' Phillip sat at the kitchen table with his head to one side and a cautious expression. He did not know what to say.

'In the barrel boy. The one in the outhouse.' She leaned over the table to him and whispered. 'Just the pee.' And then she nodded meaningfully and went about her tasks, clearing the platters and the pewter mugs from the household breakfast. Phillip had then wandered then outside and taken a peak in the barns and out houses. At the end of the range of buildings, after the out – kitchen building, he found a small planked door and just pushed it open a little. Ammonia hit him in a wave and he stepped away appalled. A farm hand came walking in his direction, under a great pitchfork of old hay, stalks falling around him as he came.

'Alright lad? Tha can go piss if tha likes, don't mind about it. We's not shy about it here!' This was shouted as he went on his way to the stables. 'Phew' let out Phillip and he closed his stinging eyes and turned on his heel away. Now he understood that lingering odour that he had noticed when he had slid off his horse on arrival in Wortley. And the bucket! He grimaced. It was a strange place he had come to. He went off to see more of his surroundings, exploring the fields, paths and byways. The village was busy with folk about their daily activities and he greeted them shyly with his soft Yorkshire accent. 'Not from round 'ere, then.' they commented, nodding. 'Folk do talk different where's tha's from!'

There were bell pits scattered on the common, on the hillsides and over the valley below. A stone quarry gaped above the Balks, and clay pits had been dug up by the windmill and down by the Holmfield Lane. The village had several wells and he stopped to drink from his hands at one that stood at the bottom of Wortley Lane. A woman had her washing there in a barrel and was pounding it with a posser . 'Watch out young'un master. There's a ghost in the well!'
Phillip peered at the water in the stone dip. 'What kind of ghost?' he enquired politely. 'Mouse,' said the villager. 'Tis haunted by a mouse. Do thou mind now!'

'I will. Thank – thank you for letting me know. A mouse. I see. Well good day then.' He raised his hat with a frown and took a few steps away. 'A mouse ghost?' he said again quietly to himself. And then shook his head and laughed.

'Settled in are we then Phillip? Now we must see about your education. Much of this will be very new to you. I think you must first learn to weave. It is not very difficult to produce cloth but to create fine quality cloth there is a great deal of skill and experience which cannot be learned from books. There are many processes to master. So tomorrow I will send you down to the workshops at the mill where the journeymen can give you your first taste of adventure. I look forward to hearing good report of you mind! We manage our workers with much vigilance and you must be setting a good example. Get Molly to give you bread and cheese for you must stay the whole day and be with the weavers and see what they do for this week. In time you must make your own length of cloth and be judged upon it.' Phillip gaped.

'I see you are surprised at this. But it is the first step for you as a Clothier. My sons and daughters did the same at your age. Only think, a man will never go hungry if he can make cloth. And a merchant must understand what he sells.'

'Thank you Mr. Bateson. I hope I will get on well and learn quickly.'

'Very well then. Good morning to you. Send my little Mary to me will you, there's a good boy. I have need of her pen work today.'

Preparations were being made for the forthcoming marriage of Sarah and John and the household and servants were hard at work all round the old house. So the morning of Phillip's introduction to the cloth trade was marked with no ceremony and little interest. He took himself off across the footpath to the mill with excitement though and some anxiety. The stench of the industry had already been adjusted to - since it permeated the air across the whole village. He knocked lightly on the door of the weaving shed having been directed there by the busy mill workers in the yard - who had looked at him with a little curiosity before returning to their work.

'Ah. Good morrow little 'un. Get in, shut door and we'un see about your edication. We like a newby, don't we Tom Wood?'

'Oh aye. Always good to get us threads crossed. So come 'ere then laddie and we'll get going. Tha takes this 'ere bucket, go down tut water meadow and in t' little shed there, is t' little coo. And then when tha's finished, tha can tak the milk and bring it up to tut dye house and give it in to 'em and that's thy first task.'

'Milk?' asked Phillip confused.

'Milk aye. It's fer the stiffening of the threads does tha see? And that's what we need. Go on then. Off ye go. Tak t' bucket.'

Phillip grasped the iron pail and descended the stone steps on his errand. He was not sure that he had expected this. He had not expected a cow to be part of a mill appurtenances so he shook his head as he wandered through the complex of brick buildings in search of a water meadow and shed. Now the labourers watched him and shook their heads.

Mary Bateson had come down the lane with a message in her hand for her father Matthew before school and she stopped in her tracks when she saw Phillip looking around him and carrying the metal pail. 'What are you doing with that Phillip? Is it full? Don't you know what its for and where to empty it?'

'No, it's empty. I have been sent to find a cow and I think I am supposed to milk it. Although I am not sure that this is what I am expected to be doing. Is there a cow then? Where is it?'

'Oh for goodness sake.'

'There's no cow?'

'There is a cow, yes, but we have th dairy maid that sees to that after she's done the herd and if she does not then I or my sisters will do it. And the cows are up there too. Look, over there. Cows. See them? Four legs, brown, udders, all that.' She made sure the bucket was indeed empty and then took it from him, leaving it by the out steps of the weaving loft. 'But this is not the bucket we use. Lord save us. Who gave you it? And if they had told you to dig up some potatoes, would you have done that?'

'Er. Well no. But maybe. I don't know much about potatoes Miss Mary. But I know how to milk a cow. We had a good herd at home you know, in Long Marston.' He sounded sad and he looked wistfully over the fields, feeling an absolute fool. Mary softened at Phillip's mention of home and she realised he was probably home sick and she knew that he was being abused by the weavers. Her soft heart was smitten.

'Come with me. I'm to take this note to my father and he'll know what to do with you. Fancy leaving you with the weavers. Whose idea was that? We all know what they're like. That's their piss pail by the way. Come on. Follow me.'

'But John Bateson sent me and said to go there.'

'My grandfather doesn't know the mill workers very well. He thinks they will be as respectful as his own weavers! But it's different down here. Times have changed. I'll go tell him that my father has you in hand and they can sort it out between them.'

And Mary took Phillip to her father who understood the situation at once and took Phillip under his wing for the time being. John Bateson was content to let Matthew take the boy on and an agreement was made to the liking of both parties. Phillip shadowed Matthew Bateson for some days to come and was able to begin to understand how the cloth industry was organised and led and he smiled gratefully at Mary at dinner time and a friend ship was begun between the two children.

For Matthew, with his four daughters, Phillip was to become something of a son certainly as far as the cloth making went. He had trained Mary in weaving and Anne was directed to the looms to begin to understand the trade as time went on. Phillip too, made his guild piece and Matthew became very proud of his apprentice, more than that. He loved him like a son.

Chapter Seventeen

Vows are made...

The hazy sun had made a little impact on the ice bound roadways of Leeds and the constant crush of wheeled carts and carriages had made a muddy mess of the usual ruts. Purchase for the phaeton's wheels was better outside some of the properties where the owners had brought out ash and cinder and spread it abroad. The carriage belonged to Old Tom Lupton and John had told Sarah they she would have one of her own as soon as they were wed. Or maybe a gig. 'Now then!' had replied Sarah tartly. 'Stick to your point John. Start as you men to go on. We'll have a carriage thank you very much, and three horses in our stables.'

'Yes my love, as soon as we can, we'll have that. You won't be riding about like Nancy Bateson!'

'No indeed. And if James and Nancy get a carriage, I would like ours to be better.' John Lupton had sighed then, unwisely. Sarah had poked him and laughed. 'A gig will do John,' she admitted kindly. 'Don't promise owt you can't provide.'

'Oh Sarah, you do tease me so.'

But here she was with her father crossing the Leeds Bridge from Holbeck, with her father beside her and John Lupton doing a good job of avoiding the other carts and carriages and beaming broadly at all around him. But there was still enough of the dark and dirty ice for several ragged children to flash across their path, sliding on the frozen midden with reckless joy, to cause him to pull desperately on the reins. The carriage stopped and skidded to halt just inches from a warehouse wall and Sarah and her father were thrown about dangerously.

John Bateson yelled at the urchins as they ran off laughing and turned to his daughter in alarm. John Lupton, blanched, turned and called to them and was reassured that they were shaken but not damaged. He drove on as directed by John Bateson at a very sedate pace.

'Are you hurt my dear?' asked the Maister still shocked. 'Why are these rogues not stopped. The same happened to me only last week but I was afoot.' Sarah, making secure her bonnet and her dignity smiled at her old father. 'I think I am alright. Well, my millinery is at any rate. And this it the most important element of this day!'

'Is it indeed? Well my dear child, your sister Elizabeth had a much more puissant creation when she married to William Lister! Far beyond yours in magnificence. And you will know how this has worked in her favour in that marriage. Of course you do. William did not have any opportunity to do other than obey her rule when her saw her wedding hat.' His eyes twinkled but his expression was neutral.

'Is that so? I wonder if it is too late to…..'

'Source a new hat? If you so much as mention abandoning this wedding and leaving John Lupton in the parish church alone, then just call to mind Old Tom in a fury...'

'Old Tom? I wonder who you might be referring to father? Well let me tell you then, that Elizabeth had not to endure the Methodists of Halifax. And therefore was she able to secure a commanding bonnet. Whereas I, with my faithful service have not been in a position where I could see the fashions of the day or know the artists of excellent bonnetry. So I have come forth to be wed in this small and humble item.'

The gig continued as they spoke and neared St. Peter's. 'So that is what we might describe as a Halifax bonnet?' enquired her father amused.

Sarah laughed and her father nodded. She said, 'This is what we shall call a Methodist Bonnet, father.' And he laughed out loud which was a rare occurrence. He helped her to alight and fortunately around the church yard, the good citizens of Leeds had distributed ashes and clinker from their coal fires, with salts generously given by the wealthy merchants, and so they were able to approach the church with confidence that they would not come to grief, disaster and sartorial misfortune.

The day was so wretched that a hasty decision had had to be made that morning and many who might otherwise have come to town for the vows had remained in Wortley. Winter weddings were often thus reduced. And so the affair was quietly completed. Nevertheless, John Lupton in his finest outfit had beamed and blushed and enjoyed the well wishes of any citizen that had had occasion to pass the church yard as he led Sarah out of the church door. Sarah in a dark and neat gown of fashion but concealed beneath her new winter cloak, wearing an elegant bonnet, had been more contained and composed. She hushed John Lupton and was conscious of her new dignity as the wedded spouse of a respectable mill proprietor.

They were all to return to Greenside where there was to be a Wedding Breakfast in the barn for the servants and employees. and within the old house at Greenside for better folk. Her father had gone to fetch a horse from the stables of the Old George. John had given up the reins of his borrowed phaeton to her brother Joseph which troubled Sarah not a little. But he was managing well and then with John Lupton's arm about her waist they set off, waving at a small crowd who had gathered.

There were on lookers that were not noticed though. One, a respectable woman in shawl and white cap, had seen the party pass from the entrance to the alley where she somehow managed to maintain a home. Mary Bateman closed her eyes and with admirable sentiment, blessed them. But what powers she used for this we are not able to tell.

Another figure, tall, dark and melancholy, watched from a doorway. He shrugged and came forth when the danger of being seen was passed, adjusted his hat, and went on his way whistling one of Wesley's great hymn tunes.

Sarah began to ponder as she watched the warehouses along the river bank pass by of the remove she must make and the loss of the new found intimacy of her family; the difficulties that might arise in her new home. There would be so much to manage!

'John? Will we take the house up in Armley? The one I told you about? I'm worrying myself now, about how it will be to stay with your parents.'

'Nay Sarah. Don't fret. There's a deal of room at Heights and mother has got it all ready for us – don't worry dearest. It will be strange for you I know but it was your wish to marry quickly. We've a great fire in the hearth in our chamber and the best things are all got ready for you.' He put out his hand and took hold of hers. 'And my darling, my father has agreed that we are to build ourselves a fine house at the top of the hill. The land is bought already and my father has given it to me as a wedding present. I was going to tell you tonight as a marriage gift. But now is good too. Whatever you wish shall be done and Mrs.Lupton will have such a great new house there, very convenient and comfortable.' Sarah gazed at John in astonishment. 'Yes,' he said. 'I shall make your happiness my pleasant duty. Dear Sarah.'

'You're very lyrical today,' commented Sarah, but her eyes were wet. She leant to him, and they were quite happily ensconced in each others arms, with the curtains down, when the carriage at last came to a halt in the lane in Wortley. There was adjusting of clothing and hats before they could step down to the greetings of their friends and family at Greenside.

The Lord of the Manor, John Smyth had been invited to the marriage feast but his health was failing. He remained in his curtained bed in the comfort of his terraced home near Park Square and his son and heir was already arrived at Greenside and enjoying the hospitality of the house. He was seated in the great parlour watching from the mullioned windows there, with a great tankard of ale in his flabby hand and a melancholy air. The Maisters wife hovered by him torn between attending to him and going outside in the cold afternoon airs to meet the newly weds and decided that her duty lay here.

'So your father is not strong sir? I will pray for him. Our time in this world is but brief.… My husband would wish to have a word with you when he comes in. Something about business I believe.'

'Mix business with pleasure. Indeed Mistress Bateson, that is what I like above all things. This is uncommon good pie.' The gentleman spoke slowly and without energy.

'It is. And you shall have another slice Mr. Smyth. Molly! More pie and fill his honour's glass for him.'

' More ale would be welcome. But not more pie for me I fear. It does not do me good Mrs. Bateson.' The Maisters wife looked astonished at this. 'Oh dear me. Well. More ale for Mr. Smyth Molly, if you please.'

Molly obliged and did so with the strongest of ale; that she guarded carefully and dispensed sparingly unless it was specifically useful. Smyth sunk himself again into his ale pot but was interrupted though, by the arrival of his Game Keeper who had come in through the kitchen without leave and had ignored the alarmed challenge of young Dan Grady sat eating yet more pie by the fire. Ben Marker was the name of the keeper and he had business to settle.

'Pardon me, tha honour! I knows tha's cum t'feast, but I 'as t'tell 'ee that what's 'appening. Me and Isaac - as is me 'elper, see? We 'as takin Turner wi' a bag 'o rabbits and we 'as takin 'im into Leeds and 'ees in the cells for t'magistrates. Just so tha's knows it for t' morrow.'

Marker looked round at those of the party who had come already within the great parlour and surveyed them with narrow eyes as if all present might be future poachers and there was a moment's hush. Molly with a jug of ordinary ale in her hand scowled. Dan in the doorway watched carefully. Smyth's face became very long and he waved his pewter mug in vexation. He said thoughtfully;

'Ah. So that's it is it? Well done, Marker! Good work! We'll see about this then, tomorrow of course. Damn me, if I don't see the rogue hang. Or transported.' He fumbled in his waistcoat for a coin for his faithful retainer and noticed suddenly that the people had turned away and were talking in low voices in small groups. He sighed. How would they understand? A man had a right to the produce of his land! Too much of this went on on his father's estate.

In the doorway Ben Marker found James Bateson who had discovered the strong ale and was savouring it away from Molly's keen eyes. 'What's up Mr. Marker? Are you come to help us feast? Kind in you! A brace of hare would have been good though, for the happy couple.' The keeper snorted but stayed in the doorway, wrapping his cloak tightly and pulling his hat further down on his head for the air was bitter and he had a long walk home.

'Came to see his Lordship sir. A little business o' poaching. Nothing for tha to worry at.'

'Well not any more Marker you'll be pleased to here' Marker grunted. James said cheerfully, 'Good night to you then.'

'Aye sir. Good night it 'as been.' Dan in the shadows crept out then and explained to his master what he had heard. James whistled and shook his head. 'Thanks boy. We'll have to see about that then, won't we?' Dan smiled.

The feasting in the house ended with music and song, while in the barn, there was a fiddler and music. Phillip Abbey distinguished himself being a good dancer, neat and graceful. Little Dan Grady watched, kneeling by the window at all the goings on. 'Now then, Dan. Tha must keep thyself warm. Come along and sit here.' Molly thrust a cup into his hands and he smiled and sipped. 'Ta ma,' he said cheekily. 'When I'm big and strong I'll be dancing too.' 'Drink tha beer,' she said forcefully, ' and never tha mind tha lip.'

Mr. John Smyth had been well cared for in Wortley and since the night was cold and chill and his condition after the celebrations was somewhat lamentable, he was assisted by Matthew and James to the Walker's house which was the greater house of the Township and had suitable chambers for a gentleman of note.

As they returned home, cutting across the tenter close, Matthew put his arm round James' shoulder.

'Oh this puts me in mind of past joys lad. I remember guiding you home one late, dark night. Only it was the other way then. I brought you home from Balks House when you were fifteen and you and James Walker had been at it all night and -'

'Times change sir. We all have our pasts – well, you don't. Oh yes you do now I think on it . Something about Mary being shall we say, born much sooner that was expected? Yes. I do recall something of the words that father had with old Hepper?'

'That was one sin. You staggered home form Walker's many's the night. Singing in the hallway.'

'Just the once?' Matthew nodded at James.

'Just the once. Or twice. Maybe -' And then he grinned.

'So do'ye think father has got him to sign owt?'

'No. But he'll have begun the thing. No point having a coal merchant for our liege Lord if he doesn't provide for us, is there? He's not the man his father is I'm afraid. Doesn't do much in the way of business like his father. More a gentleman and with those vices that come with the rank. But I hear he has debts to pay. So he may be willing to deal.'

'We won't lend him money, surely?'

' We'll buy his coal and at a premium I hope. What they've got left anyway. Thwaites was done back in '96, but they've other pits. I don't know what father intends but perhaps he has his eye set on Silkstone, shall we say?'

'He'll lend then on land security. Somewhere useful in the future?'

'Perhaps.'

They reached the old house at Greenside and bad each other goodnight, with breath misting the night air and the lights of Beeston twinkling in the moonlit night far across the shallow valley of the Wortley Beck, now made civilised by the stone courses that channelled the flow and feeding the dark mills of the western villages, all the way from Farnley to Holbeck.

'Matthew!' called John Bateson urgently across the house yard. 'Matthew come here to me a minute will you?' Matthew went to his father.

'You'll have to go into Leeds tomorrow. Turner's got himself caught by old Ben Maker and he's in the cells. Get him up before the Magistrates tomorrow before Smyth can interfere. Here take this.' He forcefully handed Matthew five guineas. 'That's more than enough for the fine - and any other expenses. Let's have him out quickly. It was only three rabbits. For God's sake!' He turned to walk away then spun round.

'And bring me the change son. Two guineas he's worth for now since we are under duress - for your benevolence to Mssrs. James and William Walker. If it's more then I'll have the pair of them make me a contribution. What are we here? The Bank of Wortley!'

Matthew stood some moments considering the matter. Then he smiled. His father was hard as ice and as soft as soap. He sighed. But Turner was a good journeyman weaver and they could not risk his loss, not now. The lad and his brother, aye, and his mother too were all reliable weavers since his father had had that terrible accident at Mill Green. The Maister was right. And John Smyth junior, future Lord of the Manor of Wortley, had plenty of lands to hunt upon. Estates in Wortley and Holbeck and Silkstone as well. Three rabbits, he told his wife Jane. She told him that if their weavers were hungry enough to risk their freedom or their necks then Matthew had best find some provisions for the workers. And oats and barley would do and cabbages if they could get some. Matthew asked her if he should go poaching in the Manor or up at Farnley? Jane told him he had better source some cheese and cheap grain. And watch at the auctions for more milch cows. She asked him what use was money to them if their workers and their families went hungry? What use the ownership of land and cottage if the people lay dead inside them? He told her she was too imaginative and that the situation was not so desperate. And then he thought about it much as he said his prayers, knelt on the cold boards of their chamber in the old house at Greenside.

It had been a terrible harsh, killing winter. Many had already gone out of business. Prices were rising relentlessly. Work was hard to find. To find extra provisions in Leeds would be expensive now. But Jane was quite right. That was what he must do and James too. Larders were emptying and it was many a month to harvest.

Chapter Eighteen

The Lord of the Manor

'That matter of which we spoke Mr. Smyth? Of course your recent bereavement has meant that you have absent from society so I have waited before renewing our negotiations. I hope we do not inconvenience you by calling today?' John Bateson took off his cloak and hat and handed them to the waiting footman.

'Ah Mr. Bateson - and son. No not at all. It is good of you to call on me. Such a burden of sadness I feel, that I cannot go about my business as I should and I find the days are long. I think I will take myself to the country for a while. Leeds is so smokey and grim that is does nothing to ease my grief. So come in by the fire and both take some wine with me.'

'I thank you for your courtesy but I do not take anything at this hour. But do please honour me by toasting my health.' The Maister looked over at the flames and wondered at a man that would burn coal in the summer! In the evenings perhaps, but by day? Such luxury. And it was warm, too warm in the papered room.

Mr. Smyth Junior indicated to his footman who poured two glasses of wine. One glass was exquisite and Smyth held it up by the light of the window. John Bateson could see etching on the body of the glass.

'Sucess to the Thwaite Colliery, and here is our family crest, Mr. Bateson. Smyth held the glass again to catch the light, hands trembling slightly. 'It was a gift – from our cousin at Heath Hall of course. My father loved this glass.' He tailed away sadly and sank into his fireside chair, lost in his own thoughts.

The footman brought the other glass, a plain one, to Jack Bateson.

'I trust we have the honour of seeing you well sir?' enquired John Bateson with a little concern. The Lord of the Manor was a sometime familiar figure at the Chapel and at the houses of the principal inhabitants of Wortley. Today, he was a different man, as if the death of his father had taken away the size, the stiffening from the man and his face was puffy, pale and lined. John Bateson wondered if he would remember what had been agreed when last they met, before his father's death had made him even more melancholy.

'I am not myself. It might be this winter that has drained my strength or perhaps the recent demise of my father has been more distressing to me than I could have imagined. And my cousin's death? Mrs. Egginton as she had become. You will have heard about it I'm sure. So much to look forward to and all now dust and ashes. So much death. So much for our brief sojourn in this sad world.'

Now John Bateson had come to talk of coal but he found he must instead give some gentle religious care to the distressed Lord of the Manor. So he told him that this life is indeed brief but that our eternal hope was never extinguished and that John Smyth junior could take heart and keep faith. Jack Bateson nodded at this father's counsel and but also gave attention to the fine wood panelling of the drawing room and the other outward signs of material wealth there displayed, which included a many branched crystal chandelier and exquisite and elaborate plaster work. John Bateson gave his son a discreet prod with his stick.

'Take heart then Mr. Smyth,' interjected Jack in support of his father. They were interrupted by a light tap on the door and the footman entered, announcing the arrival of Miss Smyth who had come down from her room to see what company had come to them in their mourning.

She had met the Bateson's many times before and was perhaps not best pleased to have interrupted her morning for such as these, cloth makers of Wortley. But then, there was a lot of money in this family and a lot of good business sense. And Jack had been widowed more than a year ago so she thought that she would be seated and give them the grace of her presence. Lydia Smyth was in mourning but the style of her dress was of the most modern fashion, being high waisted and elegant. She was in her twenties, nearer that age than thirty, a most eligible young lady with the highest of connections. There would have to be a great deal of money in this family for her to be truly interested in their conversation but she stayed non the less and amused herself.

The attentions of a maid servant and of London dressmakers had enhanced an already pretty face. Jack became even more taciturn than usual but was able to smile at the lady as she took over the management of her drawing room and the command of the conversation.

'How kind of you both to call. I know you have not come to offer your condolences because these were given us at our late lamented father's funeral. But I must have missed you then, at the funeral. No, no I saw Mrs. Nancy Bateson and we had quite a long talk. And Mr. Lister was there too. Surely this cannot be a business meeting? But do tell me how is Mrs, Bateson? I had the pleasure of meeting with her only two days since, and she was so good as to tell me so much of interest about Wortley. I was most engaged. I was only telling mamma about this yesterday -'

'Is your mother quite well? This must be a very difficult time for you Miss Smyth. Your father's death is much lamented in Wortley. He was a fine and - '

' That must be as it is,' she said brightly and becoming bored. 'My mother is of course prostrate with grief but will rally I trust. This weather is of good use to us who are sad, is it not? The sun has come back to us and the birds are nesting. So there is hope I am sure. We will be travelling to Silkstone within a few days and there my mother may be less reminded of her loss and see some of her old friends. If we can only get her into the coach without her becoming too much distressed. Distraction is always useful I find.'

John Bateson frowned. Miss Smyth had made light of her mourning and he felt this was not quite proper. Jack however smiled and nodded. John Bateson had wanted to make overtures of a quite practical nature to Mr. Smyth Junior and now needed to approach the matter at a later time. But he would see his man of business and conduct the deal by letter – all delays. He had been out manoeuvred by Miss Smyth. She turned her attention to Jack.

'Well I hear much good of you, Mr. Bateson. And that you have a good record at the Hunt! Of all things! It is quite the talk of the county! We were proud, weren't we,' she included her brother in the remark by smiling is his direction, 'to hear that Wortley is enjoying such leisure activities. Surely business must be going on well for you to be able to make your mark in county pursuits.'

John Bateson actively suppressed his dismay. 'Ha ha, Miss Smyth. A good pun and it only 11.30 in the morning. Your wits are sharp today I find.' Jack eyed his father, just a little puzzled and again smiled foolishly, but caught himself and pursed his lips and nodded, trying to think how he might best reply, and before his father too.

'Well there's no disgrace in manly sport, Miss Smyth.' he offered as his contribution to the conversation. John Bateson broke in sharply. 'I am sure you have much to occupy you Mr Smyth, Miss Smyth. It has been a great pleasure to see you both this morning and I trust we will see you again, soon, in Wortley. Ah I had forgot. Mr. William Walker wishes to arrange for some discussions around the Chapel. You understand of course. There are many people in the district that wish to see it as a Chapel of Ease and while it is for hire, we do not always agree with those that lease it -'

'Mr. Bateson. Yes. And we hear that the Methodists have completed one Chapel and are making another. Do we not brother? And it may well be best for them, that other arguments are not raised against them!' Not but what the Township likes to have theological disputes across the green. I'm sure they do, aren't you sure brother.?' John Bateson was now put out and irritated.

'Well, it is as you say. But still, Miss Smyth -' he put up his hand as he saw her draw breath to make another snipe, 'it is a fitting monument to your late father and the inhabitants are aware of this. If I might make a time sir, to suit you, or your man of business, there are other matters that I wish to discuss with you before you leave for the country. Do let me know when is convenient. For now, we will take our leave. I thank you for your hospitality.'

'Now friend, don't mind my sister. Lydia, she's always very bright, aren't you dear?' Smyth shot her a warning glance. 'You should show more respect to our cloth makers! I will send you word and you shall dine with me and we can talk over anything that you might be minded to bring to the table. Good day to you both and my thanks for your solicitude and kind advice.'

The Batesons took their leave, with John Bateson firmly putting on his hat and heading for the door, whilst Jack stood a moment, smiling and nodding at Miss Smyth. When the door was closed to the street, she fell back upon the sofa laughing.

'What is it Lydia? Why do you laugh? You should not bait old John Bateson. He's no fool you know, a man of learning as well as a man of the trade and he is very well respected. He spoke very kindly to me and he meant well' Lydia shrugged unrepentantly.

'He wants something. Some deal or other. Some favour. What a bumpkin the son is. Not at all like his brothers.'

John Smyth thought awhile. 'You liked that younger one, James isn't it? A lot, if I remember, some years ago.'

'La, yes. He is the best of them all and not so stuffy. He was quite the charmer before he married that Lupton girl. She has him under her thumb, that's for sure.. But I was sixteen then, not four and twenty and the world was a small place. Now that one, he's not a patch on the others. Hunting indeed. When a man has to spend his days watching his workers then he does not have time to hunt or shoot! They'll be enlisting with the Militia before we know it! Don't be obliging them in business John. Not now at any rate. With what you owe the estate is in difficulties and we must be careful who we make arrangements with. Don't get into money deals with the Yorkshire men dear. You know how they go on. Three months and all that kind of tedium. Don't make any promises before the lawyers have settled father's affairs and the money is secured. And Mr. Gott told me only last night, that the Walkers have not paid for their engine again. But that little brother in the Bateson family. The little Joseph. He's fun.' She had come over to her brother now and patted his shoulder to soften her reference to his financial obligations. He patted her hand.

'Now where have you seen him Lydia? Surely you do not move in the same social circles?'

'Just at the book shop. He is lively and the little boy he had with him, some young gentleman from Long Marston Hall? Well he can "do" his Maister as good as life! But I think he's spoken for. Joseph I mean. As the gossip goes. And would you guess, it's the Walkers again. I don't think our Mr. Bateson knows of it though. That might be interesting news for him - at your little meeting.'

'You imp! Do you know everything that is happening in Leeds?'

'I do! And Hull. Mrs. Osbourne has written to ask me to Willerby. Mamma says I might go and you should come too, John. I have high hopes in that direction you know that?'

'I thought I might stay awhile in Silkstone. I find company difficult at the moment. My spirits are very low. I feel weary. If I can but get out of this sooty city and walk among the trees and hills, I might find myself at peace again. Leave me now I need to rest.'

'Well in that case I will take Elizabeth. We can both find husbands and you can walk yourself into better spirits. You have much responsibility now, with your wayward sisters to manage. But we will look for you too, John. You must marry now, y'know. Lord of the Manor, all that sort of thing.'

He kissed her hand before she left the room but then remained in solitude with his father's wine and glass considering both the loss of his father and the present state of his financial affairs and other matters that distressed him. For example, that he ought to find a wife.

Chapter Nineteen

More marriage arrangements

As John Bateson brought his pony and trap to halt in the lane, the stable hand came out to help take the pony into the yard and John Bateson got down with a loud groan and banged his stick on the trap angrily.

Mrs. Bateson was watching for him from the window. 'Molly!' she hissed, 'thy Maister's home and he's not in a good mood. Put his slippers in the oven while I try to soothe him – and you children get off back to your mother's rooms. Grandfather is tired and don't want you bothering him. Shoo, shoo!'

The children ran giggling away back through the great parlour and into their mother's sitting room.

'Now then husband, let me help you with your cloak and hat. Come on and sit down. Molly's got your slippers warm and the kettle is just boiling. A cup of tea and all will be right.'

'Stop fussing me wife. I'm not a child. Oh all right. Thank you Molly.' And John Bateson let himself wearily down into his fireside chair and his wife took a stool to herself and sat beside him. The clock in the parlour struck ten and John Bateson looked at his watch, compelled to do so by years of irritation at the poor time kept by his prize possession. (Something which reminded him of his third son's vexing activities as a young boy.)

'So how was your dinner. Did Mr. Smyth feed you well.' She asked cautiously in view of his suppressed anger.

'Well in truth he did. There were many dishes. Hardly room for our plates and servings. Four removes. Very profligate I think. I wonder that gentlemen can ever finish all that is put before them. And the servants must think themselves as quality, that their table has so many fine leavings.'

'But you are out of humour, my dear. I can tell. Did it not go as you hoped?' John Bateson sat rubbing his chin and then sighed wearily.

'No in faith, but we got some concession on coals from Dodworth. Smyth's man suggested that Jack leases out most of the mill and would perhaps advice Smyth to see his way to a small investment in M. and J. He seemed to think that Atkinson might be lenient if he can get something back in from another more solvent tenant in Water Lane. But we can leave that aside for the moment. I don't think Smyth is in funds himself and in no position to invest. I fancy if we had been alone, he would have asked for a loan. That might have been useful secured by land. But then Mr. Smyth asked me if I was happy about the Walker marriage.' He darted a piercing look at his wife.

Mistress Bateson found that she now needed to look about her and rearrange her skirt and apron, as she tried to convey an air of innocence and surprise. Had she fallen from her stool and gasped, it would have been equally unconvincing. 'Walker marriage?' she said with what she hoped was a quite puzzled expression.

'Yes! Walker and Bateson marriage. Don't pretend you don't know anything about it. What do you know of this then Good Wife Ann? This might be a proper time to tell me what is going on. Why I am always the last person to know what is happening in this family, I do often wonder? It's as if you all work against me. And you too, of all people. The one person from whom I should expect loyalty and truth.

Mistress Ann Bateson looked abashed. But only for a moment. Molly came in then, suddenly, She plonked down the tea tray with threatening silence and curtseyed with menaces.

John Bateson watched her come and go with a glowering expression before turning again to his wife.

'So speak woman. What's afoot?'

'What is it?' whispered Nanny. 'What's Grandfather saying?' Mary came and stood in her nightgown unsure if she should condone such a conspiracy in the chamber above the great parlour almost certain that it was not proper. Phillip Abbey stood at her shoulder grinning. The two little granddaughters slithered back along the planked floor to the doorway and the older children made way so that they could ease their way out into the hallway and stand.

'Well?' said Mary, torn between guilt, consternation and an inability to contain her curiosity. Nanny nudged Anne who beamed with satisfaction. She looked from face to face as the little group stood in the dark of the hall, enjoying the moment and gauging how long she could make them all attend on her. Savouring the suspense and the power of it.

'Uncle Joseph is getting married.'

Phillip looked relieved. 'Is that all?' he said. Mary sniffed. Nannie said, 'We all knew that you doodle. Surely there was more than that to make Grandfather so cross. They had to put his slippers in the oven, you know. It was very serious.'

Phillip screwed up his face with the effort of his concentration. 'Do you mean he's not going to marry Gracie then? That would be a problem. I can see that being a cause of grief.'

'Why?' asked Mary innocently. Anne tittered. Phillip smiled at Mary kindly. 'They've been a courting Mary. Everyone knows it. But not you bless.' Mary blushed then but no one could see.

'Yes Grace,' went on Nanny importantly. 'I think they said Grace. And who else would have Uncle Joseph?'

'Then why is your grandfather in a dudgeon? Surely Grace Walker is a lovely girl and surely she will bring something with her.'

'Is that all you think about Phillip?' and Mary pulled his night cap off.

'No, but I know how your grandfather thinks. Well, I think I do. He'll be thinking what she brings. Divine Grace'

Anne rose up on her toes in outrage. 'How dare you say that , you --.' 'Sh.' said Nanny, rather too loudly for the import of her command. Then Anne lowered her voice and insisted, 'yes sh! They'll hear us and then you'll all know about it! Especially you Phil. You shouldn't even be down here. Take your candle and go before we are discovered being nosey.'

Nanny and Anne tiptoed carefully away to their chamber, giggling and leaving Mary and Phillip together. Phillip took a candle and theywent carefully back towards their respective chambers, talking quietly still of the evening news.

'So what is the problem then?' asked Phillip carefully.

'Walker. Grandfather does not like the Walkers. Well, he likes William Walker because he is rich and a merchant, as good as -. But he hates James Walker.'

'Is Grace some relation of James Walker then?'

'Oh, a cousin or something. But Joseph should have gone to grandfather and told him what he was about. What he intended I mean. Not to do so is both unwise and bad manners. Something like that anyway. I'm not sure.'

'Oh but if they are in love, you know. If they have fallen for each other, then maybe they can be forgiven. If some other arrangement was being made, or whatever happens, then someone should have told Joseph about it. I'm sure it will be alright.'

'Don't know much about that Phillip. I believe that people should consider others in everything. How can "being in love" excuse bad behaviour? We all owe out duty to our families too, especially to our fathers - and anything else is not good Christian duty. And I did hear -' Phillip laughed at her and put his ear to a wall and got a thump on the arm for his pains. Mary continued, ' I was told openly you cheeky puppy, that grandfather and my other uncles were trying to find a nice girl with something of a fortune. Because of affairs at the mill. J. and J. Not being properly solvent. Now that can't happen.'

'Love doesn't work like that Mary. You'll see. Love does what it likes. People don't always fall in love because someone tells them too. Are they insolvent then?' They had come to point in the hall where they must part since Phillip had another staircase to his cold quarters. He gallantly handed her the candle which sputtered in a draft. Mary hesitated. 'I shouldn't have said that but that I think you know as much as I do about it. But you must remember.' she said very softly, 'that you must not mention it, or hint at it, to anyone at all. It can only become true if it is said and so we don't say it. Confidence is important you see, and if there is not confidence, then creditors call their loans in. That is what happens.'

Phillip made a face. 'Ah I see. Good. That will save them then I think. How much I still have to learn. Good night Mary.'

'Goodnight Phil,' she said under her breath and in the flickering, dancing light of the candle flame she disappeared leaving empty darkness behind her.

Chapter Twenty

A union between the Walkers and the Batesons.

'This coming alliance between the milling dynasties calls for some refreshments my friend? James will you join me in a glass? Or even two!'

James Bateson had called this bright May morning to bring James Walker some news but Walker had already heard – as had most of the Township and a great part of Leeds too. 'Late for that,' he said. 'Old news.'

'How do you know about this Walker? I only heard three days since!' he said as he looked around him at the squalor of the untidy mill office, taking off his hat and wondering where he could risk putting it. Walker continued. 'And who told you my innocent one? By any chance was it your lovely wife?' James frowned and squinted at Walker in annoyance. Walker went on 'You're such a fool Bateson. If you took your head out of the dung barrels and paid more attention to what other people – normal people I mean - not head in the dye vats fools like you – are talking about, you would do better in business. As for me, I see many possibilities ahead. Your father I take it, he's put out?'

'I didn't come to tell you about my brother and Grace,' lied James quickly. 'I just mentioned it as I came in, that's all, before introducing the reason for my visit. And as to the dyes, don't tell me you've not had a man down our dye yard poking around and listening for useful progress -'

'Like that blue you've got Bateson. And I know how you made it.' Walker smiled disarmingly at James as he took down two glasses from a shelf and wiped them on his shirt sleeves. He uncorked a bottle of spirits that was handily hidden beneath his desk and indicated a seat to James. They were in Walker's Mill offices by the Beck and the thumps, knocks and grindings of the mill machinery echoed dully through the walls. The Boulton and Watt engine was in full fire, pumping up water to turn Walker's wheel. Soot caked the old many paned windows and the room stank of wool, ammonia and smoke amongst the many background odours of the wool processing establishment.

James took the proffered and battered chair and glowered at Walker. Walker raised his glass, still smiling at James' discomfiture. When James had heard, indeed at a late hour, that his brother Joseph Bateson at just twenty one was to be married next month to Grace Walker he had been astonished and then rather pleased too. Grace was a fine girl and James thought it would be a good match for both the young people. It might be added, that James was not the best judge of such things for a number of reasons. But he had come to share the news with Walker and Walker had immediately changed the subject. James glanced away from the miller and studied the dirty window panes for a moment or two to regain his composure. Walker watched him amused.

James said at last 'I have to talk to you about something more difficult. Money. You know that don't you? You being so prescient and all.' Walker nodded, his smile not quite so genuine now and he drew breath to reply but James beat him to it. 'So I've brought you a bill, here it is, and we would be much obliged if could settle it within seven days. It's half what you owe us for the American Deal. It would have been all, but we know you are late in your payments to Boulton and Watt. My father is of the opinion that this will satisfy us for the present time but that you must understand that the outstanding amount must be paid before the end of the year and that interest will be added.' James nodded at Walker and suppressed a triumphant smile.

Walker now looked down. He paused then nodded and looked back at James. 'James, my old friend! Yes I fully understand. Of course I do. My brother John has this in hand in Liverpool, and you'll have your money – your father will have his money I mean – in a fortnight. Just a fortnight. That is all. From one trader to another, a little understanding is appropriate, And with the forthcoming nuptials as well. Indeed we will all be family'.

'My father particularly mentioned to me that the forthcoming marriage is not going to be your excuse for leaving us out of pocket.'

Walker shrugged and pulled a face at James. 'I'm surprised your father let you handle the matter. Is Matthew away on business then?' Walker smirked. Then changing tack he asked 'What about our children Bateson? Your Thomas and my girl, twenty years hence, that would make a great match, wouldn't it? She's not so much older than your lad after all.' Walker winked at James.

' When Thomas is old enough to wed I'm thinking he'll be making his own mind up about such things.'

'Like his father?'

'You're treading on treacherous ground Walker.'

'Why? Aren't you and Nancy Lupton the best suited partners in all the world. Love's not everything is it Bateson? I think you've proved that to everyone. Anyway, she's a lovely woman and you did rather well I think, after all.'

'I didn't come here to talk about my marriage Walker, or Joseph's. Or Thomas's for that matter. What's your point'

'Dynastic marriage. Good for everybody. That's my point. I hope Matthew's little girls aren't being lost to that young apprentice your father's taken in. Taken in, being the operative word if you get my meaning.'

James' puzzlement was displayed on his face before he could control it. Walker continued the attack.

'Who's going in at the Holbeck Mill then?' James frowned now and Walker went on, 'One of your lot or maybe little Joseph. Beverley perhaps. Or does it go out of the family perhaps. Maybe I will take a look into it. And your Jack's going to be seeing the inside of Rothwell Gaol, or so rumour has it.'

'Don't know what you're talking about Walker.' James took a mouthful of brandy and swirled the remaining contents of the glass, wondering how to parry. He said, 'So what have you heard about the Holbeck Mill?'

'Atkinson's put it in the Intelligencer. New tenant, new lease, and not the Batesons I take it.' Walker raised his eyebrows. 'New tenant then, and how are you going to save your brother?'

'Do you know something Walker? This is not your business. And please don't make this the subject of chatter. It won't help any of us really, will it? What Atkinson is doing or not doing is not my affair certainly. And I know you're not a position to -'

'So that's Trade marriages for you isn't it. Shame old Atkinson's daughter didn't last the course', said Walker callously. 'Because I heard that he blames your Jack for her death. He doted on that girl'.

James was angry now as Walker had intended. He folded his arms and resisted the impulse to be answer Walker in anger and he let a silence grow. Walker waited still hoping James would be distracted and forget his charge. But James was not to be put off course. The papers that required settlement were laid on Walker's table now and James looked pointedly at them. Walker followed his gaze and shrugged.

'A week friend. Seven days,' said James evenly.

'Like I said, two weeks - because we wait on discounted bills from Liverpool. It might take my brother that long to travel back here. Two weeks then.' Walker stood and held out his hand to James, nodding encouragingly. James shook his head and he also stood. He waited. And a big broad smile lit his features. Walker blew out his breath and hesitated. 'Ten days?' he enquired optimistically.

James sighed and rolled his eyes. 'Ten days then. No longer.' Walker nodded and narrowed his eyes, again the smile that so annoyed James was on his lips.

'Good day Walker and thanks for the brandy.' James took his hat and Walker held the door for him to leave. Walker watched James as he left the mill yard, stopping once or twice to exchange a greeting with the mill hands, and turning at the great gates, he gave Walker a friendly wave.

Walker picked up the demand and said quietly.'Ten days is it my love? Oh well. Your Matthew wouldn't have given any ground on such a matter. Nor the Maister. Perhaps he won't find out. I know who will though. Guess who's going to be in bother when he gets home.'

And then Walker slumped into his seat and begun to make up his accounts and reckoning, deciding from the many demands that were piled before him, which of his creditors could wait and for how long.

The Maister John Bateson did not find out about James' adjustment to their ultimatum in the matter of the Walker's debt but he was still mightily put out about Jack's predicament as announced in the press.

The day before his youngest son Joseph was to marry Grace Walker, his eye was caught by the publication of the final act in the dissolution of the Hebdin and Walker partnership in the matter of the winning of coal from the Beeston Royds. He threw the paper down in disgust.

'What is it husband? I take it you're unhappy about something. I hope it's not your indigestion again?'

'It's nothing to concern you, woman. See to your darning,' snapped John Bateson. His wife turned back to her needle. There was little point probing her husband. She had learnt that long ago but still she waited in case he should want to speak and share what he was thinking. When he pushed back his chair and left for the back parlour, she sighed and returned to her task. There were some stitches yet needed for Joseph's new shirt for the morrow, and it was with love that she laboured. As she plied her needle she glanced up from time to time towards the study, pitying the Maister in his solitude. She hoped he would put Jack's troubles from his mind so that he might find joy in the love match of his youngest son.

Joseph and Grace emerged from the shadows of St. Peter's Parish church to the applause of their friends and well wishers. Joseph looked well in his cambric shirt and his new suit of clothes. Grace was a picture of bubbling beauty, giggling and holding tight to the arm of her lover as they braved a shower of rice. She threw her flowers into the waiting crowd to the cheers of their assembled friends.

As Joseph handed her into the hired carriage he grinned. Seated he leaned to her, putting his arm round her waist to shyly steal a kiss.

Grace teased 'Oh my Lord! Joseph! Are you bashful now we are man and wife,' and she responded with maidenly grace that belied their previous clandestine activities.

Chapter Twenty One

the deluge

It fell on the shoulders of the eldest daughter of the Batesons to shelter her brother Jack in the storm. For some days Leeds had been inundated with Autumn rainstorms that had made the harvests poor and filled the River Aire and its tributaries, the becks and other watercourses until they threatened to over top their boundaries and flood into the streets and the low lying homes and mills. Elizabeth Lister and her husband William, lived in the Park area in a new house with modern convenience and style. William was a kindly and generous man but his finances were all tied up with his iron foundry investments with Murray and Fenton, and his quarrying works in Bramley. But to them Jack would come as to a refuge which would spare him his father's disappointment and distress.

In the breakfast room of the Listers in Leeds, William Lister sympathised with his wife. 'Well n-now my darling, and so it is a good thing that we will have a lodger in our chambers! I d-declare I am most h- happy that your brother comes to stay. We can see to him and help him recover his spirits. These things happen in the affairs of men. He will b-benefit from you kind care.'

Elizabeth set down her china tea cup and looked out of the window at the insistent rain that still fell. 'I wish it was better day for him. A better day...' She trailed off and then looked back at her plainly dressed and rather stout spouse. And she smiled. 'I think things will work out in the end. This is the hardest day for him – all the handing over of property is difficult, but to be without a roof over your head. That is something else. A far more disturbing thing. We must make sure he is comfortable. I have had his things taken up to his chamber and the bed is freshly made up and aired. What else can I do?'

'Indeed my dear. And the children won't mind sharing for a while. Indeed I believe I heard them plotting all sorts of activities in their new arrangements. Such a lot of guns. Your brother I mean. The key is on your chain I hope?'

'Oh yes. Of course. Jack didn't mind. He's very low and biddable just now. You know, I don't think this would have happened if his wife had not died. So soon. It was too soon and he's not one to handle such things well.'

'No. It was a tragedy. Very tragic. I am such a fortunate man, I thank the Lord in my prayers every day, for the B- Blessings that are mine.' William Lister took his wife's hand in his and leant forward to kiss her cheek. He said 'I wonder if your father is c-coping with this. He has always believed that his name sake was the best of them. Although on what grounds – I could not quite fathom.'

'Father is not happy. He does not talk about it. But he is withdrawn and dour. I think Mrs. Bateson has had a hard time of it of late. And the rest of the family.'

'Yes well - it is his way. We all have our ways. Human judgement errs and the judgement of an earthly father is never infallible. He has never been able to see the unusual virtues of James for one thing, but he knows that Matthew is a great and capable business head. Joseph must do well now I think?'

'Matthew thinks that they can sct Joseph up. He has the Lepton works there and if you could see your way to that small loan, then it might be that Jack can work alongside Joseph with the finances held in that way.'

'Yes. But don't say anything to Jack or your father about that now. Not until our loan is arranged. Joseph must keep the books I think.'

'Yes. Joseph does so, has done so since we knew what might happen. But Jack is a very good cloth maker William. I hope he may give his attention to that now and not be after hunting and shooting.'

'We can advise him now d- dear. He would not listen to you before but I think things will change. Try not to worry, just give him c-comfort and trust in the Lord. Well I must be about my work now, much as I would rather stay.'

'Try to stay out of this wet William. It's not good to be in a wet coat all day. You won't be outside, will you?'

'No dear. I am to be inside most of the day. I have only a short walk from my dealings to the Chapel. I hope I might be home for dinner though to welcome Jack here.' William Lister stood now and kissed his wife again before calling for his hat and cloak. He hesitated a moment at the open doorway. The rain had increased and lashed the street outside, making a temporary rill on the cobbles. Then holding his cloak tighter about him, he descended the stone steps and went about his business.

By the river, a man stood watching the swirling waters and wondering what would become of him now he had lost every part of his property and brought his younger brother, newly wed, to ruin. The news had been published three days since in the newspapers and the bailiffs had been at work since then, cheerfully taking inventory of his household goods. The mill and machinery and stock had already been Indentured to Jeremiah Walker and also to Thomas Sellers, card maker of Birstall. It all remained within the Mill on Water Lane, but the yard gates were barred and locked. Rain slashed down now. The day had set in foul and the deluge was increasing.

Beneath him the dark water foamed and rushed, carrying branches and barrels, broken baskets and other rubbish. He stood with his shoulders hunched leaning on the wall of a warehouse, dejected and alone. If he had not been a strong swimmer, he would have at this moment thrown himself into the torrent! But he knew he had a chance of surviving such an action. Even with the currents and debris, there would be some chance he would survive so that would not work. Instead he turned and began walking wearily towards the bridge. From here he could see that the waters were still rising, that some of the mills and warehouses were beginning to flood. It was even some comfort to him, in an obscure way, that others would find themselves distressed in business with damaged stock and property. He was startled by a shout.

He peered intently through the curtain of rain, wiping the water away from his eyes. Another cry, this time a desperate shriek. He thought it came from upstream. He acted on impulse and slithered down the muddy bank of the river, just catching hold of an elder bush before he hurtled into the troubled torrent. Out of the darkness of the bridge a white object appeared then disappeared beneath the surface. Jack pulled off his shoes and his cloak and the fell into the moiling water; he shed his coat and calculated if he had time to remove his breeches but the object reappeared just feet ahead of him. Without thought he plunged into the flood and grabbed desperately as a body sped towards him. He held on with sudden strength born of desperation and dragged the body with him, kicking with all his last strength towards the bank and the shallowed bed of the river that he knew was just ahead. His feet hit something that had been embedded in the edge of the river, what it was he did not know, but he used it to push himself to the bank. One hand gripping some part of the body, he stretched out his arm and grabbed at a passing branch. He heaved again and again on the limb that he had caught and at last succeeded in dragging himself and whatever he had retrieved, out of the river. By now two labourers had managed to get themselves down the bank with a rope and together in the storm they dragged a lifeless body from the Aire, up the bank and to safety.

'Let me through,' commanded a deep rough voice. As Jack lay exhausted and bedraggled, he watched dully as people attended to the drowned child. A dark figure bent close over the body. After some exertions on the part of this person, the child retched and was turned over to vomit up foul water. At length it seemed that the child had been saved. The mystery man stood and turned, looking around at the crowd now gathered and his eyes lit on Jack who still lay slumped on the ground.

'My dear sir. You have been a hero this day. It was foolish, nay feckless to enter the water. You should have been drowned yourself I think. But what you have done is remarkable. Let me shake you by the hand.' Jack managed to pull himself more upright. He said 'I thought it were a gonna!'

'Nearly so I fear. But the young can sometimes be treated after immersion. In this case, I hope the child may recover. But tell me, sir, what is your name?'

'Jack. Jack Bateson.' His hand was grasped and the stranger hauled him to his feel, whilst others crowded round and clapped him on the back.

'Well Jack Bateson. It's a lucky day that you walked the river bank. It is indeed.'

'And you too sir, I think.'

'Yes. But we must all get out of this weather. You there! Carry the child to the Inn. Come with me friend. We'll seek shelter while we all recover from this escapade. Come now, come with me. I prescribe brandy and a warm fire if not a hot bath for us all'.

'I can't pay for owt.'

'There will be no payment needed I think. Not on a day like this and after what you have just done!'

One of the crowd pushed forward now. He grabbed Jack's hand. 'Sir. Thou art a good 'un. Always said it. I'm working at Marshall's sir. But when thou art set up agin, Sir, I'll be over fast as can be. Never thou be feart, man. All on us'll be coming for thee, soon as can be!' And Jack found himself being shaken by the hand yet again, before he was taken with an escort of very wet and bedraggled men, to the Inn nearest the Leeds Bridge where he was again toasted and celebrated as the hero he had been. Jack looked around himself as he sat on a stool before a smouldering fire. He shrugged. Maybe things would come right.

As William Lister said some days later, when the floods had subsided and it was safe to cross the bridge. 'Well now, so some good comes from everything. If you had not invested in your athletic activities then a child would have died. A human life, a soul, that must be of more worth than any profits and losses.'

'Ah,' replied Jack Bateson, between puffs on his pipe.

'However, I do h-hope that you will be diligent now in your labours. For Joseph's sake if not for you own. Honest labour brings dignity to man - not idleness. Let us make a toast to new beginning then.'

Elizabeth Lister lifted the tea pot to oblige her husband in this matter. Jack sighed.

Chapter Twenty Two

Nanny has something to say

Mary and her three sisters were together this January night. They had all four of them squeezed in to the wood framed bed that Mary and Anne shared in their chamber. Sarah had managed to fit herself between her two eldest sisters and was smugly snuggled there, waiting for their mother to come and find her and Nanny and to scold them and harry them back to their own room. In the winter months this was often their routine, when they were all at home. The icy winds might blow and howl down the chimneys and the freezing rain might batter the old windows but the sisters would be warm here in this little respite from the numbing cold that was endured by all folk for the greater part of the days. A coal fire glowed in the hearth and a candle stood spluttering in the drafts of the old house at Greenside. Nanny muttered and pulled on the eiderdown. 'Give up Nanny, share it. I'll tell mother.' Nanny replied, 'no, you won't. I'll tell her you took my turn in the middle and she'll believe me. Because you'll cry and then she'll think you're lying!'

'Hush now the both of you. Or I'll push you both out. I'm tired tonight.' Anne began to cough and then to wheeze and Mary looked alarmed and said, 'Oh Anne? Do you need to sit up? Here I will lift you.'

'I do – but I will not. It's too cold!' managed Anne between coughs.

'Sarah nuzzled up to Anne. 'It will be alright. You'll be better in the morning.'

'She won't. She'll always be coughing like that. Like Uncle Thomas,' said Nanny spitefully. 'And just like Uncle Thomas she'll -'

'Nanny,' said Mary sternly. 'That's enough now. You be quiet or you must go back to your own bed. Uncle Thomas Bateson had died suddenly last year, from asthma.

Mary put her arms round Sarah. Trust Nanny to be so provoking. She nuzzled her little sister's warm hair and said to change the subject 'Did you go up to see the new baby Sarah? Tell us about it.'

'I did and Auntie Grace says I may go and help her look after it any time I like. But is all scrunchy and red. Couldn't half scream an'll.'

'Small was she?' said Anne briefly, because her breathing was hard work in this cold weather

'It's only four weeks on this earth, Bless the little mite. So it will be small won't it,' remarked Mary wisely.

'She,' said Nanny. 'We ave to call it she. Mother said so. Dogs are "it", so there Mary- knows -it -all.' Mary glared at Nanny who smirked. Mary sighed.

Anne made another attempt. 'Like with her being born a bit soon and all.' She gave way to a bout of coughing and Mary put her hand across Sarah and rubbed Anne's back.

'Well I don't know about that,' she lied.

'You do! You know all about it,' came Nanny's high voice from the bed end.

'Sh! Mother will hear. It's not a fit piece of conversation for you Nanny. It's a lot better for everybody if we don't mention it. No one of us is perfect and all of us sin. But God will forgive us if we trust to His Loving kindness.'

Anne was now laughing and coughing at the same time and could not answer Mary's little prim speech.

'Why is Anne laughing?' piped up Sarah from under the eiderdown. 'What's so funny Mary? Nanny why is Anne laughing?'

'I don't know Sarah. You're an ignorant baby aren't you?' added Nanny.

'I'm not!' said Sarah sitting up indignantly. 'I'm very smart and 'twas father himself as said it. Igorant yourself Nanny -'

Mary pulled the small child back down and under the covers. 'It's nothing Sarah. You know lots of thing and you are our clever little sister.' She glared at Nanny who stuck her tongue out.

Anne was still unable to bring herself to join the teasing of Mary. So it fell to Nanny to finish the deed.

'Miss Mary Bateson. Oh wise and all knowing Mary. Now if our parents married in February …. as it says in our Bible, February the 26th. Yes? Then how are you born in June?' Nanny's little head that just poked out of the quilt was nodding now.

Anne was now choking with her bad chest and uncontrollable laughter.

Mary was brought short for a moment. For all her studies of the Bible, and for that matter her delight in the family details written neatly inside the cover, she had not made this deduction herself. Or if she had, she had denied the conclusion of the dates.

She bit her lip as she searched for something to say that would quieten her sisters mirth and restore her dignity.

'Just think,' went on Nanny. She had dived under the covers so that she could dare continue to annoy her sister. 'If our parents had not been married on the 26th February, what would that make you? You would be a -'

Mary lost control. She found a part of Nanny's leg and nipped it very hard. Nanny screamed. 'Don't you say that word Nanny. You're a very naughty girl. You hear me? You're very bad and I hope mother is coming right now!'

As if on cue, Jane Bateson put her head around the panelled door. 'Well. And what are you all doing in this nest? And why are screams echoing round the house? You had better come out right now, Miss Nanny and Miss Sarah! Indeed.'

She put her arms round her reluctantly emerging younger daughters and clucked them away to their own bed chamber. 'I will be back soon girls,' she told Mary and Anne over her shoulder. Noting Anne's struggle for breath she added kindly, 'and you may say your prayers in bed tonight. It's too cold for either of you to get back up. I'll just settle these imps and then I'll be back. Tuck Anne in will you Mary? Keep her warm.'

Mary did as she had been bad and tucked Anne in, but a little roughly. She knew her sister was coughing at her own embarrassment and she found it hard to forgive, although she knew she should. And then she relented when she saw her sister's distress and gave her pillow up for the comfort of the invalid.

When their mother returned and they had said their night prayers and she had kissed them goodnight, Mary could not bring herself to look at her mother. No child wishes to dwell upon the physical love of their parents. But that her father could have been so sinful was more than she could deal with tonight.

She lay miserably awake for some time, listening with anxiety to Anne's laboured breathing and trying to come to terms with this insight into her own birth story. And her father! That pillar of the community. That great one that she held as above all other men in his gentle kindnesses and generousness of spirit. And purse.

But tongues had wagged when Joseph Bateson and Grace Walker's child had been born a little too soon after their marriage. In the village, where such slips were treasured and shared, those who could understand the matter delighted to pass on the gossip, and the old folk recalled that Matthew Bateson and Jane Hepper had also been blessed with a child very soon after their marriage. Very soon. Memories were long for the indiscretions of their betters, especially when such folk were conspicuous by their adherence to public piety. But the remembrance was affectionate. The weavers said that such marriages were true 'uns and that those that made them were like turtle doves. Their wives would cuff the weavers and say that their husbands were pigeons and that the Bateson women were weak willed and no better than they should be and then they would laugh and taunt their old husbands about their courting days with a wink and nod and the name of the barn or location of the haystack where such wooing had been enjoyed.

But Mary found it very hard to deal with. For some days afterwards she was unable to come to terms with what she truly believed to be a flaw in her parents behaviour.

She felt herself ashamed as she walked out the next day to make her way to her day school in Leeds. She imagined that the people that she passed in the village greeted her with a knowing look in their eye. She was not able to talk to her mother about it. This was a pity, because Matthew and Jane were perfectly open about their love and her mother would have given her plenty of reasons why such a small thing was a sure sign of good and honest affection. And probably guided her too, so that Mary did not make her own errors when the time came for her to consider marriage. Her father would have laughed uproariously. But Mary kept this to herself and in fact, she prayed that her parents might be forgiven such impropriety and strove too, to forgive them!

Most country girls brought up in company with nature, would understand everything about procreation by now. But Mary was inclined to be studious. More than this. She was ever endeavouring to do what was right and good. She was known within her family for her goodness and her piety and thus did her sisters Nanny and Anne have much ammunition with which to provoke her and yet Mary bore this with patience and tolerance. Matthew Bateson noted all this and he often said to her with a sigh, 'Oh dear, Mary'. To which her mother Jane Bateson would look across at her husband and smile a little.

In the month after the birth of Uncle Joseph and Aunt Grace's little daughter Hannah, Uncle James and Aunt Nancy were blessed with another daughter, Maria. The birth went along easily, so Mary's mother told them, and Nancy was quite well considering. Uncle James though, had taken a strange mood upon him and it was known by some that he had personally attended to spalding brick work near the top of the engine house chimney much to the suprise and admiration of the mill wrights and the mill workers. These were sworn to secrecy in the matter which only increased their loyalty and affection for their adventurous and interesting master. What James gained by undertaking such a dangerous challenge can only be imagined. Perhaps the physical activity removed from his troubled mind nagging thoughts of a curse which in some ways, was proving still true and the wide view of the hills about him in a wild westerly gave a sense of control over the world which he might otherwise struggle to feel.

Nancy proudly brought the baby to show to Maister John Bateson within a fortnight of her birth and was now in the great parlour at Greenside.

'Well well. So let me hold my granddaughter. Well she's a bonny one Nancy me dear!'

'Hmm. She's coming on nicely. Your son says she looks like you sir. But she's settled quickly, feeds well and is of an even temper. So there you are. Just the spit of her grandfather.'

John Bateson sniffed at that and regarded Nancy keenly.

'Two daughters Mrs. Bateson! So that'll need some financing at some future date. You should have more sons dear. They make money not take it.' He looked up from the babe in his arms and smiled a little, but a shadow fell across his face as soon as the words were out, as he thought of his son Jack and the bankruptcy. Nancy caught this and replied quickly, 'Ah so now we hear it at last. Can I take it you think better of my James now, old father? He has your approval at last in the blessing of our son?'

John recovered himself. 'Now then girl, don't be putting words in my mouth'. His wife came over and took the baby from him and told him, 'Give up you old fool. Give me a look at the baby and be kind to your kin!' And John Bateson surrendered the warm bundle and chortled. To Nancy he said, 'The best thing about my son James is his lovely wife! Ever the best of them my dear'.

Nancy smiled and laid her hand gently on his arm.

Book Two

Chapter One

The Parade

This Thursday in May, the Year of Our Lord 1801, was a glorious fine day under a cloudless sky, calm airs and the sun shone kindly on the streets of Leeds. It was holiday of sorts - where those who could spare time for idleness of a patriotic variety, gathered and lined the route of a final parade by the Leeds Volunteers and their Command. The militia were gathered in the Cloth Hall and the sound of nailed boots marching and horse gear jangling could be heard above the noise of the waiting crowds. Not deterred by the stench of the summer drains and sewers and the bouquet of chemical and industrial odours, noisy groups lined the main streets in the welcome sunshine.

Mary Bateson and her school friends had come after lessons to watch the Volunteers as they made their final manoeuvres before disbanding in the very optimistic hope of future peace in Europe. The Treaty of Amiens had been signed some months since and the war was over. The cautious powers of Yorkshire now considered it unnecessary to keep and maintain its military force. And Napoleon Bonaparte had just been made First Consul of the French Republic. There may have been some who wondered if the disbanding of the Volunteers was just a little premature. But the Mayor and the Corporation had turned out in their best robes and were on their way to the steps of the Music Hall in Albion Street to give their thanks to the heroes, to receive the Regimental Colours with proper ceremony and to show their gratitude to their brave Militia with entertainments and sustenance and possibly with long speeches. The gentlemen officers would have the benefit of these Civic Honours but the ranks would linger in Leeds, drinking, boasting and roaring out ballads and telling each other increasingly elaborated versions of their exploits - and bothering the girls of the town with advances amorous or simply lewd. Of course these young ladies who attended the parade had been accompanied by the school assistant, one Miss Quickly – but she had developed a migraine headache and left with them with suitable advice and very little concern. Mary Bateson was there and she was a most reliable and proper young woman and mature for her years too.

'You wait till you see him. He's just too handsome in his uniform!' Amy Porter leaned forward impatiently to see if the soldiers were in sight. From the Cloth Hall the stirring strains of the West Yorkshire Militia band could be heard with flutes and drums and an out of tune cornet. The sound of marching feet and roaring sergeants excited the crowd.

'Oh do be quiet Amy! Please behave yourself with decorum. Get back out of the road, you'll fall in the gutter, you will!' Jane Rhodes pulled the love- lorn Amy back into line as she scolded her.

'Tell her Mary, will you just tell her – she'll pay some heed to you. She's after making a show of herself yet again. And all for the sake of a young man that doesn't even know her.' Amy looked at Jane indignantly. 'Of course I do. He's from our village and you know it.'

Mary nodded at Jane. They did know it. In dull extensive detail.

'I've been introduced,' defended Amy defiantly. Mother knows his mother. So there you,' and Amy stuck her tongue out at Jane. Jane retorted, 'Yes, and just a little school girl he would have thought. He must be at least 25 and you're just 16!' Mary Bateson rolled her eyes and smiled to herself. Amy had come to school in her very best gown which was made in the latest fashions from London and beyond. Fine cotton and floating, it had a high waist and short sleeves and Amy had been admired and envied. The school mistress though had been less impressed by the skimpiness of the outfit and had indeed wondered if Amy should be sent home to change into more modest clothing. But in the end the wondering had taken so much time that the day was half gone and so Amy remained in her finery in loyal readiness for the parade. The other girls, some half dozen of them, were in their ordinary clothes. They wore their wool or cotton skirts and bodices and their usual school bonnets. Most of them thought that Amy looked very fine and grown up and were even now giving her admiring glances. But Mary stood slightly apart and near to the shop fronts and stalls behind the crowds. She might have thought that such vanity and pride was a failing on the part of her friend. If this had been her sister no doubt she would have judged her. But she such not think badly of Amy who was not so well educated as the Bateson sisters. She felt only a feeling of exasperation with the girl and her silly crush on that older man.

    It felt as it the whole population of Leeds had come forth to cheer the warriors who had armed themselves and frequently paraded in defence of their town, their King and country, to the reassurance of the residents of Leeds. Even some of the workers in the mills had been let go early that they might witness this spectacle and to cheer the brave lads. The mill owners were less than happy that the Regiment was to hand their Colours in to the parish church. In such times as these, there was always the threat of insurrection by the machine breakers and the lawless type of casual labour. Those high minded gentleman that led the small army should have been more aware of the threat from inside the citizenry. So thought the owners of the mills as they took their places near to the Music Hall.

    The inns and beer houses were doing great trade with the milling labourers and around their doorways were gathered men in holiday mood and an ever increasing degree of inebriation. Mary looked about her marvelling at how great was the population of Leeds. There must have been near 100 people lining this street alone. Her eye was caught by a familiar figure from home.

    'Hello Dan. You're let out then? Oh look! I think they're coming!' Mary turned her head to look where the officers of the Volunteers had appeared now from the arch, straight and solemn on their sleek mounts, and were riding into the street in their red uniforms and glittering gold ornaments, holding her hand above her eyes for the low afternoon sun. Their flags and pennants beside them, the command was a fearsome sight coming out of the shadows. A rousing cheer went up all around.

    'Good day Miss Bateson,' said Dan Grady loudly, taking off his hat to Mary and nodding his head politely, a book held under one arm. Amy, of an age and predisposition to notice such things glanced behind her hearing the deep voice of a male. She took a step back and whispered to Jane. Jane looked round at Mary and at Dan and she blushed and quickly looked away. Amy and Jane continued to whisper and to glance at Mary and at Dan who was stood quite close to her watching the parade. Dan looked away from the soldiers and noticed the girls giggling and nudging each other so he bent to Mary's ear and said quietly, 'Good day Miss Bateson. I'll be off now then.' Mary nodded absently, still watching ahead of her and absorbed by the parade. Then she gave Dan a small smile and Amy watching, nudged Jane who pointedly ignored this childishness but could not control a covert glance at the young man.

Amy had turned her full attention back to the parade and was anxiously examining each man that passed. At last she cried out, 'There now, see him? He's on the far side.' And she began to wave her arms and to cheer very loudly, and at each cheer she made a little jump in the air. Mary had to laugh at her friend's enthusiasm. The handsome young Volunteer risked a glance at the fuss but then effected a discernable rigidity of posture, an impressive fixed gaze ahead and with good discipline resisted any inclination to return the salute of the pretty girl. But he smiled broadly and marched with renewed energy.

'Oh, oh, oh,' sighed Amy. 'Oh. He smiled at me.' Jane tutted and glanced at Mary who just laughed. Jane said in a matter of fact tone, 'For sure Amy, I am certain he was smiling at me?' To which Amy frowned and stamped her foot and shook her head. Jane pleased, stepped back to Mary's side and asked most discreetly, 'And who was that fine young man then, Miss Bateson?' Mary replied, 'Oh, no one. That's one of our weavers. He's nobody.' Jane glanced down the street. 'Oh. A working man?' she said with disappointment and returned her attention to the ranks of infantry now marching before her.

When the three hundred and fifty or so fine soldiery had passed on towards their destination at the Music Hall, the crowds began to disperse. Some went back into their shops or workshops or homes. Others could be seen heading for the ale houses having become hoarse and dry with the hard work of cheering on the parade and the unusual warmth of the weather.

'Will you come down to the bridge with me Jane?' asked Mary tentatively taking her friend by the arm. Jane shook her head quickly. 'No, we are all going to Amy's aunt's house remember? You can come too if you have changed your mind, can't she Amy? Yes you can. It'll be a real jolly. And then tomorrow… well tomorrow, that's going to be a great day isn't it? Our last day together at school and then we are all to be separated and apart. I can't wait.'

Mary shook her head now patiently. 'That's not what you mean. You mean you are excited to be growing up but will miss us all. I have to go home. It's Choir tonight and I cannot miss a practice. I certainly could not go back with you to Amy's without letting my parents know. Of course not.'

'No I suppose that wouldn't be the thing. But get across the bridge before the mills come out won't you darling? It gets so busy there later. Oh and there will be the soldiers too so don't dawdle will you? And we'll see you in the morning. I'm so excited I hardly know what.'

The other girls now intent on their own anticipated pleasure were wrapped in their animated conversations and Mary set off alone towards home. The streets were very busy with many workers idling and drinking and passing the time of day. A holiday atmosphere ruled and it was noisy and crowded. Mary made her way as best she could but when she came to the Horse and Jockey Inn she found the path blocked because of the drinkers on the street. She glanced at the midden that ran down the middle and decided against that way. She began to edge her way through the throng but was knocked and pushed as her slight figure and quiet voice went unheeded by the rowdy revellers.

'Wait now Miss Bateson. Come this way.' A deep voice made her turn. Dan Grady put his free hand gently on her arm and in a louder voice cried, 'mind thy backs now. Pardon me, but here is a lady needing way. Watch out now! There we go.' He shepherded her through the crowd with his free arm held out to make space and his book clamped in the crook of his arm. 'Oi!' shouted a big man in a grubby apron and then recognising Dan changed, 'Oh pardon me miss. How do young Grady then? What's tha reading now? Thou art scholar aye!. Watch out lads! Look what tha's doing there. Make a way for the little 'un.'

At last they came to a quieter part of the street. 'Thank you Dan. I thought I would never get through that mob. Not without beer being spilt anyway.'

'Well that would have gone down badly miss I think. Anyways there tha goes. And art thou walking home this evening? I mean now.'

'I am Dan. It's a beautiful evening for the walk but the place is so busy. Thanks for your help'

'It's my pleasure as always Miss Bateson. But I am going home now so I can walk along with thee if thou would permit it.'

'Oh thank you Dan. Yes come along then. We can be home before supper if we keep a good pace.'

'Suppers you mean?' said Dan with a twinkle in his eye. 'For 'tis to be sure I'll be getting fed at Maister Jim's and if I am very canny, I can get another bite at thy house.' Mary laughed. 'Oh yes. I forget the way things are. Yes I suppose you will do that. And you look like you need two suppers.'

'What does tha mean Miss? I'm sure I'm not so narrow looking as that.'

'I mean the height of you now Dan. What made you think to get so big? I'm sure it's not good for a weaver to have such a height on him. My father says it can cause a bad back. It wasn't a good idea was it?'

'No Miss. And I can only say I'm very sorry to put upon thee all so.' He made a penitent face. 'And the feeding of me has been a great burden to the Batesons generally. For that I am truly sorry. And also for my growth. My apologies.'

And they both laughed. Dan Grady had never stopped growing since his arrival that snowy night at Greenside; an orphan in the storm. He had first filled out and then he had shot up. And then he had filled out again and once more grown higher. And that had gone on for more than two years. He was now over six feet in height and because of his love of running and his physical labours he had a strong and slim build. His hair was dark and curling and his blue eyes were full of life. No wonder that Amy and Jane had been been curious. He was dressed in plain and mended clothes but was neat and clean. His face was strong and would have been handsome but for his nose being a little too large and his mouth a little too wide. But Mary had always though that the most pleasant thing about poor Dan Grady was that he was always cheerful and kind and never put out by others in any matter. He was resourceful and intelligent her own father always said. And Uncle James was very partial to the lad and was often heard to say that Dan would go far. In view of his height, Uncle James had suggested that building mill chimneys might lie in the future for the foundling. It was rumoured also, that the young weaver and his master were sometimes engaged in a sport that involved climbing new constructions, something that Mary believed to be only a tall tale. But she remembered herself and her decorum and the laughter faded. She set off now before him and he walked respectfully a little behind her.

In fact, Mary was very proud of Dan and felt that he had repaid her kind attentions to him over the years in the matter of teaching him how to write and which books to read. She regained her composure but continued then with a more reserved demeanour and conscious of her place she resolved that she should give some guidance.

'Now Dan you must promise to me that you will not grow any bigger because I hear my uncle James makes you climb chimneys? Which is very dangerous. Is that agreed?' Dan nodded and looked away but smiled; his height was not within his control and climbing chimneys was indeed a risky activity. Mary then enquired what he was reading and on being handed the volume scanned the spine and approved, 'This is an excellent book. You like these hymns?' They had reached the bridge and halted there.

'Aye miss, I do. But I knows one that'll like them better even than thee and I!'

'Oh you mean Molly? But she can't read though can she?'

'No but I can. So she asked me to bring her something nice to listen to and I choose this special like. Does tha think she will like it Miss Mary?' Mary beamed at Dan and agreed that it was a good choice for Molly. And then she realised something more. That Molly would be familiar with the words and would be able to say them and aid her own studies in the mysteries of the written word and that this would give her the very greatest pleasure and pride. Mary looked sharply at Dan and he gave her another conspiratorial grin. She shook her head at him indulgently.

Dan was contented this afternoon. He had been let off early from his current training in Benjamin Beverley's workshops and he anticipated a good meal and then another with his beloved Molly. And to help Miss Bateson get home safely with the uproar all about the town? That also pleased him very well. But then passive contentment was often his condition.

'Oh and is the weaving going on well then Dan? Do they treat you well at Beverley's?' Mary handed him back his book and set off again quickly towards Water Lane so Dan from just behind her said, 'They do miss, thanks to thee for asking. But it's not weaving for me in Leeds. I've been looking at the cloth finishing now and great interesting work it is too.'

'I did not know that!. You can't be changing trade now! You're much too old for another apprenticeship!' Mary stopped in her astonishment. 'Don't the finishers mind you being with them?' Dan caught up with her then.

'Sure and tha's right there. But they don't mind me. I'm just a -watching tha knows. And running their errands. But bless us all, no one wants to help out with that dyeing! Heavy work it is to be sure and a mucky do as well. But it's something we've got a good hold off back at thy mill. So it is. I take good notice you see of the other work at Mr. Beverley's. No, they don't complain.' They had fallen into step again and Mary marked it but did not now object since they were away from the town and into the lane home where the people if they knew them were preoccupied with their own concerns and would not worry for the mill owners daughter with a working man beside her. Or they would know her and would see Matthew Bateson's eldest daughter coming home from Leeds with her uncle's retainer to keep her safe. No eye saw the clothier's daughter with the tall and attractive apprentice respectfully in tow and wondered

Mary thought about this awhile. 'So you will be going into cloth finishing then Dan? Not weaving then? Oh, I didn't know that.'

Dan shrugged his broad shoulders cheerfully. 'Seems like I do most things Miss Bateson. Whatsoever is needed I think to meself. When a boy's been treated as good as meself, then I'm happy to go along and see to it. And if it's the finishing that they want for the Bateson cloth, that I don't mind at all. Not at all, to be sure.'

'This is why Molly is so proud of you Dan,' said Mary thoughtfully. Dan with tact, modest reticence and some skill turned the conversation away from himself and his business to more general subjects until they reached the path up to Greenside and then with a slight tip of his hat went homeward to the Weaving House where he would eat with the other apprentices before visiting at Mary's own abode. The child was safe home

Chapter Two

Samuel Beverley

Dan continued down the lane, to his home at the Weaving House. Mary went at once to Greenside and to the part of the house where her family lived, side by side with her beloved grandfather John Bateson.

She peered around the hallway as her eyes adjusted to the dim interior after the brightness of the summer evening. Through a gap in the kitchen door, she could see her father's coat hanging on the back of a chair and she took off her bonnet and went in to greet him. It was always good when her father was home before dark and she gave him a hug from behind before asking if there was supper saved for her but then saw dishes laid out on the table covered by a linen cloth.

'Is mother out then?' she asked. Matthew stood to greet her.

'She's gone down to Beech Grove. Aunt Mary's time has come. She may be out all night my pet, as these things go…..no day more full of significance than the birth of a child and the graduation of another. We must pray my love for the child in its journey into this world and trust that God will bless us all. Tha's late home my dear. Did tha watch the parade then after all?'

'I did stay to see it sir. I hope you are not disappointed in me. But Dan Grady was there and walked home with me. There were a lot of people in drink upon the streets and I was lucky he was there to help. They let them have the afternoon off you see, at the workshop. So he walked me home, which I think was very kind. He has told me that he is looking at cloth finishing now and I did not know?' She frowned slightly. 'He always seems to fit in doesn't he? Dan I mean. I can't think how else Beverley's finishers would let him study their trade.'

'Well yes. But it's not for thee to be troubling thyself about the Cloth Hall regulations. And aye, that's true, isn't it. He fits in with what is? That sums it up nicely. We get him to master every process child, so that he can fulfil his potential. The Lord gave him to us as a blessing. Thou must not concern thyself with such things nor draw attention to his training lest others resent his good fortune and capable hands.

'I ponder more about thee. And what about thee Mary? This is thy last day of school tomorrow. What will the big world hold for my fine daughter and what have you decided to do? Thy mother and I must know thy mind so that we may make the arrangements for your progress. I've my ears full from thy aunts all wanting thy company and services.'

'Your fine daughter needs her supper. Who knows where the Lord will send me but I'll need sustenance before any of that can be discussed.' Her father laughed. Mary sat herself at the table and raised the cloth to find ham and bread and apple tart. Her father pulled his chair to her side and watched her fondly as she ate.

'Well sometimes in the absence of obvious Divine purpose, we get to choose our own way Mary. Think more of what thou hast read in the good book. Some of us make cloth and manage the labour of others and still endeavour to walk in the light of the Lord. Not the less worthy in the sight of the God I think.'

'Of course not.' Mary pushed away her plate. 'It is just that I am not sure which way I should go given choice. I look to you for guidance father?'

'Tha knows all your aunts want you to go to them, don't you? Every single one. I think that must say a great deal about your character Mary. A great deal. But were I to decide then I would have two against me and how would I manage with such a burden.'

'I know they do. But I don't know which of them to choose. But aunt Elizabeth has the finest house. So maybe I will go there for a while.'

It was the custom for young women and young men too, those that were of the cloth making community in Yorkshire, to be placed out in other families to learn and to assist. For the young men it was as a form of apprenticeship. For the girls it would be a prelude to marriage and domesticity.

'I can see much to recommend thy aunt Lister, for there is much to be gained by a comfortable life,' her father teased. 'And thy uncle William is a wise and inspiring man. Must I think we are too simple here then and that thou desires the fine things of the town? Are we too simple here?'

Mary giggled. 'Yes. Not at all fine enough. But father, Elizabeth said she would be able to place me in helping with the night school classes.' She rocked her old three legged stool. 'And all of their chairs have four legs too. So that must come into the consideration.' Her father frowned deeply, his craggy brows furrowed. 'Four legs is it you want now? Well I never.' Mary giggled some more. Her father sighed. 'Oh I see. Tha thinks thou would like to be a teacher, like thy aunt Sarah?' Mary nodded and blushed.

'Well child, I like this thought as tha knows and I think thou art very bright and very clever. And I know thou hast a gift for such work because our Dan is the living proof of it. Thou has my blessing. As if that could ever not be the case.' He rose and kissed the top of her head. 'Now, if I'm not mistaken I can hear the sound of music up at the chapel. And thou art late for choir I think all through ogling at the handsome military! No apple tart for thee tonight!'

Mary stood up and hurried to fetch her bonnet and wool cloak. 'Father,' she called from the hallway. 'Stop eating my apple tart.' She came back to grin from the doorway. 'Hide it for me! And don't let Nanny and Sarah know there's any left. I know what you're like.' He father leaned back in his chair and nodded sagely at his nearly grown up daughter. He then licked his lips while looking at the tart. Her little sisters peeped from the bannisters giggling as she hurried past.'And don't you two eat my dinner. Hear me? Or I'll be home and eat the both of you!'

Mary ran hastily up the lane towards the Bell Chapel mortified that she should be late. She heaved on the heavy door and entered as quietly as she could. The choir were in full song and she crept to her place among the high voices.

'Where have you been?' whispered her sister Anne. 'Watching the parade in Leeds.'gasped Mary, still catching her breath. Anne said 'Oh! I bet that was fun. I wish I could have gone. Listen to you heaving! You sound like me in a bout.'

'Hem, hem.' The singing had ceased and the conductor cleared his throat in irritation. Mary, embarrassed, looked at the music in front of her to find her place. The sun glowed gold through the high round arched windows. Candles had been lit and were held here and there among the singers. Mary looked round the faces that she knew so well and a sudden feeling of happy sadness flooded her. These people in her community, this place of her childhood, would not always be here. Where the Lord would take her she did not know. But her future lay ahead and soon so much would change. A tear came to her eye and she brushed it away quickly. Silly girl, she thought, to be so sentimental. She should be braver than this.

After the practice was concluded, lamentably not to the satisfaction of the conductor, there was tea and currant bun to be had at the nearby schoolroom. Mary and Anne headed there, linked arm in arm, while Mary told to her sister the glories of the military parade.

'Miss Mary, Miss Anne?' they stopped and waited. Samuel Beverley was walking briskly to catch them up. He tripped on a stone and came to a sudden unsteady halt before them. Anne tittered.

'Hello Sam,' said Mary kindly. 'Are you alright. It's hard to see where to put your feet isn't it in the dark? Those stones are badly laid are they not?'

'Yes, yes, it is, you're right there Miss Mary.' Samuel said gratefully, 'they are'. His feet seemed to big for him at the moment. 'Come on then Samuel. Let's get our tea and buns. Your mothers lying in I hear? I hope it goes well. Another little one at your house!'

Samuel followed behind the girls, going from one side to another as he tried to fit in with their walk in the half light. 'I wanted to ask you Miss Mary? Mother said you might choose to come to us and not to Aunt Lister. She hoped you would come and stay. She's going to need help -' Samuel stopped abruptly as they came to a gateway in the low stone wall and he found his way barred by that wall. Waiting till they were through, he hurried after them. Mary took pity on him and stopped in the light of the lamp in the doorway. So Samuel continued. 'She's finding it hard to teach the little ones Mary and she knows you're good at it. I do hope you'll come.' Mary felt herself colouring at the compliment. 'I'm sorry Sam, I've got other plans you see?' Samuel's face fell. He blurted out, 'Oh, oh well. I suppose that's good. It's just -'

'But it is lovely that you have asked me. I think it is very nice. Come along and get some tea. Here, sit here.'

'No, no. I will - I'll get you some tea. And you Miss Anne of course. I didn't forget you.' Anne Bateson smiled grimly. 'Yes you did, Samuel Beverley!' Samuel blushed and turned at speed to the tea urn and tripped awkwardly to fetch the refreshments. 'Don't be so mean Anne', said Mary firmly when poor Samuel was out of earshot. 'He can't help his feet.' Realistically then, 'they do look big though, don't they? We may not get all our tea.' And they laughed behind their hands.

In the dark warm night the choral company parted and went homeward; up the hill to Armley, down the hill to Lower Wortley or even across the fields to Holbeck. Mary and Anne set off to Greenside. An owl hooted from a distant barn.

Anne remarked, 'Well well well. And there you have made a conquest Miss Mary Bateson. I do believe that Samuel Beverley's has stolen your heart too.'

'Hush now you silly girl I have enough of that with my school friends. He's a child. You do talk nonsense! I've not given any thought to such a matter. So you can just be quiet about such things. Anyway, he's just awkward, you know. He's not like his father.'

'Too right! He's nothing like Benjamin. But I saw you blush. Which means you've noticed him.'

'It does not!' replied Mary indignantly.

'Well then. That's probably so. Because you blush all the time, whenever young men speak to you.'

'Shut up Anne.' Anne smirked to herself and gloated that she had scored a point over her ever morally superior elder sister.

'Mary, come in a minute wilt thou? Go up to bed Anne, I just want a quick word with Mary. Goodnight dear. Say thy prayers please.' Matthew kissed his daughter Anne on the cheek and she took her candle from the hall stand, and went dutifully to her bed.

Mary walked lightly into the kitchen and sat in her mother's chair by the hearth. She had grown into a certain grace and she was pretty in a neat way that was something more when she smiled. She waited to see what her father wanted, thinking back to the accusations that Anne had made that were unwarranted and unwanted yet feeling slight guilty over the interchange with Samuel. But her father knew nothing of this. Not that conversations had not been had across the years by the various families. But Matthew and his wife Jane did not hold with arranged marriages. It was an article of faith with them that young people should have a choice in such matters. Among suitable persons of course.

Matthew took his own chair by the empty hearth. 'There is just one thing I want to ask thee tonight and since thy mother is out, well, isn't that the right time!' He smiled.

'On this night when thou art becoming so grown up and we are facing losing thee to the outside world I must know some things. It's a hard thing for a father tha knows, to lose a daughter.' Mary came to her father and put her arms about his shoulders then knelt by his side.

'I'm only away to Leeds father, if Aunt Elizabeth will have me. It's but a good walk on a pleasant day. It's not over the moors or anything like that.'

'Not yet. But who knows? But thou must understand if I ask thee now. Is there perhaps any one person that thou might be, let us say, considering. For the future I mean. Is there any attachment growing or anything of that kind. Forgive me Mary I must ask and thy mother is out tonight and so I pry. But I have been sat here turning over things in my head and I cannot help myself but I must ask about this.' Matthew stroked Mary's smooth hair and then went silent.

Mary waited a moment considering her answer and wondering what her father wanted to hear. But she braved an honest reply. 'No father. Of course not. I am too young for such thoughts.'

'When thou art not too young, as thou hast said, wilt thou promise me this Mary? That thou will come to me if or maybe when, thy heart is no longer thy own? I will never stand in thy way of course. But thou must always know thou can count on thy old father to guide thee and especially in such important matters as this. Promise me.' Matthew smiled with sincere thought of his child's future happiness. No one had come between him and his desired Jane Hepper. He knew nothing of complications of the heart. Or of the constraints of over riding dutifulness and misdirected intentions of redemption.

'I promise you I will always tell you what is in my heart. I am a very fortunate girl, to have such a father as you. But such things are not for tonight. Nor for some time I think. I promise I will tell you though if ever such a thing becomes needed.' And Mary too made her promise with sincerity.

 Matthew sighed. 'Ah me. Well then my child, to bed with thee after such a long day. Here, I'll hold my light for thee while tha goes up the stairs. Thy mother will not be home tonight I think. I will wait up a while though. These nights are hard nights where children come naked into the world with pain and danger.' Matthew took his candle and held it aloft to light Mary's feet upon the old oak staircase. Then he went to see that all the yard was quiet and safe and all the household safely inside and to lock and bar the many doors for the night, calling 'all's well' to his old father and settling himself to wait for news of Beech Grove.

In her bed Mary lay awake as Anne snored quietly beside her. Her father's questions had troubled her. She did not want to think of such things. Not yet. She smiled as she remembered Sam's awkwardness. Amy's forlorn hope came into her thoughts then and Dan too. She wondered if he would ever marry. And then she pondered the future. What would become of her and would she every find a soul mate? She was not sure that she would. It would have to be some very wonderful man that could be part of the life she had begun to consider, the hopes that were only half formed; the dreams and fears and the fancies too. Someone perhaps like her father? There could be very few of those in the world. Into her sleep muddled thoughts intruded a memory of the dashing young Methodist Minister that had come in search of her Aunt Sarah a few years ago. In the solitary darkness of her room she felt the blood rush to her face. She resolved to put an end to this lack of self control. She must in future be more reserved, more composed. More ladylike. And not blush. As if such things could be done by will and decision at such a tender age. When she at last dozed she wondered if she would marry with a Methodist Minister and commit her life to serving him and her God. This was a comforting thought and she constructed many little scenes of devotion, sacrifice and heroism, teaching, preaching and the saving of lives and souls, with the little ones upon her knee and playing around her in sweet harmony. Even the prospect of continued travel and an itinerant domesticity seemed to her in her youth and ignorance, to be a most pleasant prospect. To live in Manchester! Or to see more of Halifax! But she would wait with patience and see how the Lord disposed of her and her hand and she at last slept and dreamed.

Chapter Three

Two Young Gentlemen

    The short winter's day was ending at the workshop in Leeds. It was near to the Cloth Hall and here Benjamin Beverley finished wool cloth, storing it ready for shipping, smooth and pressed and wrapped in sheets of tissue. Next to the shop was a counting house when the developing interests of the Beverley House were conducted. Many of the merchants also dealt with money; loans and bills discounted in partnership with Country or even London Banks.

    Three young men were here, working alongside the Head Clerk - a man of advancing years who understood very well the necessity for the sons of the clothiers and apprentices in general to understand and practice those skills of accountancy and book keeping that would become their lot. Having spent his years in the cloth trade he also knew that the close supervision of the intricacies of cloth finishing was required in a good Clothier but that was for the manager of the workshops to promote.

    Mr Burt attended to the training of young Samuel Beverley with almost paternal care excepting that unlike his master Benjamin Beverley, he was a patient and long suffering teacher. Having witnessed and at times experienced the harsh temper of his master, he was all too well aware, that Samuel was of a different and more pleasant nature, and he bore with Samuel's awkwardness with forbearance. Mr Burt had also been given the responsibility of training the young man that the Batesons thought so well of. Mr. Abbey was also given the opportunity to learn about the complexities of the financial interests of the House. Then this week there was Dan Grady! Mr. Burt frowned. He had at first balked at the idea of a working man in the counting house, for such was Dan Grady. But he had been impressed by the boy's ability and his pleasant manner. Mr. Abbey too, with his brother now establishing so they said, in London, well Mr. Abbey was a good natured young gentleman and he understood things very quickly. Mr. Abbey had been in Hull in the warehouses and he was quite familiar with bills and figures. That he was not quite so dedicated to his set tasks as the other lads was noted. There were some three under clerks in the counting house and offices and Mr. Burt managed all these with fussy diligence and fastidious care.

There was also a monosyllabic overlooker whose toleration of the young masters was not remarkable. Had Mr. Cooper been inclined to be more articulate, he might have had much to say – about the urgency of orders and the delays to such orders that were a risk when the place was nominally in the charge of a mere child, albeit the son and heir of the House. But he restrained his irritation slightly and restricted his observations to the occasional tut or ill natured grunt, which the workers in the finishing departments understood only too well. On occasion, Mr. Burt would peer over his wire rimmed spectacles at the overlooker, with slight disapproval and a pronounced sniff which might be enough to remind the overlooker what their responsibilities might be in regard to the young master, Mr. Samuel.

Mr. Harris was the head dyer and Mr. Walker the main man for the pressing room, both of which processes had their own buildings across the cobbled yard from the main workshop. Mr. Harris had developed a particular liking for Dan Grady who would volunteer to put on his smock and apron should there be urgent need and was a consistently cheerful and hard working young man and regretted this time lost to the training in the counting house.

This night, near to Christmas in 1801 there were upon the long counter wax candles and the ledgers of the merchant whose business they were studying. It was late and dark and they bent close to their work in the pools of light cast by the flames. One of the three looked up at the clock.

'Coming down for a beer Dan?' Phillip Abbey stood and linking his long fingers together he stretched his arms above his head. He grinned. 'Ouch. I've been sat that long on that chair, that my arse aches. Come on. Time to knock off.' He slapped Dan on the back and went to fetch his hat and cloak from the passage leaving Dan Grady perched on a tall stool at the table where they had been attending to Benjamin Beverley's books. Dan, smiling and watching the young gentleman whose attention so quickly wandered when the workshop clock showed the hour of six o'clock. Samuel Beverley stood and tripped. He followed Phillip into the passage and hissed in his ear. 'Can't do that Abbey. Can't drink with the workers. My father -' He nodded meaningfully back at Dan who stood now calmly watching them.

'Oh rot!' replied Phillip loudly. 'If we can sit at labour with Dan all the day long I'll be dammed if I can't share a draught with him. Besides. He's got coin in his pocket. You'll stand us a beer, won't you Dan?' Dan smiled a little in reply. 'I'm off to the Three Legs for a wet. You can come too Sam or you can stay here all night for all I care. Dan's not a worker, are you Dan? He's family.'

Samuel Beverley, who was most consciously the son and heir of the House hesitated, looking unsure of himself. He looked at Dan briefly and then looked away. Everyone liked Dan. But he did not want to go the alehouse after his duties were finished and fraternize with the labour force. Phillip turned to Dan. 'You're one of us, aren't you Dan?' Looking back at Samuel he said, 'And he'll have his own finishing shop before he's done. Won't you? Or better idea, you can come finish my cloth when I set up. See Sam? That's how things go.' Samuel shook his head at this and frowned and wondered that Dan did not seem put out. Phillip felt sorry for him momentarily for being such a stickler for things and such an unfortunately spotty and awkward boy as well. He sighed and turned to go.

Dan put his work place neatly in order and he said pleasantly, 'No sir. Mr. Abbey I thank thee for thy offer. But I'll be finishing cloth for Master James and Master Matthew. Or the dyeing. Now that's where the best wages come for the likes 'o me. Tha can find thy own finisher I think. Mr. Beverley will assist thee I'm sure.' Samuel looked blank for a moment then realised that Dan had inclined his head at him and nodded slightly with a worried scowl.

Phillip laughed. 'Have it you own way then Dan. Let's be off now. And mind, you're buying the ale. A little short of cash right now you see.' Dan agreed. 'Isn't that the way of it then sir. Good night Mr. Beverley.' Samuel gulped and said his good nights.

In the corridor Dan shouted down the length of the building. 'Night all! See you bright and early,' which brought shouts of good night and laughs of derision. It would be an hour before they too could leave.

Samuel Beverley sat glumly staring at the dark shutters that covered the window before him, waiting for the night watchman to arrive and take the keys to the workshops from him. He returned to the figures in the open ledger before him. An hour, and then all to be put in order to secure the premises. He could have left it to the overlooker but he did not want to ask the man to help him, and if he had been honest in his thoughts at that moment, then he would have had to admit to himself that he held the man in some fear. The overlooker was a surly man and had tarred Samuel with the same brush as his demanding and short tempered father. No, he would not ask Mr. Cooper to do his duties. As his candle burned into a guttering stump, the rest of the workers and the overlooker included, departed just as soon as the clock showed seven, giving him little more than a grunted 'Night sir'.

He felt the unfairness of things – that Phillip and Dan were popular and easy with the men but that he, as the son of Benjamin Beverley, must remain aloof and be on the receiving end of any grumbles or complaints that the work force might have. He stared again at the barred window before him. One of the barely expressed grudges was that Dan Grady was being allowed to learn the mysteries of cloth finishing and at the advanced age of 18 too. And he was a weaver by trade. Some of the men had muttered about this to Samuel and Samuel had not been able to find anyone that he could counsel him. His father would not like to have to discuss such a difficult situation. And yet so well was Dan liked that he had been soon been accepted and nothing had come of the unrest. Yet. But these were dangerous times. Benjamin Gott had of recent months had his windows broken in the night and had resorted to placing an armed guard around his house! Samuel shivered.

The watchman arrived, stumping up the stairs wrapped in an old and tattered coat. 'By gum, this'uns a cold 'un, right enow, and my poor rheumatism's playing up bad. Tha's ready?' Samuel startled, then jumped up and knocked over his stool, and fumbling for the great ring of keys he gangled down the length of the workshop to check that the building was safe for the night, all candles snuffed and all lanterns cold. The night watchman shook his head and called after him testily. 'See tha in the yard then - sir,' and stumped back down the stairs to where his little shelter stood by the great wood gates. Samuel locked and made sure all was secure for the night and found the watchman busy at work by the scant glow of his lantern, lighting the brazier in the dark yard. He looked up and back at the shuttered and barred workshop. It was only four months since, that Gott's mill had had every window broken after the arrival of a gig machine. Samuel stood with his shoulders hunched checking there was not light anywhere in the two storey workshop. There were few glass windows here anyway, and they didn't think to bring in a gig machine. Not now or here, at any rate. Perhaps in Wortley.

'Keep a good watch now!' he said intending it to sound firm but instead sounding querulous. What the night watchmen said in reply to this was inaudible and Samuel felt foolish. He let himself out of the yard gates and dejectedly waited to hear the gate locked and barred behind him.

The evening had come down early following a dreary grey December day. It was dark now and grey wisps of smoke curled above the wall where the watchman nursed his fire. Outside in the street, Samuel pulled his cloak tight about him and his hat down over his face and he set off home to Beech Grove in Armley. His recent thoughts of industrial sabotage led him to see danger in every shadow and dark doorway and although he berated himself for it, he startled at every dog bark, every rustle and every distant voice. He tensed as he passed any stranger in the dark streets fearing attack and knowing that he could not put up much of a fight in his defence.

Phillip and Dan had by now nearly reached the Three Legs Inn. Phillip had been working through the books, reconciling orders and stock, and making accounts for his Master, John Bateson, whose cloth was now in Beverley's warehouses either in Leeds or in Hull. It was arduous work. Mind numbing. But he cast this reality aside and thought happily of the Inn, some good ale, good cheer and the company of his elder brother Henry. The card rooms in Leeds were open tonight. Henry was always up for a game and wager. Liked a risk or two. He was in Leeds for a few days and Henry had engaged in a drapery business in London in partnership with John Wells and with the hope of commissions for James and Matthew Bateson and Francis Sowry and other Wortley cloth makers.

On their way to the inn they had happened to pass a man who had worked for Beverley but now worked for Benjamin Gott, muffled against the chill damp air with a rough cloak pulled over his face and seeking the shadows, hurrying from an alley in the direction of the town. Phillip gave the figure a second glance and thought he recognised the man.

'How now then! Pullan isn't it? How are you man? Hey, do your fancy some ale? We'll stand you ale for good gossip from Park Mill!' Phillip winked at Dan.

'Can't tonight sir.' Pullan halted and shuffled his feet and looked up and down the lane uneasily. 'Got to go somewhere else see?' Phillip now intrigued, demanded, 'where's better than the ale house man on a night like this! What's up with you then, turning down a jug of beer! Our other lads are down there - or will be when the gaffer lets 'em go. Catch up on the gossip for old times sake. Look, here's Dan your own sort of man, and I'll not stand on ceremony with you. Get yourself down there and get some ale in you!'

Pullan coughed, looked at Dan, and then mumbled his defence. 'Going to the night school sir. All the same to thee, ain't it.' He suddenly stood tall. 'I'm learning my reading sir. And I'm doing really well. I can read the Intelligencer now. I know what's happening in the world see. Nowt like it.' He stopped suddenly, self conscious of his pride and how he must appear ridiculous in front of the gentleman. Phillip laughed out loud and Pullan looked away his face hidden by the shadow.

Dan hesitated, then taking a small step towards said quietly. 'Good, aye, good is that! It's good to see thee too. I think that's excellent Robert. I admire a man that can bother to get learned. It's what's needed, aye and so it is We all 'on us, we need to know what's a going on in the world. I remember it well learning to write and only like yesterday and hard it was.' Robert Pullan had turned to Dan when addressed and he nodded.

Dan added, 'See you on Sunday Robert.' Pullan nodded then doffed his hat to Phillip and scurried away disappearing into the shadows of the night. Dan glanced at Phillip Abbey and noted him smirking.

'Should have persuaded him Dan. He's working for Gott now. That was your chance to find out anything that might be of benefit to your masters. You missed a good chance.'

'No sir. Dan's a friend and I know he's not one for idle words. If you can catch my meaning. There's no need for fear of sedition - you know that? The Batesons and indeed Benjamin Beverley are well respected and in the case of the Batesons, you'll find they're well liked too. We don't need to bribe the workers to find that out. It's in the air.'

'Oh is it really. I suppose it might be where you hang your hat. But you'll have to mind yourself then, you will. And make your mind up who you serve!' Phillip cautioned half in earnest. At which Dan just roared with laughter.

'So if thou were to pay for our beer tonight thou would have the chance to find out what's in the air from those that are in the know about such things, and yet since tha's not paying for the drink, art not thou missing out thyself on such an opportunity for bribery as thou just chided me for missing?'

Phillip looked confused. 'Am I? I don't know what you mean. Say that again.'

'Stop blethering on and get thyself moving man!' said Dan amiably. They moved off together and Phillip remarked, 'That's my Mary you know, do-gooding. That's where she is, teaching one of these night schools.'

'Encouraging the labour to rise?'

'Ha ha. No - but being a good soul. Doing what's right and all that.'

'Miss Bateson you mean sir?' enquired Dan, his face blank.

' Miss Bateson. Yes of course. Oh sorry. Yes you don't get to call her Mary do you.'

Dan thought for a moment. He shrugged. 'Aye sir, Miss Bateson is a good girl. Nothing surer than that. And clever too. No, not clever, intelligent like. But then she's much as the rest of them tha knows being apprentice and all. Tha don't need me to tell thee. And being in the town now, I see a bit of this and that here and there, with me knowing who I work for as tha so rightly say I must. So yes, Miss Bateson is a fine young lady. Tha knows she taught me the writing don't tha, because tha was there at the time and mocking her. She's helping the men go up in the world, it seems. Rising.'

Phillip Abbey caught out, 'You don't need to tell me Dan. I know her like my own sisters. She has the kindest heart.' Relenting, 'Lord and she's saved my bacon many the time. What do you mean, rising?' Dan said nothing but smiled at his companion and Phillip gave up the battle to understand.

'We'll go drink her health then. Come my talented friend. Come and be merry for Christmas is upon us and there are fortunes to be made!' Dan put out his hand and stopped Philip as they approached the doorway, 'a word for thee sir if I may and it's to go easy Mr. Abbey, wilt thou, on Mr. Beverley. Mr. Samuel I mean. He's my age but not got me life's road and the knocks I've had, that can give a fellow a hard skin, if tha sees what I mean. He's young for his age and he takes everything very hard. He's not as grown as his father thinks he should be.' Phillip Abbey raised his eyebrows and replied. 'Well thanks for the guidance. Our little Samuel's alright and I believe he takes it all in good part. He must be used to it with an irascible father like that. Not our fault Old Benjamin's so pernickety is it? No wonder he's no fun though.' Phillip poked Dan's arm now. 'We're best off out of it and you'll be best when you get back in Wortley. Me though, I'm off back to Hull as soon as. And then Mary will have the minding of Samuel perhaps.' Phillip was curious. Dan smiled and nodded in agreement. 'As you say sir, Miss Bateson is a kind heart.'

Within the Three Legs Inn there was a roaring coal fire and tallow candles lit the crowded public room. The landlord stood before it, his hands behind him and his apron covered belly before, lordly in his domain. He looked up as Phillip entered with unchanged expression and a curt greeting, but when he saw Dan coming on, he smiled and called out "good evening". Henry Abbey, sat in a screened booth by himself, raised his glass to his brother Phillip and called to the landlord. Dan shrugged his shoulders with resignation and laid out some coin on the nearest table. Enough for Phillip to have a jug of common ale and he asked for his own ale with a smile. He wandered over to a group of shabby men who were playing dominoes and thanked the maid who brought him his own welcome pewter pot of ale, watching the game, sipping, wiping his mouth on his sleeve and glancing occasionally over to where Phillip and his brother were bent in conference. He left after he had had a few games and called his good night to the Abbeys who barely glanced up as he departed.

The Abbey brothers were sat in enthusiastic conversation until the hour was reached in which the landlord wished that no more drink should be available - deep in consultation over matters financial and commercial with a little gossip thrown in for light relief. 'Time please gentlemen. Time to get tha selves 'ome.' Men stood and drained the last of their ale and began to drift away to the door.

'Is that the time!' noticed Phillip. 'I'm locked out at my lodgings. I know I am. Oh lord, I can't face knocking in the street till the old bat deigns to let me in. I'll have to stay here,' he said casually, stretching and yawning. 'Landlord, find me a bed will you?' The host was gathering the jugs and pots and gave Phillip a scathing look. He growled 'tha can share thy brother's bed then, "sir". We've nowt for thee that's not spoken for already by them's that pays their way. Bill outstanding Mr. Abbey!' The landlord pushed Henry's feet from a stool as he bent to clear the table. 'And thyself Mr. Abbey. Still owing me for the last time thou was up 'ere, begging thy pardon. So thy brother here can settle with me direct in the morning. Then one of thee will be straight, right? Don't do to be keeping folks waiting, see?' Henry smiled smoothly. 'Now, now, Joe, Mr. Wells will be here tomorrow. Please be so good as to wait till then. There is no problem with this at all. Don't I always settle with you as gentleman should? You have to be patient my good man.' The landlord retreated to the back kitchen muttering about gentlemen, debts and other basic economic facts. Henry turned to Phillip and made an outraged face at him. 'We'll away to our beds then. My bed I mean. Shame about the card game though. We should have got ourselves out and about this night Never mind, it will have to wait upon other matters. I have the coach booked after I've done my business.

Phillip replied with true regret thinking at that moment very much of the cards. 'Yes sadly. And I am due a win. I've had a run of bad luck just of late and so it's time the pendulum swung back in my favour. What time are you meeting with John Wells? If I can, I'll come along.' They gathered their hats and cloaks and crossed to the hallway, perhaps a little unsteady on their feet. Henry continued. 'We'll be meeting over early dinner at his house. Come if you can - but they don't think to have much of a spread. But once we have the cloth suppliers signed up, and the imports in hand ,well, who knows what can be achieved? Just think. South America! China. Cargoes across the world. See yourself as an international agent Phillip? London! I can't wait to get out of this hole and back into the world. Leeds is a pit of stinking self righteous bible thumpers and foul smoke.' He continued as he hauled himself up the bare treads of the stairs, his eyes as bright as his words of hope. 'But this is going to be the making of us all. Yes. Even your Batesons. It's going to make all of them very rich men. And me - expanding the market. Oh yes'.

'London and the streets paved with gold then?' called Phillip from behind him as they reached the top of the stairway. Henry laughed and put an arm out to his brother to steady himself. 'Paved with Yorkshire stone more like. And there's another opportunity and that one's open for the game. And there's our good friend Will Lister with a stone quarry all his own and a fortune that likes to be investing, know what I mean?' He punched his brother on the arm. Phillip said with resignation,'one of your stinking bible bashers though. Just like my Matthew Bateson'

'I thought Lister was a Baptist? Sure you said he was. But then our James is for the High Church so I hear around the place. They cover all the possibilities do the Batesons. Very cute they are'. Henry Abbey swayed as he tapped his finger on his nose.

'One or the other old Lister. Can't remember. Mr Matthew, he's for the Methodists. He's very astute Henry - and very well respected. But you know, he's been very good to me. If the old man had been like him! And James is a good one too, when he stops talking that is. Not such a prig as the rest. He'll help you get things off the ground. Sharp in business all the while he's prattling on. I'll do my bit and keep your company in their minds. For a consideration of course.'

Henry took off his coat. 'You want to make sure of one of those girls brother. It's been understood from the start of it all. They will be well dowered and you'll need the money. Didn't want to mention it in the public rooms, not with that lout hanging round, the one you have in tow. Ears and all that. You're in bother at home are you not? Saw the old man two days since. If I was at this time sober, I could give you the full benefit of a verbatim recount and the tone of his voice too. Then Mrs. Fisher was at me on the same theme and that husband of hers too. Things I do for you Phillip.'

'Yes yes. I'll get nothing more from him. He's made that clear. But the other? That is never going to occur. Not a doubt but that the governors all had that in mind when shaking hands on my fate. But you know how it it is. There's other nice young ladies in Hull, don't you know. Belles that like a little fun and know how to amuse a fellow without wanting a man's signature on the dotted line before hand. Pretty girls on every street corner. And money too. Well endowed in all the areas that please a man like me.' Phillip was amused at this and sat on the side of the rickety inn bed grinning inanely.

'Fun is it you're after? Damn me Phil, what you need, and the both of us need, is a prime match and away into the big money. Don't you be messing about with passing bonnets and just make sure you find out the prospects of the ladies before turning any heads.' And he added as an afterthought, 'or breaking any hearts.' Phillip yawned and dragged his legs off the floor and onto the bed. He mumbled, 'you sort it out with the old man. Speak up for me and I'll see you right with the cloth. I've had a run of bad luck, tis all. I can do better than the Bateson clan I think.'

'So you keep saying. It's the same tale told again. You've no chance of anything from that quarter, not after the last little meeting he had with his attorney and bankers. You've make a bit of a mess of the money side of things as far as the old man's concerned anyway.' Henry sermonised to the wash stand as his brother closed his eyes.

Phillip sighing, made a face at his brother's back. 'Methodists. Long sermons…… could do with getting over to Hull again. London…..' he mumbled to himself and then was fast asleep in a few seconds. His brother looked with exasperation at his feckless junior, then took off his own shoes and those of his little brother, blew out the candle and joined his brother in easy repose.

Chapter Four

Of love and passion

Christmas was upon the good people of Leeds. Although there would be much of interest and delight to be seen and heard in the town of Leeds, Mary had decided to go back to the village of Wortley for Christmas Day to be with her own parents and sisters and with her beloved grandfather too. Although she was comfortable with her aunt Elizabeth Lister, adored by all the little Listers and a favourite with Mr. William Lister, she wished to be where her sisters could love her and taunt her and to see the sun setting over the fields, pastures and hills. The spoil heaps of the mines and quarries she would not notice, so familiar were they to her eye.

Mary and her aunt Elizabeth were sat close together in the front room of the tall terrace house with the drapes drawn across the sashed windows and working beside the bright coal fire.

'Aunt Elizabeth, do you have a little brown paper? I want to wrap up these things for my sisters.' Her aunt looked up from her mending and smiled.

'Certainly. Just go down and ask our Judy where it is kept. Oh, is that the purse for Anne? It's so sweet. Here let me have a closer look.' Mary left the little treasure with her aunt and wrapping her shawl more closely left the bright warmth of the room closing the door carefully behind her, and made her way down the back stairs into the basement where the kitchen lay, all bright polished brass and familiar smells. Mary went to the dresser and found scraps of paper and ribbon and returned.

The bundle of papers were on her lap and her aunt smiled at Mary's animation as she began to wrap the little gifts she had made.

'How many are coming to you on Christmas Day aunt?'

'Too many! Your uncle likes to be sociable. And we shall have the pleasure of a professional singer – specially invited from the Music Hall – to entertain us in the evening. Now you're sorry you are not to stay with us for the day, aren't you?' Mary shook her head and then giggled. 'No at all. I want to be with my sisters. We fight a lot you know? Tell me Aunt Elizabeth. Did you fight with your sisters when you were small?'

Elizabeth Lister's eyes opened wide. 'Oh my dear child, not at all. The very thought! Your grandfather was a tyrant to us you know. He's mellowed now the frost has come to him, towards you and your sisters, compared to how he was when we were small. He was so strict. And remember, we were so spread in age, so many years between us all, that we always had a care for one another. For instance, I was a mother to my brother James. And your father was always a peaceful child you know. Always pleasant and kind. And Jack, well he was just busy running about and playing scur. Well - there was one time and a problem with a hunting gun. But best forget about that I believe. And your Uncle Joseph was poorly at lot, too much of a - I mean too fragile to be naughty. Although James was not always kind to him, there were never real troubles because James has a very kind nature under all his nonsense. And we all had too much to do to be bickering with the baking and chores. But since you and your sisters have become such fine ladies and been to school, then I suppose you must squabble - as young ladies do.'

'Well I am sorry to say that there is discord on occasion - quite a lot. And Nannie is very saucy you know? On the quiet - when there's no one to hear her.' Mary laid out unbleached tissue across the small table and smoothed out the creases.

'Oh indeed. I've noticed that one. She's a great watcher and listener I believe.'

'You have that right. She bides her tongue when she's with company, but my, can she give Ann and myself some impudence. She knows more than is good for her. Always. But Sarah is my pet. I love her dearly. But she and Nannie are bothersome when they are together you know.'

Elizabeth Lister smiled at her niece and knew who she thought the best of Matthew's daughters.

'And so who might be at Greenside? I wonder if your uncle and aunt Lupton will come down? Or perhaps your grandfather will have a guest or two come over. James Wood for instance. If he comes to you, will you give him my best wishes and a general invitation to supper with us here?'

'Of course I should be sure to do so, and I hope he shall come too but perhaps he may be too busy in Halifax. I shall give your love to them all. Especially that little boy of yours, Uncle James.' Elizabeth laughed now.

'Yes and tell him to be good too – from me. I know just what he's like. And if he climbs on the furniture at all, just you tell me straight away, you hear.' Elizabeth kept a straight face.

'Well Aunt Elizabeth. Certainly,' said Mary with no expression for some seconds and then bubbling with laughter until speechless. There was a silence. And this being a close moment between the loving aunt and her favoured niece, Mary made a hurried decision.

'Aunt Elizabeth – may I ask you something?' Mary frowned and hesitated and Elizabeth waited looking down quietly and continuing her stitching.

'Did you know -?' Mary halted again and struggled to find the words that she needed for her delicate enquiry. She blushed with memory of the shame of that her parents had brought open her. But at last she came to a decision and said quickly and quietly

'Did you know that I – I was come so soon after my mother and father were wed?' Elizabeth suppressed a smile and put aside her work. She took Mary's hands in hers, amused but sympathetic 'Little Mary my dear. This has troubled you I think. Of course, it was not so soon after they were wed by the Methodist minister you know? Then the marriage at the Parish Church was later and that's the record made in the bible - that is the legal record.' Mary nodded but could not look her aunt in the eye. 'But child, it was no worry to anyone. Well your grandfather put upon him that face that hides his feelings and we walked on tiptoe for an hour or two. When your father first told him but not after that. You should understand that your parents were very deeply in love and so no shame attaches to their – their precipitation. If you see what I mean.'

' I see.' Mary processing this, hesitated. ' Although aunt, maybe that is not the right word to use? Perhaps. But was it not wrong in – in my father to be so – precipitous? I mean -.' Mary looked up suddenly at her aunt and met her eyes. Elizabeth held her gaze and gently said, 'Mary. When a man and a woman are truly in love, feel passionately for each other. Hunger.' Elizabeth faltered in her turn, wondering if she had misunderstood the nature of Mary's enquiry and that perhaps she should ask other questions. Mary looked away and the blood coloured her cheeks. Elizabeth hoped she did the right thing and continued confidingly. 'If such is the case, well, then let no man part them asunder'.

You see my dear. This is the foundation of a strong marriage. A partnership in life that can carry man and woman through all the vicissitudes that the world can throw in their way.' Mary looked up and into her aunt's beautiful but lined face as her aunt continued with certainty, 'so my love. Now you know that this is a good thing - that your parents loved each other well. No marriage is complete without desire, one for another. For of such base appetites come the children that are wanted and the life that is full of tenderness and contentment Your mother would agree it seems. But I will say, if it helps, that such is my experience and such is my – my – joy. Does that help?' Elizabeth now fanned herself. 'Oh Mary, I am embarrassed. Look how you have made me blush!'

' Yes. I suppose it must, I don't know. I - I am sorry aunt if I have embarrassed you. But you have given me good advice. I think.' Elizabeth Lister fanned herself some more. 'Oh Mary. Goodness. What a thing to be talking about. But if you ever need to come to me, to talk about anything that troubles you, then come and I will do my best to help. I shall think it good practice for when my own daughters grow up and should I ever need to talk to them about – about such things. Dear me. But do my lamb, do come if you are ever in need.'

Mary let out a breath, not quite a sigh. 'Yes. Yes and thank you. For all you do as well to help and guide me. I hope I may be as happy as you and William make a good a wife. One day.'

Elizabeth finished. 'I think precipitation *was* the wrong word to use. But into every life a little rain must fall! Put this from your mind My dear, for now. But I am here for you always.' They continued their small tasks together in amicable and comfortable close conspiracy.

Chapter Five

A Widower

But Christmas at Greenside was shadowed this year by the human condition. And the complications of trade. So well do we all love Christmas and the good things that come with the feast, that the pains of life are magnified by contrast with the general expectation of rejoicing and merriment. Such expectations can make those who are sad feel alone. and grief can seem heavier. So was Mary's uncle, Joseph Bateson, made sad by the celebrations of his family and all the games and singing and the business of the large household. His step mother had told those that needed to be told - and these in the main were Nannie and Sarah, that they were to go carefully around Joseph and be minded of his recent loss.

Grace Bateson his beloved wife had died in September and the gried had brought him low. He had now a little motherless child to see to and so had come back to live with his father and step mother at Greenside. His stepmother Ann Bateson had seen to the little one, baby Hannah and taken delight in doing this. And Joseph had turned with new diligence to making cloth with Jack to keep dark thoughts at bay.

'Oh Mrs. Bateson, oh Uncle Joseph. Here you are.' Mary kissed her grandmother and then her uncle on the cheek. Joseph looked thin and pale and Mary resolved to be extra kind to him. Then she went immediately to the other side of the house to take off her outdoor things, calling out that she was come to her sisters and her parents. She found her grandfather sat in his carved chair in the great parlour and she threw her arms around him, kissing him on the top of his grey head.
'Well Mary,' he said, 'and home for Christmas Day. Come here

by the fire and sit with me. It's a long walk you've made I take it?'

'No sir! I came with the carter as far as the crossroads and just walked up the Holmfield Lane from there. What time is the Service?'

'Plenty of time. Come now, tell your old grandfather just what you've been up to, away there in the town. Are they all a reading and a writing or is there more work to do?' Mary sat on a stool beside her grandfather and entertained him with stories of her labours and gossip of the town amidst the bustle of the household until it was time to leave for the service in the Chapel.

The Methodist Chapel was a modest building recently built, which lay across the roadway from John Smyth's Bell Chapel - that good building that had not been commissioned for the parish because the Lord of the Manor and the Archbishop could not agree on the patronage, but was instead of service to any of the many groups that wished to worship together in particular form.

Just then the Bell Chapel was in the use of Episcopalians, much to the entertainment of John Bateson - but the Methodists would vie with them for a good crowd this Christmas morning. Had they an organ they would have rivalled the Bell Chapel for music too. But that was not the case. However, in the hearty singing of Wesley's fine hymns there was no competition.

Jack Bateson joined the family group just a little after the service had begun. John Bateson looked up at the interruption and his face told nothing but he marked the fault. The prodigal son, he thought to himself. Well. But here he was in the Chapel and that at least that was the right thing. He gave an imperceptible shrug. Only the most perceptive of observers would have noted it. Mrs. Bateson noted it. She gave his ribs a sly prod and bending her bonnet close to his head she whispered, 'all the family then my dear. Praise the Lord.' John Bateson snorted just after the preacher had finished stating the theme of his sermon and several of the congregation looked round astonished to think that John Bateson had expressed disagreement with the good preacher, John Bateson had to find his handkerchief and make as if he had a head cold. Mrs. Bateson smiled around and nodded at the family clan gathered there together, dressed in their Sunday good clothes and with white linen starched and clean. She took stock of her blessings on this auspicious day. There was her step son Matthew with his kind heart and generous hand. And there was James his partner and a good natured and affectionate lad he was too. But he was not attending to the service. Instead of this he was making something out of paper from his pocket to entertain his son Thomas. So she looked away. Poor Joseph. To be widowed so young and the marriage had been such a good one, for the sake of both the Walkers and the Batesons. That union had been sorely needed what with the competition between the two Houses, and now? Well, time would tell. Poor baby Hannah - but then to Mrs. Bateson, childless herself, the care of the child was yet another blessing. And there was Jack too. Back within the bosom of his family and although he was not his step mother's favourite she could find much to recommend in his forthright manner and simple speech. Yes indeed. Some of these around her in the simple pews could talk a great deal too much. She glanced at James again. And the girls, Mary and Ann and little Nanny and Sarah. So proud were Matthew and Anne of their family although the son they had so wanted had never happened. Mrs. Bateson sighed. But now Nancy and James had yet a third daughter. And her husband John Bateson who chided his sons for this proliferation of woman kind but adored each and every of his granddaughters. It had done no harm to the cloth trade and the profits. She looked down then, and admired the fine leather gloves that had been her gift from John Bateson this very morning. Yes life was good. She had thought her lot was to be a servant in her family and to live her life as a spinster but then the Batesons had needed her and here she was the centre of it all by a comfortable hearth. And there was that handsome youngster, the Clothier's apprentice, looking very fine this morning in his fashionable rig. So here she was, middle aged Ann Robinson, mistress of a fine old farm house, in the midst of all these good god- fearing and educated people and prospering. Yes God was good. Oh yes, things were very good. With a start she realised that all had stood and opened their hymn books for the next hymn. Flustered she rose, dropping her book in the doing so. James' son Thomas scrabbled around the skirts and shoes until it could be retrieved and handed it back to her. Dear me. She should pay more attention. She was getting as distracted as James.

    James meanwhile had lost interest in his furtive paper modelling and was listening intently between verses of the current Methodist Chapel singing to see if the Chapel over the green was singing the same number from their common hymn book. That there was an organ there made this more difficult and was sometimes a problem for services. The book was a special selection of hymns dedicated to the people of Wortley by the Rev. T. Bennet and James tried not to draw attention to himself as he surreptitiously thumbed the pages. When the Methodists' last chord still hung in the air a distant chorus of The Holly and the Ivy could just be discerned. James broke into a grin and he nodded to himself; his brother Matthew gave a smile. His distracted brother was a distraction in itself.

Fortunately but without intention, the ministers of both the congregations concluded their rites at almost the same time and the people left together and called Christmas greetings to each other across the green and then waited for neighbours to share the walk home. Of course the rivalries of the Dissenters were passionate and keenly felt by the inhabitants of the village. But this was not the morning to be churlish or lacking in Christian charity, to renew theological debate - and the host of people who were now gathered across the green were prepared to act as though such difficulties did not exist for this one morning at least.

Mary was a little surprised to see Samuel Beverley emerge and make his way towards the Batesons across the damp grass of the common, lifting his hat and making a small, fussy bow.

'Christmas wishes Mr. Bateson sir, Mrs Bateson and all. I hope I find you all well?' John Bateson replied, 'Yes Samuel, and the seasons greetings to you and yours. Please convey such to your father.' Samuel nodded obediently and John Bateson continued, 'But young man, I am a little surprised to see you come from the Bell Chapel. Have you made conversion? What would your father think of this? Merry Christmas Mrs. North. And Merry Christmas Mr. Walker...'

'Oh,' said Samuel innocently while doffing his hat to the passing good folk, 'I was late coming down the lane and when I looked in the door of the chapel I could see there was not room. So I went nearest you know.' Samuel did not mark the blank expression that John Bateson had and misconstrued it. He addressed Matthew now. 'Have to build a bigger chapel sir. There was no room at the inn.'

'Ha ha. This fine building of ours is only just made. So do you think we need a larger just to accommodate your good self when you can't get yourself out of bed? Perhaps we could add a porch for you. I think so. What do you think youngster?' Matthew shook hands with Samuel who visible relaxed. Then Matthew turned to Dan who stood respectfully at a little distance and included him in the conversation.

'What do you think Dan? Will we be knocking down the chapel to save our friend from the evangelicals next door?' Dan approaching nearer considered the matter with apparent gravity. 'I think so sir. Although I may need to give this more thought.'

'A wise answer. Now come up to the house young sir and join us for some ale and chat. We have some music planned and you'll be needed for your voice. You can then tell your mother what fun she has missed at home. Come now, you all, lets away out of this damp dreary day to have fun and enjoy the fireside. Come on girls. Don't be talking all morning with your old father catching rheumatics.' He took his wife's arm and waved his large hand to the girls to shepherd them along. They set off down the cobbled lane as villagers streamed away home. Samuel, given the lead by Matthew's inclusion of Dan in their encounter, walked with Dan and James. 'Congratulations to you Mr. Bateson,' he ventured. 'My mother tells me you have another babe. Sarah, isn't it?'

'Yes exactly that. Sarah. Come here Tom, keep up now. Yes a girl. That's three daughters I have now. A whole tribe of daughters.' James sighed and looked at Dan. Dan said, 'never mind Maister Jim, I get 'em on the weaving and they can pay their way, so they can.'

'Well my thanks Dan. That's the best plan. Otherwise I don't know what I shall do with them all. The weaving sheds it is then! But do you know, I have mentioned this plethora of girls to my dear wife Nancy and she was not at all pleased.'

'I can well imagine that sir.' replied Dan and he winked at Samuel and missed the shiver that James could not control for beneath this banter James was troubled as he recalled past troubles and past prophecies. He had son Thomas that was true, but still he would that he had more sons. Just to be on the safe side of any superstitious nonsense. But it *was* all nonsense. And he shook himself and made an effort to change his thoughts.

'Are you headed for Greenside Dan or to the Weaving House,' ventured Samuel for something to say to the tall boy at his side whose manner was so easy. He felt even more self conscious beside Dan - this worker was self assured and was evidently so well thought of by the Bateson family, while he, with his better education and prospects, was always blundering and tongue tied. Samuel was not sure now, if he had offended John Bateson with his casual justification of his attendance at the evangelical service. He knew his father would not care. But John Bateson and his father were partners and Samuel was wary of them both. His anxieties were interrupted when Dan said cheerfully, 'both! I am home you see, at both houses. Don't let my master hear me say this.' Dan glanced at James and grinned. 'I will go home with Maister Jim, play with Thomas and the little girls and chatter to Mrs. Nancy. Then I will sit at table and eat me full of what is on the board. An'then, I shall make me visit at Greenside and I shall tell Molly there, that I am not fed properly at my master's and she will oblige me with a second spread. So that is how it works.'

Samuel was astonished and inclined to be disapproving. But James chuckled. 'It's what he's been about since he came to us and an excellent plan too. And we'll need your voice too, Dan, when we get going with the music this afternoon. And you too Samuel. It will take all of us to drown out my father's fiddle.'

Samuel hesitated as they reached Greenside House. He dithered a moment as James and his apprentice continued towards the Weaving House, then turned off to follow John Bateson into the yard. Mary and Ann were beckoning him and Ann said to Mary, 'oh dear. Samuel Beverley. He's such a child. What is the matter with him?' and was shushed by Mary who knew how to behave.

To Samuel's relief Mary waited outside the door to bring him inside and ease his awkwardness. She helped him out of his coat and guided him into the great parlour, giving warning looks to Ann and her little sisters too. Such was Samuel's reputation in the family that the sisters would think him fair game for tricks and teasing. 'Oh Phillip, there you are. Come and talk to Samuel will you, for a minute? I must go to help in the kitchen.' Phillip came with a ready smile and threw himself into a chair. Samuel struggling for conversation said, 'Dan Grady is to come along later. Did you know? Master James seems to think a lot of him. I didn't realise he was become such a part of the family?'

'Yes indeed. They treat him like a son sometimes. I tried to tell you you know, but you would have none of it. And don't say a word about him to Molly neither, not if you know what's good for you! But he's a good sort. The god's have favoured him I think.'

'There is one God, Phillip. You mustn't talk of plural deities. Especially not in such a household as this one is. And on Christmas Day of all days. I don't think Miss Bateson would like it. I really don't.'

Phillip put his head back and laughed and Mrs. Bateson looking over, was pleased to see the young folk so happy. Samuel's eyes were wide at such levity and he began to worry at his shirt cuffs in his discomfiture.

'Oh Sam,' Phillip said dismissively, 'don't be so stuffy. They are God fearing here, but you know, they're not ignorant. It was just a figure of speech and I am sure our Mary would think nothing of it. And here she is. Mary, settle our dispute will you.' Samuel looked truly alarmed and began to stutter and mumble, 'it's alright Miss Bateson. There's – we have no argument you know.' Mary looked round and found a stool and angling it between the young men, sat herself down with a quick firm movement.

'Now then both of you. I'll have none of that now. You see, how well I can rule here? Now Phillip you have promised to tell me about the houses you have visited in Hull. And then you Samuel,' she paused thinking quickly, 'you can tell us all about the sermon that you have had today. And we can all get on very well I hope. Come Ann, join us over here while we have liberty to talk. There'll be a great deal of clearing up I know later on. Let's be merry while we may.' And Ann joined them and brought a stool to the left of Phillip Abbey and quite far away from the unfortunate Samuel Beverley.

When the dinner had been had and the women went to help clear and tidy in the kitchen, Phillip took Samuel out into the garth where there was a good view of the valley on a clear day but in the grey light of December the landscape was blue and blurred. Dan joined them.

'Hast tha enjoyed thyself sir?' he asked Samuel. 'Tha's a good voice for the parts sir.'

'Thank you.' said Samuel gratefully. 'It's a sign of a gentleman I think. Oh, I didn't mean, I'm sorry, I ….' Dan grinned. 'No offence taken sir. I've the humble origins, that's no secret to be sure. But a man can enjoy his music no matter his degree in life and be welcome because of it and this is a house where welcomes are many.'

'Yes that is the truth of it,' interjected Phillip enthusiastically. 'Yes. We are made welcome and as for you,' he turned to Dan, 'you seem to be welcome everywhere. There's chances for all us of to make our way forward and make something of ourselves. You're the best one for it though Sam. You've got a head start over me and Dan.' Sam looked nonplussed. Phillip continued with energy but with his eyes fixed on the misty view, 'your father is very well placed now, but watch out for me too. I won't always be here I think, in this little place and you know my brother Henry is concerned with an important drapery and more plans for business. Hull is the place to be – or better still, London.' Dan nodded politely and stifled a yawn, leaning back on the old stone wall that edged the garden and studying Phillip, noting that drink had left him a little incoherent.

'That's good to hear,' he said, 'very good to hear. Because the next time we get into the Three Legs, thou can buy t' ale.'

'And I will,' promised Phillip, fully intending to do so and sealing the deal by shaking both their hands.

'I think I should go now,' said Samuel, restless and fidgeting with a stick he had picked up. 'I'll wish the both of you good evening and must go and say goodnight to the family. To John Bateson I mean. Well...'

Phillip took the opportunity of teasing Samuel in reminding him that there was no Cloth Market the next day which Samuel was well aware of and took some offence at. He protested much about this and then hurried into the house to thank his hosts for their hospitality. Phillip turned to Dan. 'Poor Sam. I don't know why he's always in such a state.'

'He's young sir, that is all. Be kind. If tha has a harsh father then it can make a man go like that. Worried I mean. It appears that I must remind thou of this regularly.'

'I had a harsh father but I know how to carry myself in company and how to make polite conversation. I can't see that it's an excuse for being a fool – which is what Samuel is. '

'Maybe he has something on his mind? But since he is my better – while I am working for him anyway– then I won't say ill of him for his clumsy tongue. Or feet.'

'You never have a bad word for anyone do you? And you know, I like that in a fellow. I really do.'

'I've been under good influences and so I have, to be sure,' said Dan matter of fact and losing interest. They watched Jack Bateson come out to use the barn privy and Phillip remarked, 'now there's a few a bad things might be said about that one.'

'Don't say so sir. And it's not my place to judge.' Phillip raised his chin to look at Dan and tried to decide if he meant to rebuke him, but could not see his expression in the fast falling night of the short day. He decided that no offence was meant and therefore took none. Dan continued without haste, 'and they make amends. It's going well now. And the Maister? He's happy enough at any rate. They're going to build on what they got and move slow - but they'll do well now. Sometimes it takes a few mistakes before a man can get himself right. That's what I sees anyway. So we all us will have troubles but it's how we get out of them, that's the thing to look out for.'

'Well quite right. Very wise. Let's go drink to that. Mistakes and successes and plenty of both! Let's get back in the warm – there's dancing. I'll beat you to the prettiest girl!' Dan watched Phillip rush laughing to the back door and sighed.

Dan stayed by the wall, his hands on the cold grey stone and watched the light fade from the clouded day, keeping his thoughts to himself. That one was a shallow vessel. There was more to this life than trade and making money. Now there were many who met in Leeds, in the Chapels or in the Inns or at the loom even, who would question the foundations of trade and point out the injustices of the age. There were some who told of the new order that had come just over the Channel in France and the equality that was aspired to when the old regimes of royalty and aristocracy had been destroyed. There were militant radicals who worked to rouse the populace holding meetings in secret places and writing pamphlets that their masters would not enjoy reading. He spoke to the old artisans that worked for Benjamin Gott and the other manufacturers and heard them complain about the new machinery taking their work and the new ways upsetting the old order when men could come along now and take employ in the Cloth trade without they had served their time since childhood. And he was one of those that had come into the cloth trade late and had done well. But he kept this fact to himself unless others mentioned it. And all these ideas were new to him and he was considering them well.

Seventeen is a difficult age for us all. It was all very well for Phillip Abbey because he had been born a gentleman blessed with good fortune and he had been trained to undertake dealing and bargaining and thinking so much of money and Dan did not envy him for this but that only that Phillip had that time at school, where there is the opportunity to learn so much to help one understand the world. Dan had only gone from one family to another, from one labour to another, picking up what he could learn along the way. There was movement in the yard behind him but Dan kept still in the shadows with the cold air to clear his head, considering all he was learning.

At last he wandered back into the warm old house and watched as the young people danced, the young ladies and gentlemen that they were with the expectations of society to fulfil. Not all the Methodist families would have allowed this he knew. Dan tapped his foot to the music but did not presume to join. This was not his place nor did he know much about dancing.

'Come in or go out Dan!' said Nancy. 'Don't stand by the door loitering. 'I'll go see if I can help Molly,' replied Dan, with a quiet smile.

Jack was in the kitchen sat lumpily at the old table and talking to Molly about pigeons. Dan took off his coat and hung it on the peg by the door and rolling his sleeves up, nudged Molly from her post at the sink and took over her task.

'Tha's a good lad Dan!' remarked Jack. 'Will thou come down the way there and help us out?' Dan grinned. 'Of course. Does tha pay well?'

'Oh aye.' Molly cast Jack a dark look. 'Tha needs a wife Jack Bateson. Sat in my kitchen and should be talking to the master about finding a nice lass. Or looking thyself, round about the place. Plenty o' nice lasses here would suit thee fine.'

'Aye and nay.' Dan explained. 'I think Master Joe must find a wife before Jack, ma, because of the baby. It's not a good time just now to find a wife for both the lads. See what I mean? Is that right Master Jack?'

'Aye, tha's right there Dan.' Molly thought a while. 'Maybe both had better wait on then. I had not thought of it like that. I was just thinking of the poor boys and not a woman to guide them both.'

'Aye,' said Jack, now animated. 'That's just it Molly. Tha has it right.'

'What's right then sir? That the roof's not water tight or that thou lacks for a woman's guidance?' Dan grinned mischievously at Jack who thought about this with effort.

'Seems the way of things boy. I've realised something. Business goes to pot when there's not a wife to rule.' Dan and Molly exchanged a look and smiled.

In the great parlour the party were tired now and Matthew sent his younger daughters to their beds. Phillip sat with Mary by the window. 'It's been a good day, hasn't it?' she remarked.

'Why yes Mary. Church and then, er, prayers, more prayers. I enjoyed the readings too.'

'Oh dear. You do prefer the dancing and feasting don't you? But the two go hand in hand. The Word of the Lord brings us joy, does it not? What will the year bring I wonder?'

'Hull, I hope. I have asked your father if I may return there and act as agent. It's by far the most interesting aspect of the cloth trade.'

'Why is that?'

'Why, all the buying and selling. It's exciting. And the great ships coming into the harbours and all the merchants – and the wealth and fine houses. You should come visit – get your father to take you to look at Hull. It's twice as busy as Leeds. And the theatre! You would love it!'

'Why, I'm very happy here in Leeds. And occupied you know. There is a great deal to be done here. It is much as I like it you know? To be busy and help others. If I were to come to Hull I would do just that same as do here I believe.'

'Yes, but you should travel. See a little of the world. It changes things you know.' Mary smiled at Phillip's enthusiasm.

'Have you been home - to Long Marston I mean?' Phillip became quiet. 'Yes, I went home in October.' He looked away and at the flames of the fire for a while. 'They were all well,' he said at last, effecting a pleasant expression.

Mary went to say good night to her parents but her mother was gone upstairs to the younger girls.

'Father, I have come to bid you good night. I have enjoyed my day very much.' She sat in her mother's chair.

'Yes. We have been gathered as one today I believe. If it were not for thy uncle Joseph's grief it would have been perfect. Thou hast worn Phillip out at last?'

'I have. Well he's retired I think. He was telling me how much he wants to be placed in Hull. Will you send him there?'

'Yes I think so. To be honest with thee, I'd like to keep him here but we do need a trustworthy representative in Hull. So alas, even as we are one family, we must lose him again.'

'He'll be back though, won't he? If he is happy there then it is well to send him?'

'Yes true. And he is a good agent and we are blessed to have him working for us. I miss him though and had hoped that he would begin to take some of the burdens from my old shoulders in the manufacture. Thy grandfather is growing old and there is ever much work to be done. But good night my dear. Come kiss thy old father and wish him Merry Christmas.'

'I wish I could help you. But then there is Dan, isn't there? And he is always to be making cloth?

'Yes, that's true. We are doubly blessed then. Goodnight Mary.'

Chapter Six

Agent in Hull

Phillip Abbey arrived in Hull stiff and cold. It was a bright February afternoon but even with the aid of a his blankets and shawls Phillip had not been able to enjoy his position on the outside coach bench which he had optimistically believed that he could endeavour to do so, in the commendable cause of gallantry and more dubious cause of juvenile bravado. He had been provided with funds for a good seat in the public stage coach but had given in both to pitiful pleas from a damsel in distress and to his current fiscal difficulties and given up his inside place to another.

He rubbed his numb hands and cursed under his breath as he made his jump down off the high vehicle but swiftly his expression changed as the object of his amenable displacement alighted gracefully from the body of the coach and catching his eye, began to renew fulsome thanks and blessings for his sacrifice. Phillip begged her again, as was polite, to think nothing at all of the matter. He avowed that he had been quite comfortable and had enjoyed the excellent views of the scenery. He thought, as the words slipped glibly from his mouth, of the mile upon mile of bare field and water meadow, punctuated by dyke and ditch and the bleak waters of the Trent as they struggled sluggishly to the North Sea. But he smiled and bowed and he noticed again that the maiden was expensively and fashionably attired and accompanied by a well dressed maid. He dared to introduce himself and was rewarded by a name and an address. He made a mental note to find the young lady's connections - in case this opened to him some interesting social opportunities.

Society in Hull was wealthy and sophisticated. A new contact could provide him with interesting introductions or invitations. The gentlemen at the George Club would know who had arrived in Hull and if they did not, the waiters and ostlers would find out for him. He smiled as the young lady was bustled away by her maid, looking back over her shoulder at him and smiling shyly again and he made another bow.

But as his fingers regained some feeling he looked around him happily. Now he would be comfortable and entertained, away from the restrictions of the good Clothiers of Wortley. But as a good agent he went at once to the warehouse by the private staithe where Benjamin Beverley, John Bateson, Messrs. M and J Bateson, and other Leeds cloth makers stored their wares under the patronage of one of the great Hull merchants.

He liked to attend at the warehouse; it was not a burden to him. Within this place he was established as a significant operator and as the representative of a number of Leeds Cloth Houses, he was of some importance. He strode briskly along the streets and the waterfront, his hat held to his head with one hand and his coat flapping in the ubiquitous wind feeling his spirits rise at the joy of freedom. Around him the inhabitants of Hull swarmed about their business or their pleasures. Many languages mixed in the town; Russian and Dutch, German and Swedish. Even the drawl of some Yankee sailors who were issuing from the doorway of a shipping office with their pockets full of ready money. Phillip grinned at the sight of these last and their rowdy anticipation of the pleasures of the Humber waterfront, spilling across the thoroughfare and holding up the busy carts and carriages.

As he reached the tall warehouse, the watchman nodded in greeting and the workers inside looked round warily but then relaxed as they recognised one of the proper persons who could be admitted. Once arrived in the drab building he was met by Jem Collins who ran to greet him with, 'Sir! Mr Abbey, such a thing as we has found. Such a lack, oh dear, yes. It is as well you has come for we don't know what 's to be done!' Alas Jem had spent this day repeatedly counting rolls of cloth and checking dockets in a state of wild panic.

'My word Collins! What amiss to engender such a greeting? Is Mr. Coleman not to be found?'

'No sir. He's been taken with distemper. Not been in the office for a week and the other has gone up to Selby. There's been no one and I don't know what's been happening. Come quickly sir and look at this.' Collins pleaded, under the misguided perception that repeated checking would provide for missing wares. Phillip smiled reassuringly and followed the agitated clerk up the rough stair that led to the office glad to be at last out of the bitter cold of the February day and relentless winds of the low lying port.

Collins showed the young master the lading bills and went through them methodically, explaining the obvious and then wringing his hands at intervals. Phillip listened to all this with restrained impatience and at last, when the recitation was completed, asked to see the consignment and somewhat reluctantly went below to where the batches of Bateson and Beverley cloth were stored ready for export. They spent some time together checking the rolls with the lists. There were two rolls missing. Fine wool cloth this, in a finished condition and a lot of money gone.

'What'll we do sir. Has we to get up the insurance? I never seen this before. Such a lot astray. Oh Lord, oh Lord.' Collins again wrung his hands and glanced left and right. But there was no one in the vicinity and the discrepancy could remain private.

Phillip scratched his head. He considered the problem for some time and then came to an optimistic conclusion. 'Well now, Mr. Collins. No need to fret. Leave this with me and I will sort it out for you. Indeed I will and as soon as I can. You have no need for alarm. I shall personally vouchsafe for your own honesty and, if needs be, I shall inform Mr. Bateson that he must raise an insurance claim. Please be calm Mr. Collins.' Phillip flicked some dust from his sleeve. Collins thanked him repetitiously and Phillip reminded him emphatically that he himself must be the one to handle the loss not the senior agent and at last Phillip was able to extricate himself and head for the inn.

This was a complication he had not encountered before and he did not know what he should do. Perhaps the cloth had been delayed and the other man in Selby would find it? Or perhaps he should write to his masters and begin a claim? He didn't know for sure. So he put it from his mind and went eagerly in search of his evening meal.

Phillip found his way back into the main streets of the town and was turning the corner into Mytongate when he found his way blocked by a small crowd of people who gathered in order to assist a private carriage that had come to grief. The crowd were assisting by watching the interesting event. Phillip felt obliged to join them and moving some urchins to the side, edged his way to the front of the audience. The incident was now made more interesting due to the arrival in the street by a heavy cart laden with provisions that had made the corner at a good pace only to find it necessary to immediately halt. There was loud cursing and other signs of annoyance and the small crowd turned their heads, appreciating the drama and the entertainment. Phillip now in the front row at once recognised the arms on the carriage and also found that he knew one of the occupants - who had alighted and was encouraging his driver to 'do something' by taking his hat on and off and stamping his feet.

It was the Lord of the Manor of Wortley. Phillip stepped forward and approached the distraught gentleman with a bow.

'Mr. Smyth sir? I am Mr. Abbey, sometime of Wortley in Leeds. Agent to the Bateson House in Hull you see. If I may assist?'

John Smyth turned his woe begone face to Phillip but looked past the young man, hoping for substantial help. A voice from the carriage called peevishly. 'What is happening John. We are all on top of each other. Ow, my hat. Oh Lord!' There followed a little screaming which sent a ripple of excitement through the onlookers.

'Mr. Smyth, if you would permit me to remark, there is a blacksmith's shop just on the next road.' John Smyth looked at Phillip now and finally decided to fix his hat to his head.

'Thank you. Thank you – what did you say your name was young man? Well thank you Mr. Abbey.' Smyth looked up and down the street as if a smith would materialise without further human agency. Phillip realised that he must be of more effective assistance. He called to the coach driver. 'You there! Come here.' Phillip grabbed an urchin by the shoulder and thrust the ragged child forward, explaining the need for a smith. A little party set off to seek rescue. Several interested parties came nearer, to more closely examine the accident and in case there was anything horrid to be seen. Phillip took John Smyth by the arm and led him towards the carriage.

'Sir. We must help these others from your carriage. You and I may do it and – wait.' Phillip beckoned to a muscular man nearby. 'Come on now, there's a good fellow, lend a hand. Go to that wheel and put your shoulder to it. And you. Steady there! Now don't move any of you....' Several volunteers had come forward and without very much discussion, the carriage was righted to the point where it was possible to evacuate the passengers, but not without some yelps and protests from within the vehicle.

'Mr. Smyth,' said Phillip. 'We shall help the ladies come out now.' John Smyth shook himself and his eyes regained some focus. 'Yes. Yes of course. And thank you. What did you say your name was again?' Phillip shook his head at this and nodding at the emergency crew by the wheel, carefully opened the carriage door and peered inside. Lydia Smyth was already on her feet and ready to be brought out, clutching her bonnet which was askew and reaching her other hand to Phillip she made it safely to the street. A small cheer went up. Miss Smyth, unlike her brother, was fully in control of herself and managed to adjust her head gear and nod in a dignified manner. She beamed at Phillip. Her brother led her away to the shelter of a porch, and to Phillip was left the further rescue. He brought forth a whimpering and trembling maid and an elderly lady who was weeping and shocked but able to comply with the advice of her hero and so to reach the safety of the cobble stones but not able to respond to the final cheer that accompanied her emergence. Phillip guided her to safety.

Having accomplished so much, Phillip saw the crowd disperse and he watched as the repairs to the wheel were begun. The man who had lifted the axle remained stood to one side of the road as if there was something that had been forgotten. Phillip felt in his pocket for a coin. 'Mr. Abbey?' He turned to see Miss Smyth beckoning to him. 'Dear Mr. Abbey. Thank you so much for your assistance. I am so grateful How fortunate are we that you came along to take charge.' Phillip beamed and bowed. 'Miss Smyth. It was my pleasure. And I did very little you know. This man here, he did the heavy work. Perhaps?' Miss Smyth glanced at the docker and smiled her thanks. Phillip was them himself obliged - to give the expected remuneration. He sighed inwardly as his savings on his coach fare were lost. Miss Smyth continued. 'We are to be in Hull only today and then we are to make our way to Willerby. But perhaps we might see you there? Do you know the Osbornes at all?' Phillip shook his head. 'No matter. I will send a note to you and then we can have the pleasure of seeing you again and my brother might be able to express his gratitude to you in the proper manner.' Phillip could only bow at this.

Miss Smyth said confidingly, 'he is sometimes a little easily distracted. One might wish for more composure. But anyway, where are we to send our note?' Phillip thought quickly and decided not to name the Black Swan as his address.

'To the George Club if you please Miss Smyth – it will reach me from there.'

'Very well. The George Club - I will remember.' Miss Smyth gave her hand to Phillip and also a brilliant smile. He was a fine looking boy, she thought, and well made. She doubted that he was entirely of the proper class to bring into her society, but he had excellent manners and would pass himself off creditably she was sure. And it was good sometimes, to give others a step up in the world. Besides this, it would be entertaining to see how people reacted to her rescuer. Sometimes, society could be so dull.

Chapter Seven

At Willerby

'Well la! What have we here?' Miss Smyth leant around her companion to study the new arrival that had been remarked upon. They were sat in an alcove by the elegant windows, occupying a cushioned window seat and arranging themselves well within the velvet draperies while maintaining bored expressions. Miss Smyth sat back and laughed.

'Well?' demanded Lady Catherine. 'Do be so kind as to expand on your amusement. Who is that fine looking young man.' Her eyes moved again over the new arrival but her head remained still.

'Really. Your Ladyship won't be interested in such as him, I do assure you. Not for you, me dear. You keep your eye on your prospects and leave the flirting to me. Look at that Admiral over by the orchestra. That's your target,' the stout sea dog saw the attention of the ladies and bowed, 'I may play - but you may not.'

'You are so sure of your mark Lydia? Has he asked?'

'He has not. But never fear. I will take him when I am ready and I not ready just at this moment.'

' To be so sure of yourself? In your position I would march at once and secure my prize. So your bills have been settled? Your brother has found someone to extend his credit?'

'Something like that. Some business arrangements. He wishes always to tell me about it, but it is so tedious.' Miss Smyth yawned and hid it behind her fan. Lady Catherine sat frozen as the object of her interest walked past them, looking around him with refreshing interest and curiosity. But then he stopped, thought and turned, and came back to them smiling broadly and without affectation.

Oh! Miss Smyth, you must forgive me. How good to see you again!.' Phillip Abbey bowed gracefully. His eyes met Lady Catherine's and he smiled even more. He continued to look at the aristocrat as he said without hesitation, 'and your companion. Might you introduce us?' Lydia Smyth was very amused. This was delightful. 'Of course Mr Abbey,' and the introductions were made. It would have been kind, in the circumstance of Lady Catherine's predicament, to have given some detail as to the position of the young man in the world, as Miss Smyth certainly understood it to be. She told herself that there had not been time. That it was not for her to interfere and that she had already given something of a warning. It was for others to heed what was said, was it not?

'Might I have the pleasure of a dance, Lady Catherine? I would think your card will be full already because you must surely be the most beautiful lady here - but should you have a little space for me, I should be greatly honoured.' Miss Smyth cleared her throat. 'And Miss Smyth.' Phillip bowed and took another liberty, 'It would complete the enjoyment of my evening if I might also have the pleasure of partnering you. I must say, you too look extremely beautiful tonight.' Miss Smyth could not help but respond with laughter. 'Oh Mr. Abbey. But of course. Lady Catherine is resting now. Come with me.' She stood as the band began the introduction to the next dance and took Phillip by the hand.

'So many people to meet. Good contacts for you I think,' she whispered in his ear as she led him away to the space that was clearing on the dance floor. She wondered if she should warn him about Lady Catherine but decided against such a course of action. Fair was fair. 'My dear Mr. Abbey, you should not dance tonight with my friend I think,' was all she said which Phillip took as a challenge. As the dance progressed Phillip gave her his full attention but Lydia looked back to where her friend still sat, beautifully arranged on the window seat. She smirked and Lady Catherine gave her at least one quick scowl.

There were many important personages that attended the ball in Willerby. The great merchant families of Hull were well represented and the county gentry were there. Phillip knew that he had been allowed entry into a world that he had glimpsed but not dared to think would be his just yet. His appreciation of the opportunity was not reduced by thoughts that such an invitation might never come his way again. He was all optimism and animal enjoyment. He had gone to great lengths to appear well dressed. As well outfitted as as a young Clothier could be in his present circumstances. His coat was fashionable and well tailored for a friend who was very similar in height and build and his linen had been secured by barter and promise. He had laid out more than he could easily afford for lace but paid with kisses for the stitching of this to his shirt cuffs

Some of the newer dances were unfamiliar to him, but he was a quick learner and his hesitation and then happy adaptation was endearing to all that noticed him. Lady Catherine noticed him a great deal. Phillip was permitted many opportunities to dance with her and to whisper in her ear. Eventually his flirtation was interrupted by the approach of a tall and thick set young man of obvious quality who waited impatiently for the set to finish then took his partner's arm, whispering to her,

'Cousin. A word if I may. Not here, come out with onto the terrace.'

'One moment Mr. Abbey. I shall return. My rude brother does not care to be properly introduced. Stay here do I beg of you.' Lady Catherine allowed herself to be led out of the tall windows and into the cool night air. Phillip watched the well built abrupt gentleman lead his friend away. He shook his head and shrugged. But it was late and he would put it down to experience and retire to his room at the local hostelry.

Her Ladyship frustrated demanded, 'What do you want Thomas? What are you about now that you expose me to the chill of the evening. Be quick and tell me.' She shivered on the stone terrace..

'Just to remind you my dear coz. Our circumstances being as they are. You have been dancing all night with a pauper. You know that. And I had arranged for Mr. Cowpen to be here and he has wanted for partners. You should make wise decisions on such matters. You understand me?'

'I do. And I did give Mr. Cowpen my arm for a dull minuet. He has bad breath. Go away now and let me enjoy myself while I still can.'

'As you wish.' Thomas grabbed her arm and gripped it tightly. 'Don't bother with that young man. You know the one I mean. He's merely an agent, and you are a valuable commodity.'

'Dear Lord, Thomas. I know my situation and my circumstances. Please let go of my arm. I only amuse myself with the boy. He's an innocent, he really is. It is the folly of a moment and you should not begrudge me one evening of innocent pleasure.'

'Very well. But you have had your pleasure. Now go and find Mr. Cowpen my dear.' Lady Catherine leant to her cousin's ear. 'How much does he have again?'

'A thousand a year. Pay attention. You know this. And coal under his land and no persuasions from his friends to make any advantage of it. So about your work dear.'

'Are things that desperate with you then Thomas? As if a thousand pounds could straighten you. It would not keep me in gowns!' Lady Catherine twisted her arm from his grasp and quickly walked back inside. She knew that the young man would have gone and realistically knew that she was not likely to meet him again. She went to find Miss Smyth and see what other options her friend might suggest for the advancement of her marriage plans. If only that brother of hers would look in her direction. He had a complicated fortune once his affairs were straightened and could maintain her and her friends in the manner to which they were accustomed. But all he did was mope and moan.

Chapter Eight

The London Attorney

The fine port of Kingston upon Hull was enjoying a renewed prosperity and increase of commercial activity in this interval of Peace that had come upon the merchants, the manufacturers of paint and oil, and the ship owners, since the Treaty of Amiens had been signed. New warehouses were even now being hurriedly built upon the banks of the Humber estuary. In these edifices were stored great quantities of West Yorkshire cloth, and the tools, stoves and other manufactures of Sheffield. Corn and cheese bound for London arrived by river and went away on the coastal routes to feed the south. Timber and iron stores were in healthy supply. The ship yards rang and boomed with renewed activity for once not in the interests of the Navy. There was plentiful work for all the people and the water front was thriving with international trade.

The stone -wharves were all astir and the coastal roads to London had taken the harvest of Yorkshire stone and clay pantiles with voracity and demanded more. Free from the fear of harassment and piracy on the part of France and her allies, the good citizens of Hull waxed fat and contented.

A small vessel arrived with the rising tide and the with the assistance of a river pilot was making her way into the estuary as the sun set over the sprawling town and the fort on the far bank.

'Well sir, here we are and we have made good time. You will let us down upon the shore before much longer I trust? I for one have had sufficient entertainment from the efforts of your crew to keep us afloat and so I shall be glad to enjoy the comparative peace of Hull port.' Mr. David Parr glanced at the young man who had spent the last three days bawling and cursing, wild eyed and frantic, at the sullen and lubberly seamen that were his crew. The Master had been a junior naval officer left on the beach when his frigate had been laid up at the cessation of hostilities with the continent, the first lieutenant of a battered frigate that had limped into Portsmouth, discharging scores of wounded men and paying off the valiant crew, including most of the officers. As a married man of limited means and no connections at the Admiralty, Lieutenant Brown had had no option but to seek employment onboard any merchant rig. To his lot had fallen the charge of this commercial cargo hauler, this lubberly and antiquated Sophia Louise- and his understanding of the leadership of free men was impaired by his training and expectation of immediate discipline from the volunteers and pressed sailors of the His Majesties Fleets. Mr. Parr, an attorney with business in Hull, had observed the frustration of the Master and the resentment of the rough but capable crew. Between the master and his mate was an intense dislike born of the deep knowledge of the coastal highways of the latter and the foolhardy decisions of the former whose navigation had been in the blue seas of the Atlantic.

'Crowther!' The mate rolled aft to see what their fool of chief wanted now. The man at the wheel met his eyes and grinned. 'Stow that,' muttered the mate as he hauled himself up to the raised deck and stood within ear shot of the helmsman. 'What is it now?' shouted the mate, still keeping his eye down the boat and looking from the ship's wheel to the sails and to the pilot's boat ahead.

'Well and good evening to you as well, Mr. Crowther. Would it be too much trouble for you to find the means to call a boat for the passengers. If you please. Before we have to unload them with the cargo?' Aside and into the wind he remarked, 'Certainly they have seen quite enough of our unusual ship handling. As have I.'

'Pilot'll show us – as is the custom of course,' yelled the mate now with his back to the Master and that so all might hear. ' We don't just stop in the lanes! Give your passengers a warning and they'd better be set to go. They go off when the lighter comes out and the Customs Johnny has been. Not before.' The mate leapt down and made his way back to his post angered at such blatant ignorance of traditions of the Humber port.

Parr watched the exchange with interest and smiling to himself went below to see that his belongings were brought up onto the deck. Ex First Lieutenant Brown clung hatless to the rigging and glared at the sky.

An hour later Parr and a few others were landed at the rough timber jetty known as the ferry staithe and made their way up the weed covered steep steps to dry land. Here, among the laden carts, idlers and noisy dockers, young porters waited for their custom. Parr beckoned to a nearby lad with a barrow.

'Where to mister?'

'The Swan Inn -'

'Ooo, look at that lugger! She's buggered is that one!'

All eyes had turned to the river, where the Sophia Louise had fouled and been taken aback and was coming round sideways across the channel - threatening to ram two small fishing boats or a coal barge whichever way the tidal currents took her in charge. Men could be seen running up and down the craft, hauling on ropes and the sail was undecided as to answering in time. Climbing up the side of the unfortunate craft could be seen a sodden figure which Parr recognised as the unfortunate Mr. Brown; raising a fist and apparently yelling and then instantly clinging on for dear life as the boat began to slowly swing back into the proper course. If ex Lieutenant Brown could hear the laughter from the West bank he would have let go his hold and allowed the dark waters of the Humber to carry him to oblivion…….

'Dear me,' commented Parr.

The landlord of the Swan Inn was pleased to find a bed for a gentleman just arrived from London. 'This way sir and it's a clean house we keep here. Never fear! There's them's as don't keep it all spotles but this here, well, we 'ave ever so many gentlemen as chooses our establishment above all the rest. The traders from London allays look to us first and we've gentlefolk and all. And people from Leeds.'

The inn keeper protested the supposed cleanliness so often and in so many ways, that Parr began to doubt the veracity of the claimant. He surveyed the proffered chamber quickly from the doorway and then with rapid steps approached the stout wood bed within and whisked aside the blankets to examine it. Meanwhile the landlord stopped mid flow and watched as the attorney sought the proof of his claims of good housekeeping, his gaunt black clad figure bent over the linen almost as if he were sniffing it. The landlord stood with his mouth open as Parr turned and smiled with all his wretched teeth revealed. Recovering his wits the landlord asked doubtfully, 'It meets with your approval then sir?' and then, more in anger than in hospitality, he went on to recite the facilities of the house re private rooms and dining areas and the tariff of additional charges and the expectation that accounts would be settled immediately. Parr nodded his head at all this and his eyes swivelled from left to right assessing his temporary domain in a way that was of further annoyance to the land lord.

'Please see that my chest is brought up and a bath made ready.' Parr turned his back to the waiting host. This was a lodging room at the front of the house and he was desirous of seeing if it commanded a good view of the thoroughfare below. It was a feature of a room that he enjoyed. He half turned his head, and said; 'Is Mr. Abbey dining here tonight? Without waiting for reply he added, 'Let him know I am come and let him know that I will be joining him, would you? And good sherry if you please.'

Mr. Samuel Crawford, owner and proprietor of the Swan Inn plodded noisily down the wooden stairs having formed the opinion that he did not like Mr. Parr nor welcome his custom. But young Mr. Abbey was a good lad, and as he explained to the wife as she berated him for agreeing to private hot water at this time of the day when the kitchens were completely given over to the provision of good and substantial suppers, that they would put up with the attorney and his insults for the sake of the regular lodger that they had formed a fondness for.

' Mr. Abbey sir. Phillip if I may take the liberty? We are all friends in this enterprise I must assume? So Phillip. We will proceed with the documents now. It will not take but a moment. Here is an extended credit document. You will know from your experience that such things are not readily come by.'

Phillip Abbey who had enjoyed the good sherry quite adequately, took the papers from Parr and made as if he was studying them. Of course, this arrangement represented a loan of good long standing and additionally of substantial worth to himself. He should have enquired, had he read the proposition with due diligence, what interest would be payable and when. Parr knew this. He knew Phillip would not bother to consider it carefully. Henry Abbey and John Wells needed a signature and he felt sure that the young man would carelessly co operate. Extended credit would be for the supply of imported wool and was a most desirable commodity. All Wells and Abbey and Co. had to do was ensure that their associates would provide quality raw wool in quantity and everyone would benefit. But it could not be done without credit and credit had to be secured. Nothing could be more straight forward, he explained to Phillip.

'So I must get Mr. Bateson to sign this?'

'Indeed yes. Or maybe. No I think not. You yourself with your good prospects might be able to benefit from this in the longer term and Mr. Bateson will certainly do very well from it. It's nothing really. We will organise everything from our end in London.' Parr leaned across the dark oak table and poured the last of a pint of sherry into Phillip's glass. 'It's not late my friend. We shall make a good night of it I think. What is there to amuse a gentleman in Hull?'

Phillip glanced up from the papers, distracted now and he chewed his lip as he considered this. 'I go to the George Club for cards. And they would welcome me tonight. I did so well some evenings since, that there are some who wait to have vengeance!' Parr laughed. He liked this boy.

'Well put your mark here and we'll be away to please the gentlemen of Hull.'

Phillip took the proffered quill pen and dipping carefully into the provided ink pot that Parr, as a cunning and accomplished attorney, kept carefully in his pockets, Phillip Abbey signed a paper which he had not read and did not know the consequences of. 'But even though I have been lucky at the tables my purse has shall we say, many needs? Henry has sent me some immediate funds I hope?'

'Oh yes Phillip. Your brother has paid some funds into your account in London. You may enjoy yourself tonight without anxiety! And to show my good faith, I will foot the bill for all of our amusements tonight.'

Phillip Abbey relaxed. 'Come on then Parr. Let's please the town and ourselves.' The gentleman of the George Club were indeed relieved to see Phillip again and a few hands were played in the well lit card rooms. Phillip's luck held good and he and Parr were very satisfied. They found themselves at last with no offers of gaming and sat by themselves with some hot water and brandy.

'They are not glad I think, that you have again had such good fortune this night. Let us depart now and leave them to reconcile themselves to their losses.' Phillip Abbey smirked at his dark friend and they left to relieve themselves in the stable yard. Parr fastened his breeches. Phillip laughed. He had won a year's allowance this night and taken into his possession an IOU of some significance. To the winner the spoils he thought.

'What say you we take a stroll around the town? A pity to curtail such an auspicious evening? Yes. Let us take walk my friend. We are in drink and must needs have fresh air to clear our heads. A walk will be of benefit. Let us go to see the river and for the benefit of our constitutions.'

Phillip acquiesced to this plan, feeling elated, intoxicated and triumphant. But he also felt confused, as if the games that he had played had not been within his control, and something jarred but why spoil the evening? He shrugged. It was the sherry. He followed Parr and caught up with him as the attorney strode off into the dark night and they went towards the river.

The docks of any port are like to provide interesting entertainment to gentlemen of a certain disposition. Hull was no different to the other port of the kingdom. Along the waterfront there were attractions that did not exist in sober market towns –at least not with such organisation and finesse. Parr found what he sought. A red lamp glowed over a dark doorway which was otherwise a well painted, clean and seemingly respectable entrance and he nodded to Phillip. 'Shall we? This is a suitable establishment I am told. The clientele are mostly gentlemen,' he insisted with a slight but encouraging smile. Phillip was familiar with the waterfront attractions because his work would bring him to the quay-sides at night and he had always good humouredly rejected any number of offers. But he had heard of this establishment and there were one or two at the George Club that had recommended its services.

He hesitated one step away from the door but in delay was his downfall. Parr hid his teeth and nodded again with lips pursed and an expression of smug invitation. Phillip weakened under the influence of the wine he had drunk; Parr's eyebrows high in enquiry. So Phillip stepped forward. They entered the doorway into a hallway of modest appearance and a door opened before a stairway to issue forth a plainly dressed matron of middle years. Her gown was dark and of plain wool and she wore a white cap and collar, much as would an elderly aunt. She quietly bad them welcome and ushered them into a parlour which was furnished with a number of matching carved chairs and a wealth of plush red velvet. Distantly could be heard the sound of a flute being played rather well. A coal fire glowed in the hearth and they sat themselves before it.

'What happens now,' enquired Phillip faintly and cleared his throat. Parr again raised his eyebrows at Phillip but said not a word. The creak of the door made Phillip startle and turn on reflex to stare at the door. It was the matron.

'If you please gentlemen. We are ready for you. Follow me.' Parr smiled and put his hand under Phillip's arm to encourage him to stand. Phillip felt his legs weaken but managed to follow the matron and Parr up the stairs to where a corridor branched off and further stairs led to off other floors.

Their guide opened the first door slightly and for one moment of horror, Phillip imagined that he and Parr would be trapped and imprisoned with the kind of woman that hid in alleys and called to the sailors, dressed in faded finery and rouged to hide a poxed face. But Parr nodded and thanked his hostess and disappeared behind the door. Phillip stood in confusion and his knees felt weak. But the matron simply went on down the corridor to another door and looked enquiringly. Phillip had little choice now. He must either retreat in cowardice or continue and discover what lay behind these doors. He took a deep breath and went to turn the door handle and cautiously pushed the door slowly. He could not retreat for they way behind him was guarded by the expressionless hostess. He entered. The door was pulled shut from behind him. Phillip glanced once at the figure that lay upon the curtained bed and then behind him as the door was closed. He half expected to hear a key turn in the lock.

'Good evening sir,' said a quiet sweet voice. A girl stood now and Phillip noted that she was very pretty and very clean. Her hair was loose about her shoulders and she was clad loosely in a cotton wrap with lace about her neck. Phillip was transfixed. She came towards him slowly and told him her name and that it was her pleasure to meet him and other such ordinary pleasantries, but at the same time she began to help him undress with the skill and dexterity of an experienced manservant.

Nothing was said between the pair as they walked back to the Inn under the northern stars. Each was content with their own thoughts. Phillip wondered if he should thank Parr both for the introduction and for providing the funds for such activities. Or if it should be good manners to continue without making such reference to their dissolution? Phillip did not know. Certainly he would not have done such a thing in Leeds but then when in Leeds he was continually reminded that God was with him and that a man must do what is right. There were not grey areas of morality within the bosom of his employers, or with his friends even in that town. But was it wrong? Had he done the wrong thing? Such thoughts were very difficult for Phillip to handle unaccustomed as he was to question himself or his actions. But then when he had been in Leeds, well, he had been a child. Now he was a man and had certainly caught the eye of a sophisticated lady. Was it perhaps better than he should become a man of the world and know more of such things? He told himself that this was in fact the right thing for him to do and that there were many ways of living that the Methodists of Leeds did not have the opportunity and means to experience. In Hull, that more cosmopolitan hub of society, a gentleman could have a game of cards and take his wine without being judged as a rake. All this passed through Phillip's mind as he and Parr strolled home together.

Parr broke his reverie. 'Cigar?' Phillip took a havanna that was proffered and waited for Parr to secure a light from a nearby lantern. They stood on the banks of the Humber, enjoying their tobacco and neither spoke. So this is the good life, thought Phillip to himself, this is how it should be with his purse bulging and a feeling of intense comfort, and he warmed to his odd companion.

'I don't like it Mistress. Not him. Don't bring him to me again. And I don't think he's clean ma'am. You get a lass off the streets an' he frequents us again.'

'But, Mrs. Greenhow. You know this is your particularity. There's always some that have special preferences. You are our young lady for just that kind of thing. So if the gentleman should visit with us again, you just be firm with him, see? And more to the point, dear, at your time of life you're lucky to get any custom at all. As for certain infections, we both know your Mr. Greenhow is near his end with – a certain little problem. It's a risk we all have to take. This is your work m'dear. That's all.' The matronly madame ended the interview with her most mature employee by folding her arms which her girls knew to be the signal that she would make no more concessions to their fancies. Mrs. Greenhow grunted but understood that the facts were as they were. Someone had to see to the less desirables and at least - at least the youngsters were protected from such – problems.'

Parr stayed up that night and was at the port offices by the harbour masters office when that gentleman arrived promptly at ten in the morning. He followed the official into the harbour office. There was a particular business that he was interested in and time was pressing. The official gathered his papers and knocked them straight upon his desk.

'There's not much today and I don't think there's much tomorrow. You could try the Blackbird but she's no cabin space that I am aware of. If you wish to make your own arrangements then do so. It's all the same to me!' He put down his papers and reached for his log books as if the interview were finished. Parr leaned forward and took the log book from his hand. 'Come sir. There are many loading at the Legal Dock. One of those will be bound for London.' The official's plump face grew red. What an insolent man! Finding that this appeal was not effective, Parr took out a handful of coins and laid them on the desk. The harbour master looked at this for a moment then sighing, reached out a plump hand for the bonus and recited a few boats that were for the coastal waters by the evening tide that also - carried stone.

    To the southern end of the waterfront Parr found what he had been looking for. The Yorkshire Rose was low in the water, heavily laden with massive paviours for London streets. Parr thought this would be an interesting voyage and looked forward to finding out as much as he could about the trade in such commodities. Henry Abbey was very interested in such details.

Chapter Nine

Coffee House

'Mr. Abbey?' Lady Catherine had seen Phillip below from her place in the private box of her friends and now outside spoke his name in a low voice that would not be heard by others.

The play had been tedious. It might be that the players had been celebrated in London, but by the time the troupe had reached the provinces, it was clear that some of the glamour and gloss of the performance and the costumes had been lost. Lady Catherine had occupied herself with watching the audience and making inventory of society that were present, her eyes darting about the place behind her fan. She could not but note that her new acquaintance was below but also that he was in the common area of the theatre. But he was enjoying himself so much! Oh to have such innocent delight in the provincial performance of a jaded play. She sighed. Oh well, it had after all been a passing fancy - and an evening to remember when she did manage land the catch that she must angle for - should the nights be long and dull.

But as the audience streamed out into the lamp lit street she found that she was close to him and her heart knew it. He turned and she saw his eyes sparkle and his fine mouth smile. 'My lady! What a pleasure to see you again! Tell me how did you enjoy -'

'Hush,' she said in a husky undertone. 'I can't stay to speak to you here. But tomorrow -' she looked about her to see who might overhear. He said hurriedly, 'tomorrow? Where?' Lady Catherine whispered without looking at him. 'The Coffee House that looks over the water. At three.' And then she gathered her skirts and went swiftly across the cobbles to the waiting coach. A man in livery turned and looked towards Phillip and he withdrew into the shadow behind him. Tomorrow! Tomorrow he had an assignation with a beautiful aristocrat! He did not know her pedigree entirely but still, she must have connections and influence and that could only be good for him and his ambitions. And if such connections could not be harvested, well still, that was a shapely ankle he had seen a glimpse of as she had stepped into the coach. But he should of course, make enquiries as his brother Henry had recommended. But not at the George Club. Not just at this moment. That could wait.

It was entirely possible for Phillip to organise his working day so as to accommodate unexpected meetings and appointments. Such was his role. To be called when a consignment of fleece had arrived at a wharfe from London, let his superiors know and make his compliments to the Wool stapler before even the Customs Officials had been finished their work; before others could interfere with his masters' requirements for Spanish fleece. To be at the markets when a Merchant was making an order for wool broad cloth, magenta dyed and to pursue such an order with quite some authority around terms. To be at a private staithe to sign for a shipment to Hamburg that sailed with the tide before dawn - that was the nature of his work. Much of his time at the office in the warehouses was given to reading the newspapers and broadsheets with his feet upon the desk. As we have seen, his accounts, inventories and stock control were not always conducted with diligence and accuracy. But his correspondence with Leeds and Wortley was regular and detailed thus he was well thought of and also well rewarded in commission even if those rewards did not quite cover his outgoings. Some leeway as to working hours was always permitted. And Phillip had made this known as his right upon his arrival as the Clothier's Agent last year and now he was given charge of various aspects of the business his status has risen and none would challenged his whereabouts..

    He had left the Clothier's offices at two o'clock making some plausible excuses, and had returned to his lodgings at the Swan Inn so that he could shave and change his ordinary shirt for his finer linen. He put on his second best waistcoat and his only other coat -that which had been given by a kindly sympathiser at the George Club. He peered at himself in the small mirror over the rickety washstand in his lodging room. He nodded with approval. She will like what she sees - or she won't; let luck be with him even so. And then he went happily through the streets, holding back his urge to hurry, anticipating a pleasant afternoon and feeling as if the world was his own to command.

    He waited outside the Coffee House until the Town Hall clock struck three. He believed it did not do to be too eager and based this on certain advice that Parr had generously given him. So he studied the window of a book shop until his impatience got the better of him and he could bear do to so no longer. Yes, Parr had told him in a moment of patronising intimacy something of the best way to handle women according to his own wide experience of such matters. Not too eager and never too soft. It was Parr's advice to his young disciple, that woman liked mastery and a strong grip. Not that this was foremost in Phillip's thoughts at this moment. However, he felt himself to be now a man of experience and certainly able to manage such as Lady Catherine. But the lesson might have taken root in his subconscious. After some minutes had passed, Phillip approached the entrance to the Coffee House, adjusted his neck cloth and pushing the door wide, strode inside. Lady Catherine was sat with another young lady near the front windows.

'Oh, Mr. Abbey! What a surprise to see you here. Pray come and join us.' She smiled her best smile at him. 'Call for the waiter my dear, do. I will have more coffee if you please.' Phillip gestured to the waiter who came with shuffling steps and a sniff of disapproval. He did not think that ladies should make assignations in his premises. Such modern goings on.

Phillip asked carelessly, 'would you care for anything else? Some cake perhaps? Your friend………..'

'No. When I asked for some coffee that is what I desired. 'What else might I desire that I have not asked for?' As Lady Catherine asked this, her friend removed herself discreetly to another table. Phillip was confused and stuttered foolishly. 'they have biscuits I believe?'

Lady Catherine laughed out loud. 'Oh my poor lamb. Not cake nor biscuits please. Oh my word. Do you think that I am so lovely without I can resist sweet pastries. Not at all. Such attractions as I have are entirely due to self denial. In the matter of cake certainly. One has to consider one's complexion and one's figure. It might be necessary for those of us that have to undertake physical labour to keep up our strength. That I understand.' Phillip immediately jibbed at the bait.

'Nor do I have need of sweets pastries Lady Catherine!' answered Phillip somewhat indignantly. 'My labours, as they may be called, are entirely sedentary. I assure you I do not move from morning to night at the counting house. I mean my office.'

'I wonder that you are here then. But no matter.' She glanced out of the many paned bow window and continued, 'Perhaps I should not have agreed to meet with you!' Phillip thought to remind her that she had suggested the coffee shop appointment, but perception won and he swallowed his pride.

'Trade Mr. Abbey. I am not used to mixing with those of your class. Pray tell me all about it. What may I *count* on with this meeting?' She looked him straight in the eye but he did not flinch from her challenging gaze. He had quickly recovered his composure. She looked away first.

'You may count on me, my lady. Be assured. I am your obedient servant. For myself I believe that I will continue to make my way in the world - and to be the agent of some noted Leeds Cloth Houses, is not an insignificant position in the world.'

'I am so pleased to hear this said. When I wish for some wool cloth I will be sure to come to you Mr. Abbey.' There was a silence. Phillip began to think that indeed he should not come and that he was being made a gull of. Lady Catherine was certain that she should not have come. She liked him; more than that. This much was true. In other circumstances she might have been able to consider furthering the acquaintance. But really, it did not do at the moment. It did not suit. If only such nice young men were to found in the circles in which she moved and if only she were free to dispose of herself. Phillip was silent and then continued pleasantly. 'Where do you stay in Hull? I hope you have comfortable accommodation?'

'Somewhat. But we shall be in London soon. I am tired of the provinces and long to be back where there is something to to amuse me.' She yawned quite prettily.

'I am sure you will be missed when you depart. Your person has added grace to the society of this town. How can that not be so.'

'I pretty compliment. I thank you.'

The coffee pot arrived with fresh cups and Lady Catherine poured for them both and recanted. 'You are such a treasure my dear. If you were to know how much I do like your innocence and youthful enthusiasm. Well, that is enough encouragement I think.' She did like his fresh youth, but there were other attributes that he had that she admired. And a basic attraction that she could neither own nor act upon. She placed the coffee pot on the table and as she did so, Phillip reached out and grasped her hand. He pressed it hard. Lady Catherine laughed and pulled it back.

'Take your coffee sir. While it is hot. We have not much time.'

'Is that so? I have time. What presses you Lady Catherine that you make conditions? We should enjoy the moment I believe.'

She studied him over the edge of her china cup and then sighed.

'The coffee is good at this moment.'

'It is made better by your presence.'

'Of course you must say so. What a glib tongue you have in you. Perhaps not so innocent after all.' She adjusted the front of her gown of habit, drawing attention to her charms.

'Tell me more about what you do then Mr. Abbey. I believe I have a few minutes to waste with you after all.' Her friend had taken up a news paper and was seemingly engrossed in the editorial and Phillip and Lady Catherine did let down their guards and find shared ground in their different places in the world. He did have great charm and was a good conversationalist and his world was very different from her own. They shared their appreciation of popular theatre and commented upon the various fashions of the day. Lady Catherine discovered that the Abbeys were an old established family and had some very good connections, and that Phillip was something a sportsman and claimed to be a good shot. That he was a dedicated card player. They had so much in common! She began to think that he could become something more to her but that thought must be suppressed - and to defend herself from this realisation she said., 'but my dear, look at the time. You must go I believe. I have another appointment. And it would not do for that gentleman to find you in his seat, would it?' As the words left her mouth, she hated herself for saying them. Loathed what she was and how she treated those who did not have influence in her world. Thinking of these things made her angry at the circumstances of her life and her mouth was hard and her eyes glared at her victim.

    Phillip was startled and put out at the sudden change in her expression and felt himself grow hot around his neck. There was a moment's silence between them. Then he stood quickly, forced a smile and said with affected carelessness 'If that is the case then I find I too am engaged. But I thank you for a pleasant interlude. I hope that we may meet again.' He bowed.

    Lady Catherine waved a hand at him dismissively and so he turned on his heel and quickly left.

    This was something. What was he to make of her? He was of an age when such things were much in his thoughts and were more so since his recent introduction to satisfaction. He was sure that she liked him and he was also certain that his feelings towards her had become more fixed. There was something that drew them together, he knew it! Yes that was it! With this glad thought he began to whistle to himself and by the time he had reached his offices he had vowed to himself that if their paths crossed again, as well they might do, then he would continue the liaison but with nonchalance too. Yes, this was the right way to think about it. Luck might be on his side. Of course, he did not think about Lady Catherine as someone who would in the future be his loving wife. No, that was not what he thought of. He thought of playful entertainment and delightful flirtation and other more dangerous advances. The joys of the chase.

As he took his seat he saw that letters had arrived for him in his absence. He took up the top package recognising the writing and the seal. It was from M. and J. Bateson. This late in the afternoon the sun had gone from the windows and he called for a candle to be brought by one of the clerks down the hall.

Phillip found that Matthew and James wanted to increase their order for dyes and commissioned Phillip to attend to this. Also Matthew had enclosed a private letter for him, with news of all the family in Leeds. Phillip had a brief pang of guilt. about the missing bolts of cloth that he still had not addressed. He chewed a pencil while he thought about it but came to no conclusion even though the pencil suffered badly. The next paper on the pile though, went some way to resolve this problem. The cloth was to be shipped on the morrow. Phillip pushed back his chair and went to see about dispatching the consignment calling to Collins to come down with him to the warehouse floor. Collins, when he heard which batch was to be sent out, became alarmed and flustered. He trailed behind Phillip protesting in a low voice.

'But Mr. Abbey, sir. It ain't all there. What's going happen at the other end sir, when they finds it short? It'll look bad on us won't it sir? On the house I mean. We're known for us trustworthiness sir. Reputation is what we have.' Collins continued in like vein as Phillip did his best to quieten him before he sent for assistance with moving the cloth to the waterfront.

'Hush now Mr. Collins. All is well I do assure you.'

'But these amounts is wrong sir, you know it as I do.' Phillip struggled then said:

'There will be more to follow and it is best not to keep the customer waiting, isn't that it Collins? Late or short. It's one way or the other. I will of course write to explain the problem. The shortfall will be made good at the next delivery. Of course it will.' He was relieved then and believed his own lies.

'You've arranged that then sir?'

'Of course. Nothing to worry you at all. Here, help me lift this one.'

Phillip had done nothing of the sort. He had not liked to trouble his masters in Wortley. All the action he had taken had been to warn the night watchman to keep a close lookout with some energy, which warning had caused resentment in the diligent watchman. But the cloth had been lost on the journey down the Aire and the canals and river. It would have been stolen, or damaged or fallen into the water whilst being loaded and unloaded.

There was one more opportunity for Phillip to address the missing cloth when it came time for him to sign the lading documents and Customs agreements. But he did not hesitate in the just breaking light of dawn to add his signature to the others on the papers. Of course there would be some fuss about the discrepancy. But that would be sometime in the future and by then, well something could be done.

Chapter Ten

Robert Wood

By way of Long Marston and a difficult interview with his father Henry Abbey, Phillip travelled back to Leeds in the summer. This was to be a short holiday for him but also a time for him to discuss business affairs with his employers and their associates. But never the less he anticipated the visit with pleasure, intending to frequent the theatre in Leeds and the summer season of dances. He could spend a little time at the card rooms and catch up with old friends. His father's words still haunted him. The old man had said that he would lend no more to Phillip and that Phillip had better not borrow from any other source. He warned of signing arrangements with "disagreeable" persons. Phillip in fact had such an agreement on his person whilst his father made his threats. But he knew that it was quite a usual state of affairs for gentlemen. And since Phillip knew himself to such and he saw no harm in it. His father could be harsh and even rough so some caution might be necessary. But his brother Henry would soon have plenty in the bank and would be ready to give Phillip a hand. If not, then he would certainly have to find himself a rich bride and go into the cloth trade, something that he had for the last year at least, hoped he might avoid.

He was welcomed home by John Bateson and his wife Ann Bateson at the long low house at Greenside. Matthew and his wife Jane made much of him and his first evening in Leeds was spent with their daughters, Anne, Nannie and Sarah. The girls squabbled less than they had been wont to do. Anne was now fourteen and had become tall and slender and rather pretty. She was witty and lively and Phillip was glad of this. The household too were pleased that he had come. Molly embraced him with floury hands and laughed to see him grown taller and so fine a gentleman as if she had not seen for years instead of months. She made him sit by her as she thumped the dough before her, and between efforts she told him all the news.

'So my Dan has been a doing great work and he's back with Maister Jim and Mistress Nancy has been a telling how well they think of him in their house. She don't want him to be off working in Leeds. He's a great one with the children tha knows. Him and the master were making kites on Sunday – tha knows it were a big wind last week? - and little Thomas loves Dan so much tha knows? She pounded the dough and rolled it. 'He follows him everywhere and they go down the dye shops together and he says he wants to be a dyer too, just like my Dan. And they was racing too. Went out to run over to Bramley with Jack Bateson. Of course Dan would a won of course, only he was stepping back to bring Thomas along. So now he goes to the choir with the young ladies as well because he's home. Sometimes I hears 'em singing in the great room there. Him and Miss Mary. He's a lovely voice has Dan. John Batesons says he's as true as a fiddle and who's to know better than he about such like.'

Phillip becoming a little tired of this. He agreed with the accolades made because Molly insisted that all should agree with her on all matters and the household were were used to bending before her opinions. It was not for him to upset her.

'Well I'm glad he's back home Molly. I can see that you miss him when he's sent away and I've missed him too. I don't have such an honest friend when I'm in Hull. There's just the old men in the offices and I don't get to have much time to myself.' Molly left off with her kneading and grabbed Phillip's cheeks.

'Oh don't tha worry my pet, because there's plans going on to entertain thee while thou art here. Why, Mr. Wood is coming over as well and tha'll be dining with him. What does tha think of that?' Phillip now had two floury hand prints on his face.

'I look forward to it. He's an interesting man and, and, good company for all he is -'

'Aye, a very learned gentleman is Mr. Wood. And a fond father as well. He's the best preacher I ever heard, I do declare.'

' - a man of the cloth,' continued Phillip. ' I can't wait,' he added helping himself to raisins and getting a rap on his knuckles for this transgression.

The anticipated encounter with the Reverend James Wood was not such penance as Phillip feared. Young Robert Wood was brought over to Leeds, home for the summer from his school and he was a lively companion for the young Misses Bateson. Of course, there were many prayers said and solemn readings of scriptures. To have such a leader of the Methodists among them was a great event and the great man could not be kept for the Bateson's sole entertainment. Callers were many, including James Smith from Armley and Benjamin North from Silver Royd. Fortunately for Phillip, there were social activities arranged too, for the purpose of occupying the young people. Some of these were musical soirées such as old John Bateson loved where the family gathered with their friends and sang together. There were walks with the youngsters and various young ladies and also opportunities to make calls around the district, which although not quite in Phillip's preferred line of social activity, nevertheless passed the time pleasantly enough to distract him. But in those moments of reflection, which were few enough, he did think of Lady Catherine and sigh a little for the loss of her capricious favour. His lack of interest in this social set did not lessen his charm though, and he was much in demand and much admired for his interesting conversation and his accomplished manners. There were some eligible clothier's daughters that watched for his comings and goings and felt the beating of their hearts.

A visit was organised to the Theatre in Leeds where there was to be a performance of some note of various popular numbers from Sacred Music. Matthew had invested in a light carriage that could both transport and contain his daughters as they began to grow up and what with the improvements to the fortunes of the Bateson Cloth House and the dangerous times in which they lived, he and his wife Jane thought it a wise investment. It is not to be supposed in general that, Anne, Nannie and Sarah did not in fact prefer to walk about the lanes of the township and enjoy the company of their neighbours and friends but that since their status was rising, then that status should be marked by suitable transportation. Matthew's wife Jane was careful that she should not feel wordly pride in this possession and Matthew found that a source of merriment.

So Mrs. Bateson carried her excited daughter Anne to the Theatre of the town of Leeds and waited with them in contented composure in her best wool mantle on the steps of the Theatre, nodding at those she knew and scrutinising unfamiliar faces. Anne were animated and excited. They were soon met by Phillip and Robert Wood and another young gentleman from Wortley. Samuel Beverley had been included at Mary's insistence and her sister Anne had protested but then agreed that there might be some additional entertainment to be gained by his attendance. So it was Samuel that had escorted Mary across the summer streets from the Lister's house, stumbling and mumbling and generally failing in his attempts to match Mary's composure and grace.

Mary was enchanted by the grand musical performance. The glory of the music and the beauty of the choral harmony made her eyes sparkle and shine in the candle lit interior of the auditorium. Phillip too, quite enjoyed the music and when his attention was not thoroughly engaged by the performance, made a good use of his time in watching the others of the party enjoy themselves and of studying others in general. Samuel Beverley had trod on many toes as he made his awkward entry into their seating. But Mary had kindly moved and indicated that he might find shelter beside her good self. Anne smirked at Phillip - and Robert Wood catching this expression smiled inwardly. For himself, he had no favourites. But sat close to Phillip, he wondered to himself, which of the daughters of the family Phillip might admire and in the future, lay claim to.

Although Robert was only 15, his nature was perceptive and his outlook mature. He could not see at this present time, that Phillip had any particular interest any of the young ladies that were of this party, but during the course of the evening, he did begin to suspect that Phillip had an interest in young ladies in general as he noticed that the Clothier's eyes were ever darting around the galleries.

'Here you are,' whispered Robert, taking from his coat pocket a pair of small opera glasses. 'Use these. You'll be able to see the – the chorus, so much better.' Phillip took these and did use them to observe the performers in greater detail, but from time to time the direction of the glasses wavered and scanned the young ladies directly opposite.

'Robert Wood!' accused Anne Bateson, when they were moving in the interval. She poked him on the arm. 'You gave those glasses to Phillip so that you might see where he spies. What a horrible thing to do. I think that is so bad of you.'

Robert made a puzzled face at his friend. 'Oh yes so bad - and I saw you laughing at it too. You just keep a close eye on that one.'

'Indeed I do. Because there are people like you around who like to tease and taunt others. I shall be sure to tell your father. And how can I keep a close eye on him for that matter, when you have let him have your opera glasses. You should have lent them to me so that I could as you just advised see him in all his glory.'

'Come come Miss Anne. You won't tell my father. That will never happen. I'll get to him first and tell him all about it and you won't be able to run fast enough in your frock to win the game.'

'Have some cake Robert. Oh sorry, it's all gone.' As she said this Anne put the last large lump of their treat into her own mouth and they both giggled

As the young men strolled home together in the cool summer air there were further opportunities for them to become acquainted, the ladies having all been removed by carriage. Samuel had only to walk to Armley and would leave them at Beech Grove. Robert and Phillip had to walk another mile down to Greenside. It was Robert Wood that led much of the conversations with his curiosity about the town and about these new companions. Still at school, he was an intelligent and interesting companion, easily able to hold his own with these young clothiers. He probed them for what they knew of the various workshops and premises that they passed and when they came upon a chapel he would ask what they knew of that too. Samuel was able to provide answers since he was mostly in and of Leeds. 'Tell me, both of you,' do you ever get up to the Mill Hill Chapel?'

'I do Robert, when I can. I like to go to the different places you see and hear what each has to say for themselves. I heard a good sermon last week, but not at the Mill Hill. Where was it? Oh yes. It was on Albion Street. A man come down from London was there and he was a great speaker. Everyone said as much, so it must be true.'

'What was his text?' asked Robert Wood, now curious and wondering if he knew the preacher. Samuel looked puzzled for a while and then abashed. 'I think I have forgotten,' he said apologetically at which both Robert and Phillip laughed. Robert went to speak but Phillip was quicker.

'Dear me Samuel, you should have just made something up quickly. Here is our own child of the Connection and you have made yourself look a fool. Unless he is very mean and goes to seek the true information, you might have told him anything. Is that not right Robert?'

'Indeed, you have a point of your own there Phillip. Samuel might have given me a text that was convincing, and would then have appeared to have given more notice to the substance if not the purpose of this notable sermon and would have profited from it. But that this Minister did not leave a lasting impression is a revelation of itself.'

Samuel protested. 'But I would not do that! How might that be! To claim something that I know not what of!'

'What of?' scoffed Phillip. 'What of what Samuel?'

There was a moment's pause. Robert followed with, 'Is that what you would do then Phillip? Would you be able to convince others that you had taken notice of a fine speech, when you had in fact been gazing about you.'

Phillip glared at Robert and felt hot. 'No, of course I did not mean just that. But I would wish my hearers to be comfortable. That is what I meant. But that which I mean to say to Samuel is fair advice – for a man in business. When we do not know the facts, then of course, we might say we have not our ledgers to hand but will find out and be on the matter straight away. Something to that effect. Samuel is always quick to own a fault when there is none there.' Robert whirled round and faced Samuel. 'Next time you find yourself lost for the references, just tell me that the text was most admirably suited both to the congregation, the liturgical cycle and the sermon. That way will you be beloved of all the ministers sons!' He hopped on one foot and turned on Phillip. 'Is that it then? Did I do it right, like a business man?' Samuel had halted and looked astonished. Phillip said, 'Yes. That's the way An excellent answer. Samuel you must learn that by heart. And you Robert Wood, you will go far.'

'In business?'

'You will be for the church I think?'

'I hope so. I hope that God will call me and that I may serve Him. It is no secret. But I fear Phillip that you do not think that of much account, do you?'

'Well someone has to do it.'

'Indeed yes.'

'And I respect that too. It won't be an easy life if you follow in your father's footsteps. I can at least see that.'

'You mean he would be a hard man to follow.'

'Yes I mean that and more. You would not have a home or much hope of wordly goods I think.'

'We believe that God provides Phillip. We look to the next world for our rewards. It might even be that yours is the harder way.'

'I don't see how that can be. The rewards are there for those that work hard and can be trusted. I hope so anyway.'

Samuel interjected here, 'No Phillip, that's not what he means. He means that you will have more difficulty in entering the Kingdom.' Phillip laughed at Samuel's simplicity. Robert studied Phillip but made no further comments and the crossroads were before them. They made their good nights.

'Good night and God Bless, Sam. I hope I will see you again while my father is in Leeds.' Samuel smiled and they bowed and shook hands. As Samuel walked out of hearing Robert said, 'Come on Phillip Abbey, I'm wanting to know more about your thoughts on business. Most interested am I, and you to be a Clothier. You have been in Hull. I want to know all about Hull. Tell me all about what there is to see and to do there and about the great ships that sail to make your fortune. I won't ask about the Chapels. I see this is not your particular interest.' Robert Wood settled to learn what he could of Phillip and listened with interest to the young gentleman who began.

'Of course. Well, Hull is a much more sophisticated place than Leeds.......

James Wood and John Bateson were sat outside in the garden when Robert and Phillip arrived at Greenside but John Bateson was fatigued with the heat of the day and retired. Phillip followed his lead and Wood and his son were left alone.

'Did they make good work of it then son? I trust you enjoyed your night out in the town?'

'Yes father. It was a good performance – and the walk home was interesting too. Sam Beverley was telling me much about the industries and the place. I've taken a liking to him. There's nothing complicated about him.'

'I'm afraid the young ladies do not speak well of that one though. It's a pity. He is solid lad even if over earnest.'

'I've been learning a lot about business in Hull – from Phillip Abbey. He had a lot to say about that - more than can usually be got from a general conversation.'

'He seems a pleasant young man and he at least is not rejected by the Bateson girls. I believe he may do well and be prosperous and in time may be one of the family as well.'

'Indeed. He believes very much in himself and his possibilities. He has a great confidence about him and an ease of manner that is attractive in itself.'

James Wood waited as Robert paused and reflected. 'But I shall be courageous tomorrow night and dare visit with Benjamin Beverley that I might know Samuel the better.'

James Wood understood. 'Mr. Beverley is at home but he is not to be feared. There is much good about him in many ways and it will be interesting for you to meet with the family. But young Mr. Abbey? Matthew Bateson loves the boy, you know? They lack a son and heir and Phillip has been something of a substitute. He is trusted to do much of their business even though he's short in years - in Hull - and does so very well I hear. I believe he will be part of the family in some way for years to come because Matthew wishes it to be so.'

'I'm sure that will be well. And it is well for him that he has this family to care for him because he will be guided by them where his own beliefs might lead him to error.'

' Quite.' The Woods retired then themselves with candles, for they would both read the Gospel and pray, before they laid their heads to rest.

'Hello there.' Dan Grady was chopping some wood for his Molly in the garth at Greenside when Robert Wood came out to see the morning sun come up.

'Hello thyself. A good night then, at t' Theatre? Were second violin sober? It can spoil the whole thing if it aint all of a tune.'

'I think it was all of a piece. Why, have you heard it then?'

Dan chopped down on a round of oak and then looked up. 'Aye sir. I was there the neet afore ye. And it were most of it delightful. But there were a bit of clash from that second and it it was hard to ignore.'

'You must have a good ear then Dan. It is Dan, isn't it? We've not had the chance to speak before but then Molly has a lot to say of you, and all good. I know so much of you that I feel we must be friends!'

'Oh Mr Wood, I'm such as is friends with all men.'

' I hear as much.'

Dan put down his axe and stood his full six feet, extending his big hand to Robert Wood. 'Here's me hand then sir. I hopes as thee and I will be good friends then. I was a talking with thy father only yesterday down at t'mill.'

Robert took hold of Dan's hand and shook it firmly. 'You know I want to know all about how you came to be here Dan It's very romantic what they tell me.'

'And so it is, to be sure. Here am I, an orphan out of the storm and adopted by the Batesons and the one they love the best.' Robert laughed.

'Do they? How is that then?'

'Because they rescued me. Because I can run faster than Jack Bateson. And because Molly insists upon my virtues and proclaims them to the world. And because I repay their trust in me and serve them well.'

'You live over there with James Bateson, don't you?'

'Aye, that I do. It's where I call home, except when I'm here, and then I call that home too. And here am I, a chopping of wood for the ovens, and others still abed.'

'That's diligence, to be sure.'

'And if a storm comes and ought else fails, I believe I will still be a chopping of the wood sir. And mind, next I must be away at the dyeing at the mill.

'You owe them gratitude Dan?' probed curious Robert.

'I owe them everything sir. Miss Mary as much as any, for she it was that taught me to write and gave me so much as I have of real education.'

'Taught you? Oh, Miss Bateson? Did she give you lessons?'

'Aye, she did that sir. She's a good heart that one. None better.'

'You're like a brother to her then. Or a cousin. Is that it?' Dan didn't answer. He chopped two more logs and put them in the stack by the door. 'Like this Master Wood. I'm her good servant and always will be, where I can be of service that is. Now does tha take up the rest of these logs and bring them into yon kitchen where we can get something to eat from my Molly.' Robert gathered as much of the oak as he could into his arms and followed Dan thoughtfully into Molly's domain.

'

Chapter

The Loss of The Neptune

A faint clack and rattle could be heard from the weaving room as the weavers plied their shuttles above. The sour smell that hung over the Beck and the fulling mills along its banks, was not overpowering on this day. The prevailing breeze came up from Farnley and took the smell over to Beeston and beyond.

'You look well Phillip. I have been admiring that waistcoat from afar. I think the tailors in Hull get first pick of the good stuff,' remarked Nancy Bateson as she supervised the burlers in her workshops, with her baby Sarah on her hip and little Maria toddling under her feet.

'They do Mrs. Bateson. This stripe came from Manchester, from a firm that brings its products to the same warehouse as our own.' Phillip's hand admired the expensive fabric.

'What! You can take you pick?' Phillip laughed at that absurd idea. 'No but samples are to be had, if you know the right people to ask.'

Nancy sighed. 'Oh, just bring me a bit of that then dear, will you? No I have a better idea. Take my husband with you back to Hull and let him find some nice pieces for me and the children. His head in the dye vats all the day and never a thought about anything else.' She smiled at her baby and tickled her chin.

'He has good diligence Mrs. Bateson. It is admirable. I wish I could find it in me, to be so fully engaged in any of the manufacturing procedures.' Nancy pursed her lips and regarded him with narrowed eyes. How strange, that the Apprentice Clothier was not passionate about all aspects of the cloth trade with it many complex processes and its woven relationship with the people that made the fabric of their world from it all. Or yet, it might be that she had spent too much time with James' eye for detail and complexity and that there were other views of the world. And other fabrics. She touched the Manchester velvet of Phillip's vest and sighed. No cotton for Wortley. Only the Marshall's bleach fields provided relief from the endless working of the fleece. But Phillip had stepped forward and given his professional eye to the work of the burlers. He nodded and smiled at the lass that stood at the sloping table with the cloth across it for inspection. And Nancy was reassured. It was evident Phillip did know his trade.

'Come and take some tea. And yes, you lot may all take a break. A short one. Tea! You won't believe how much tea these here can drink in a day. That's what the cloth trade uses. It's tea. Never mind all your other requirements. It's not teazles and fleece that will bring about our ruination. It's the bill at the tea merchants. I'll send a jug up. Mr. Abbey come down to the parlour and bring Maria with you.' Phillip followed Nancy down the outside steps, carrying Maria and bouncing her when safely down to see the toddler laugh. When the little girls had been given to their nurse, Nancy and Phillip went to sit together in the domestic quarters of the weaving house and waited for their refreshment to be brought to them.

'So I hear that you are enjoying your rest in Leeds?' Nancy poured tea into china cups.

'Yes indeed. And tonight there is hope for entertainment at the Assembly Rooms. I believe you like the dance, Mrs. Bateson?'

'Well I did once upon a time, mainly to provoke my father to disapproval, but now I must be the good Clothier's wife and stay home and see to all things. And twice more than that again. You know James. He has been climbing chimneys you know? But I have put a stop to that. I think it good that you young people are out and about and have company. The village is very well for me and always has been and that is my contentment and – and security. Never mind that now. But you and Mary, and Anne too, you must be about in the world. I hear that you are to act as trusted escort to Mary? Take care of her now! Do you dance well Phillip?'

'I have been told that I do, although I am not quite up on the newest steps – but no matter, I can learn them almost at once. It wasn't part of my training Mrs. Bateson was it? Rings in the barn at harvest time and the occasional formal affair at Greenside to train the young ladies.' From the hallway came the sound of a noisy arrival and the maid knocked and announced Joseph Bateson.

'Ah, here you are Phillip,' said Joseph, flustered and wiping his nose on his handkerchief. 'They said you would be here. I've got some bad news, I am sorry to say, and sorry to be bringing it.'

'Well don't keep us hanging Joe. What's up?' Nancy has tensed and her cup hung in mid air.

'We had a letter this morning from Hull.' Phillip put his own cup down carefully on the saucer and listened, holding his breath. A small voice deep in his unconscious mind made a warning.

'We have lost a cargo. The Neptune was fouled getting into Rotterdam and although there was no loss of life, the cargo was spoiled.' Phillip let out his breath and took up his cup again. 'Just to tell you. And so Matthew will have to put in the papers to the insurance. If you would step along when convenient and our Nancy has tired of you. He's at the counting house at the mill and needs you to sign and so on. Otherwise that's all. Is there tea? '

'My goodness,' said Nancy. 'That's terrible news. But lucky that no lives were lost. Yes, sit down Joseph, I'll get you a cup. You sit here and let Phillip understand the better way you're going on now.' Phillip picked up his tea and crossed his legs.

'Terrible news. But this is why we pay such a great deal for insurance, is it not? So all is as well as it can be. I myself signed for the consignment. At least no lives were lost. How are you. Maister Joe?'

'Better than I was, certainly. We have three more looms now and the books balance. I make sure of that. No risks for J. and J and co.'

'What about yourself though. I know you're down at the Lepton house with your Jack. Will you there long or are you looking for your own house?'

Joseph's face fell. He remembered his unhappy loss. Phillip regretted the remark which he had meant for conversation and felt a brief stab of remorse. 'I am so sorry. I did not mean -'

'Don't apologise Phillip. I come here off and on, many the day - and to my father's where the food is best. As for unfortunate remarks, well, you're not in the same league as James! They are damned lucky that he has you in Hull with the merchants. And you stick to Hull because it won't be long before me and Jack will be sending out our cloth and all.'

Phillip whistled and Joseph beamed at him. 'Well good for you then Maister Joe. And all credit to you, I think, that affairs should be going so well. You'll keep the stand at the cloth hall?' Joseph nodded.

'What works is a good book keeper. Jack can do all the other stuff, but without knowing what's in and what's out, then there's no progress. Take that as good advice from me sir. And yes, Jack will never part with the cloth stand nor my father. Nothing more sure than that.'

'I will heed your advice Joseph. Here's to good book keeping.' Phillip raised his cup to Joe, the strong light from the large windows shining through the transparency.

Chapter Twelve

The Assembly Rooms

It was not for Mary, such an evening as this. She did not feel herself to be old enough even, at just seventeen, to be going out into society in Leeds. In so thinking, she did not count her services among the Methodist Society and did not consider that in teaching others the rudiments of education she demonstrated great maturity and some confidence. She had been raised in expectation that she would rule both her domestic household and a small army of journeymen and apprentice cloth workers and such as she did now came quite naturally to her. But she had become very anxious when her mother had agreed with Phillip Abbey urging that it was quite the thing to do, to see that her daughters attend more of the social activities in Leeds. Her mother, and her father too, could see then see that such was the way for their daughters. Growing wealth and a strong sense of social duty that came from the rock of their Methodist faith must mean that the daughters of Matthew and Jane Bateson should engage with the world as it was now and be brave as they did so for society was changing and people must change with it.

Mary believed her sister Anne would have no such qualms as she did and would have been ever so much braver. Mary was not ever sure in her own mind, that to dance in public, was the proper thing to do - but her mother and aunts had prevailed and so she must prepare herself and be ready to be seen in the world. 'You have had the lessons my dear, and all the extras. You must now put them to use, as they were intended or the outlay will be wasted,' she had been told wisely by her mother.

Her aunt Elizabeth Lister had helped her to dress and her new gown was lovely but still she felt uncomfortable. She looked back at herself from the mirror and frowned. It was not so much that she did not enjoy nice clothes and dancing and music. She did. But she already believed that it would be all so trivial and so false. She would meet with some of her school friends, grown a little, but still silly. And there would be gentlemen to dance with her that she did not care for, know, or respect. Strangers who might later mock her quaint ways and plain speech. She did not anticipate a good use of her precious time. It was all vanity.

'Come along now Mary. You are of an age to enjoy yourself and meet with people. This is part of your social duty, as much as working among the poor. You work so hard that you have the right to a little pleasure.' Her Aunt Elizabeth cajoled her and fussed about acting with affection as a lady's maid and reassuring her beloved niece that she might go to a Public Ball without bringing herself into disrepute.

Mary looked at herself again in the tall glass 'Yes I know. It is right to be seen about in the right places and all that kind of thing. Wearing the right clothes and pleasing other people. But I don't seem to enjoy myself in a crowd. I don't think my mother understands that you know. And neither do you Aunt - you don't even like to be at Chapel if it is busy, so don't be hard on me because I like to be quiet. You know perfectly well that you prefer home, family and simple ways against all this ceremony. I am only in your likeness to choose my own friends from among the Society. It's your stance to the world that I have adopted. There now, stop poking at me. I'm done and if it does not please, then so be it.'

'Oh this is nonsense Mary. Why - I could step out with the best of them when I was your age. Time enough to stay home and do the chores. There now, you look beautiful. You go on and join in and be young and carefree for a change. Too much duty is not good for young people. One can be too dutiful and it makes for a dull person. Don't be dull.' Mary tutted at her aunt who smiled gently in return. 'And be kind to old Mrs. Walker and make sure she has someone sat by her. It is very generous of her to offer to chaperone you.'

'It's not quite what I heard aunt. Something about her making you promise that she could accompany me? Her dying wish, make an old woman very happy perhaps?'

'Oh you minx. Well let that tell you that there are some folk very glad to be at the Balls. Think of it as a kindness to her if you will. There, now, it's duty.'

A bell was heard announcing the arrival of the others of the party.

'There's Mr. Abbey. Take your fan dear. Oh my, I am worn out with getting you dressed and must fall on the bed quite drained.' Mary put on her wrap and took up her fan. 'I could believe that if I did not know that you have invited all your friends this evening and that Mr. Lister is hoping for music.' She went to the door and passing through, made a stately descent of the fine staircase. Had her aunt seen her face she would have understood that Mary intended the effect to be comic. But Phillip Abbey saw a slender young woman in a new and fashionable gown and was surprised.

Phillip made an elegant bow and complimented Mary on her dress and taking her arm led her out and handed her into the waiting coach. He settled himself opposite her on the leather seat. To Mary's astonishment the carriage was empty. 'Where are Miss Cooper and Samuel?'

'Miss Cooper sent word that she was indisposed. As for your Samuel, I know for a fact that he has been detained by an urgent matter at the works. Mercifully we are spared his ongoing confusion and disaster. You look nice, by the way. It is good to see you so well dressed.'

'Well dressed? This dress is so flimsy I think it might not last the night.'

'It might last till dawn.'

'I really don't want to be there that late Phillip. I hoped you would bring me away before midnight. You should have let my aunt know that our party was reduced. It might not be the right thing that we do.'

'Oh tish. Your Mrs. Walker is there just for you as soon as we alight. There is certainly no impropriety at all. And I am as good as your brother you know.' Mary doubted that this might be thought the case in the circumstances.

'But you must be excited to go to your first proper Ball. You'll meet lots of people there, that you will not see in your usual circle of friends. That will be interesting.'

'No Phillip. I am simply terrified. I was before and now Miss Cooper does not come, I find I am alone and you must stay by my side.'

Phillip put out his hand and took Mary's little hand into his own and gently pressed it. The carriage jolted on a rut and she fell close to him and moved quickly away.

'Don't be worried. You worry too much. I will be there and you will not come to harm. Perhaps you may enjoy yourself. There now, try not to fret so.' He saw her large bright eyes and thought to himself, that she was a most unsophisticated girl and so immature. She has such simple country ways.

'We can come away whenever you feel that you wish to. Perhaps that might be the best thing. And then another time, you might feel more comfortable. Yes. That is the way. Think of it as a beginning and a small venture into society. And you may know some of the people there? From your school perhaps, or from the chapel.'

Phillip had reluctantly agreed to curtail the evening if Mary's anxiety required that to be done. But he was easy around this. He would enjoy the evening certainly but as he knew that he had hopes in other directions, it would be as well that he did not play the field. Not just now. Just a little maybe. In fact, as he thought of this, he blessed his circumstances. It was fortunate! He was free to do as he wished tonight without any real need to impress or to attract. He could see advantages in such a position. And there were always other pleasures that might be enjoyed later on such a fine summer night for a gentleman on leave from his duties. The billiard rooms would be open late, or there might be a game of cards to be had if he was lucky. He smiled at Mary and adjusted his expectations so that his Master's daughter might be accommodated in her awkwardness.

'Don't worry,' he said, squeezing her hand again. 'I'll keep close and if you need me, just wave. And as soon as you wish to leave, just say the word. You will find something to amuse you, if it's just the band and watching the dancing. ' Mary felt some relief at these assurances and managed to produce a faint smile.

The Assembly Rooms were reached and the couple took their turn in the queue of coaches and alighted. Mary stood trembling in the harsh lantern light. Phillip offered his arm and sighed inwardly and managed to bring her inside without much in the way of disaster. It was only Leeds. Here though, would not lose status by being seen with Miss Bateson. In fact, perhaps there was something to be gained. Mrs. Walker was waiting, proudly installed with other familiar matrons of the town and she nodded to Mary when she saw her arrive.

'That's the girl you've to mind, is it Bella? Mrs. Lister's niece isn't it.'

'Yes indeed. But she's such a good girl you know. She won't need much supervising. So what about your condition dear. Have you consulted Dr. Morgan? No? Well you should.'

'I was about to tell you that our Ruth has recommended a great man from London, but you will interrupt dear. Oh look, she's given that young man the slip already.' Mrs. Walker leaned forward to see where Mary had got to, but since her vision was very poor, she could make out little more than a yard before her face. 'Has she? Well, good for her. Perhaps she has a plan already. Good luck to her I say. Oh to be young again!'

'Quite so. So I was trying to tell you Bella about my discomforts but you are so distracting…… and then she came right out and told me….. she sat there just as you are there now…… I never heard such a thing in my life…..'

But now the Ball was in progress and Mary could not see Phillip at all. He had melted away with the crowds and she stood with a hand on a column feeling both singularly alone and that everyone would be staring at her. Mrs. Walker was surrounded by her coterie of old friends and she would not retreat to such a haven, and yet she did not know what she should do. She began to panic now and she could feel her hands sweat and tremble. Here she was, alone in a sea of strangers in their very best attire and she could hardly stand upright. She felt acid rise in her throat and feared she would vomit, right there, on the polished floor before the whole of Leeds.

'Might I ask for the pleasure of this dance?' Mary jerked into the present and turned to the question. 'Yes.' she said timidly, because there was no other course of action open to her. 'Yes of c -course. I would be delighted.' Mr. Gott was a familiar face and she had no other choice. He had observed both her abandonment and read her position and her posture with perception. He guided her onto the dance floor and smiled encouragingly and although she at first thought she might in fact faint, so hard did her heart beat, by the time the dance neared its conclusion, much of her acute distress had gone. Mr. Gott enquired,' I thought that Mr. Abbey was here?'

'He is sir, but I am afraid I have lost sight of him. We have been separated.' As the dance came to its close, Mr. Gott nodded slightly to a young man nearby who was obliged by favours and connections, to notice this, and Mary soon found herself very much in demand and engaged for every dance. In fact, her evening was very fully occupied with the joy of being active and almost popular and she had something of a change of heart, about the interest of the Assembly Room Balls. She enjoyed the music. Her eyes shone, and her cheeks were pink and she became animated and very pretty as a consequence of this. And though not all her partners were handsome young men, she found that all were considerate, lively and companionable. And so the evening was not so desperate as her imagination had painted it and she thought that she might come again. From time to time, she looked around her to see where Phillip might have gone, but he certainly had not taken to the dance floor.

'Oh just look at that young lady over there. Oh, she's lovely and she dances with just anybody. What a model of civic duty. She's even had a dance with that old Colonel Brumby and everybody else made some excuse when he held out his hand. Such delightful charm and innocence!'

'Where? Oh, that's Miss Bateson – you must know her? The eldest of Matthew Bateson of Wortley. I'm glad she's enjoying herself. I am supposed to be keeping an eye out for her.'

'Are you really! How very gallant of you. She' very nice though. I fear you have neglected her then. Did you not mean to escort her? You are a rogue!'

'I was called away for something as we arrived as you well know. Business. I will tell her so and she will understand. And when I returned I could see that she had found herself quite popular and so I thought to myself, Phillip, you just let her find her own feet. Now she will be confident in herself and that won't do any harm. It's what she needs.'

'Oh I see. That was very thoughtful then. But do you not consider her then, at all? I mean for the future and your prospects? There's a good dowry there if I'm not mistaken and a way into a partnership. Or are you mine dear.' Phillip laughed in the face of his friend. 'I'm my own man. And she is nice as you say. But not for me. Rest assured dear heart, I am free for you.' Lydia Smyth bowed to accept the compliment. 'Silver tongue Mr. Abbey. So come on then introduce me, you pup.' Phillip agreed and took Lydia Smyth by the arm and they made their way through the crowd to where Mary stood, a little bewildered and breathless from the last dance. Mary caught sight of Phillip as he approached with a fine lady on his arm, and she smiled in welcome.

'Oh there you are, Mr. Abbey!' she said, still breathless. 'And what happened to you? I did look for you but I find, I find I have been altogether rather occupied. I hope you are not disappointed that I did not wait?'

'No, of course not. I hear you have been much in demand as a dance partner. I had to talk to someone about business. I do apologise but it was most urgent, so of course, I had to see to it, but I concluded it as quickly as I could. Then when I returned, -

and it was almost immediately - you were spoken for and then so much in demand that I have not been able to see anything of you.'

'Oh I'm sorry. I wasn't sure you see. Oh I see. Of course then. And your friend?' Mary turned to Miss Smyth, smiling and with a nod, to include her in the conversation. Phillip remembered the purpose of the exchange. 'Yes of course. But this is the sister of the Lord of the Manor of Wortley who will have last seen you as a child!. Miss Smyth, this is Miss Bateson, of Greenside House, Wortley.'

'Oh my dear Miss Bateson. How well you have danced tonight with all comers. I have been watching you and have been enchanted by your efforts. Pray, do give my compliments to your father.'

Mary considered this for a while. 'I am obliged to you Miss Smyth and I shall of course, convey your compliments to my father. I hope that you too have enjoyed your evening.' Then turning with dignity aside said quietly to Phillip, 'I shall go home now I think. Would you be so kind as arrange this?' Miss Smyth studied her victim. Phillip made the very slightest of shrugs and Lydia Smyth understood the gesture.

'Of course, Miss Bateson. We must go Miss Smythe. Good night.' Phillip bowed as he said this and she bowed gravely back to him. As Mary stepped away Lydia Smyth reminded Phillip. 'Business? So convincing. But don't forget what I have told you about our mutual friend.' Phillip made another small bow and Miss Smyth found she was tired of the evening after all.

'Miss Smyth was a little impertinent I think. I am not sure that I like that.'

'She was just teasing you. I'm sure she meant no harm.'

'Do you know her well Phillip?'

'Well enough to know that she intended to be amiable. You must not take offence so easily at those who are higher placed in the world than you. It was not meant unkindly.'

'Perhaps you will be so good as to find our carriage. I will just say good night to Mrs. Walker. And her friends.'

Mrs. Walker was still fixed in her comfortable seat in an alcove. 'Mrs. Walker, I have come to thank you for your good help tonight and to wish you all good evening.'

Mrs. Walker awoke with a start but made a quick recovery. 'Oh, very well then my dear. I hope you have enjoyed yourself. Good night.'

Mary looked out of the window of the carriage and the journey to her aunt's was quickly over. Phillip helped her into the house and wished her good night.

'Thank you Mr. Abbey,' said Mary stiffly. 'I hope I have not spoiled your evening.'

' Not all Mary. And I think you did very well.'

'Thank you,' said Mary expressionless. But Phillip did not perceive this as he had already turned to leave.

Mary lay awake reflecting on the evening and wondering if she really ever would consider a public Ball as enjoyable. She considered Phillip's advice well as to the advisability of not taking offence at persons of high station and any conditions that might be imposed on such feelings and she thought rather less of Phillip Abbey than had been the case before he had so spoken. Having made such a discovery, she felt it incumbent on her to keep such a judgement to herself. It was bad that she should hear him betray himself, but it would be worse to accuse him, because might he not learn better ways and have it in him to change and to be a better person than that? Being the kind hearted Christian that she was, she then put her mind to the sourcing of some improving reading or perhaps even some

future comment that she could make, that would remedy
Phillip's fault and turn him to the right way of judging others.

Chapter Thirteen

A fox among the chickens

   Some days later Elizabeth Lister sent Mary with some pamphlets to Greenside. Molly was bringing in the eggs and called that the kettle would be boiling soon and Mary went at once to find her sisters about the house. She knew where Anne was because the sound of a pianoforte, being played very well, could be heard from the hallway. Deciding to leave Anne to her practice, she found Nannie and Sarah at their lessons with their mother in the parlour and she joined them for simple pleasure of being home in the old routines with the sun slanting low across the dark oak table and then undertook a walk with all her sisters across the village fields with the background sounds of the weavers shuttles and her little sisters bright chatter. After supper and before it was time for her to set off again on her walk into town, she sought out her father alone and reading in the parlour and she took the liberty of interrupting his activity to have a little time with him.

   'Well now love. Has tha time to sit with thy old father at last? I have been waiting all the day for thee to notice me!'

   'You were not here till just before supper and then the little ones were all over you. Then you went to say prayers with them!'

   'Well I might own that is the truth of it. But tha ran out straight away and went to visit with thy grandparents. Thou had best made the most of it now Mary. I will be nodding off before long.'

   'Why? Is that a very dull book that you read?'

   'It is. It is an excellent thing for an old man like me to have an aid to rest.'

'You're not an old man father. That is grandfather you are thinking of there.'

'When my child has left me and gone about the world alone, then I feel old.'

Mary put her arm around her father's shoulders. 'Poor old man,' she said, but not sympathetically. Matthew laughed.

'So Mary, thy mother tells me that thou art busy with the young men, dancing the night away at the Assembly Rooms.'

'Oh hush father. The both of you arranged it and I went because it was my duty to do so, since Mrs. Walker wanted to be watching the young men dance.'

'Phillip told me tha was beautiful and that tha was much admired.'

'He has a great deal to say sometimes does our Phillip. He was in much demand from Lydia Smyth, perhaps you should know that.'

'If I did not - then I know it now. But I don't think that much will come of that – from all accounts she is to be the bride of a very nice man in Hull. But otherwise it's good. We like our agents to be favourites with all the county.'

'Good for business you mean?'

'Yes why not? And good for Phillip too. I am happy that he enjoys himself, but I sometimes worry about thee my love. So much duty, always, and perhaps that is as it should be. But then we are only young once and it is important that thou mix with thy equals as well as with the poor. It's balance Mary. Phillip balances these things well and he serves the House well in doing so. Not least because he has apparently found favour with the Smyth family. We like their coal. But I like to think my daughter can walk with her head high no matter who the company around her and believe herself their equal in all respects.'

'I can father. I did enjoy being there and I might even consider attendance at the dances again. The music was very good. And indeed I spoke to lots of interesting people that I might not otherwise have encountered. But I think I will always love the hearth better than the world. And as for equality? You need not fear for my confidence. I know myself as good as another – in the sight of God! But I prefer a quiet life'

'Well there's no harm in that love. But thou must see more of the world before thy hearth days. Thy life is before thee and many paths lie open. Speaking of which, young Sam Beverley seems to find a lot of reasons to call here.'

Mary smiled at her father but did not trouble herself to reply. It has become a joke within the family that Samuel was sweet on her and she recognised provocation when it was put before her. There came a knock upon the parlour door and Dan Grady put his head inside the room.

'Ah, Dan, - come in lad. And here's Mary come home for thee to talk to for a while.' Dan held out a book. 'What does tha think?' asked Matthew. 'Excellent sir. That's one I'd like for me own shelf one day.' Matthew stood and gently brushed away the returned volume. 'If that is the case - it is thine,' he said warmly.

'But sir I must not take it from thee because it is not what I can afford and I don't have any good place to keep it. I know where it is if I need it. Not to take now at any rate. When I am settled, I may take the liberty of the loan again, and then I shall remember - and forget - to return it.' Matthew smiled at this and took the book from Dan. He handed it to Mary. 'See dear, this is thy work. Teach them to read and then they come and borrow books from their employers.' Mary opened it and studied the title page. 'I see I have caused the spread of sedition then,' she smiled, 'for this is a work of rousing morality.'

'I have need to withdraw, children. Thou must entertain my daughter for a moment Dan. And there is but half an hour Mary, before it will be too late for thee to walk back to Leeds.'

'Tha's away to town? In that case I will walk back with thee Miss Bateson. It's a fine evening for a stroll.'

Matthew left them together. On invitation Dan sat himself down quietly in Matthew's chair and asked Mary how she did and enquired of the Lister family in Leeds.

'They are all well. And what else are you up to Dan, apart from being in my father's good books and borrowing them too?'

'The usual I suppose Miss. Good sales at the cloth stand I believe and some orders from Hull which thy grandfather mutters about. No idle looms for the outworkers. We've set on a couple of nice lads from the poorhouse. They've settled in well. Michael and David they are. Two brothers from Kirkstall.' He leant back and stretched his long legs before him. Mary frowned a little so he straightened immediately.

'I'm glad for that Dan. And you'll be seeing to them I expect. Keeping an eye out and all that.'

'Aye, I will. They'll not get the run round while I'm there, not at all.'

'When Phillip came to the village, there was only me Dan, to protect him. They were after sending him to milk a cow with the weaver's pail. You know what I mean.' Dan looked aghast and then chuckled. 'He had thee though to defend him, tha says. I tell thee, there was worse to happen to a little 'un when they set me on with the weaving.'

'What?' said Mary, troubled. 'Did you have such a bad time of it? Oh now I remember. It was the lads at the Grammar

School. One in particular. Still, they won't catch you now will they?'

'Well that's a fact. Now I realise why I'm the best runner in the village!'

'Can I ask something?' Dan kept still in Matthew's chair.

'What is it Miss? If its aught about the cloth then I can tell thee. Otherwise for most things, tha'll know more than I do.'

'Do you ever hear the men, well complaining? It's just that sometimes, when I am among them in Leeds, I hear the odd word, here and there. Some complain of the gig mills and others I know, find it hard to feed the bairns. And then, you see, I get to worry about the village and if we look after folk properly.'

'Aye miss. There's a lot going on there in Leeds. Gott has to watch out. But we are a happy bunch here. Maister Jim never misses a day at the mill and can do the same as any of the lads. He's both respected and liked. And your father makes sure that the old 'uns and the widows get what they need to keep well. There's nowt for thee to worry about here. Jack and Joe, their team don't grumble. In this village we look after our own, that's what tha'll hear. Walker's crew make a lot of noise but that is the way Walker runs things. But its not to be marked, is that '

'Why not, Dan?'

'Because they complain there about being called upon to do owt. But believe me, Miss Mary, there is nothing so terrible in this world as when tha has to do the same thing, day in and day out and long hours just watching the machines and them too loud for chatter. I tell thy father that, and Maister Jim. I say that if the labour moves around, tha can get good cloth and happy workers. But then they say that they can't pay a man the different rates for the jobs if they move around. There's rates for skills does tha see?'

'Yes I know that. But Walker manages it.'

'No miss. If they have to leave their work they they get a piece rate that don't reflect their skill and then they have to tighten their belts. Thy folk, they pay less overall, but they pay every week so folk can know what's coming in and that pay goes over the lean times as well when others let go and care not. It's not that the men don't grumble – they do, but step back and look and things usually work out fair.'

'Oh. But Walker's men get paid more? But nothing in the hard times! And our workers get a regular rate. I understand. I never thought about all this before. That's strange isn't it. To be a part of the family and not know such ordinary things that are so important to other people.'

'Like tha knows a lot of other things Miss, instead. When thou has a minute free next time tha's over, come down and I'll take thee round t'mill and thou can talk to the workers and see what's up for them. They take right warmly to Mrs. Nancy coming down. I'd take a bet that they'll like to see thee down there too, because it's not all about cloth is it Miss? It's as much about people.'

'You're right Dan. I will do that. It's a good idea. I was - I should ask my father shouldn't I? About these things that I am learning about. Ignorance is not a good thing, is it?'

'No Miss. But thou knowst more than most already. Now tha had better get thy things and step out. We'll need to get going if tha's to be home before dark.'

Mary and Dan were setting off along the lane as her mother came home and waved goodbye in the gateway. In the kitchen Jane Bateson shook her head at her husband as she took off her bonnet and shawl. 'Don't you be letting foxes in among the chickens husband.'

'Never a fox my dear. Not that one. That's a man that knows his place and will never give cause for concern. But the place will be bigger afterwards. That's all. Mark my words.'

'Oh riddle me ree. Hear him puzzle. Thy wisdom man, can be vexing.' Matthew smiled and took a bite of apple from the bowl on the table.

'We should not worry about either our weaver or our daughter - for the both of them are going the right way in the world.'

'La la la And to do the right thing.' and Mrs. Bateson looked out of the kitchen window at the evening sky and for just a moment wished that Dan had been their apprentice and that he could have been better placed to make one within her own family. 'And Phillip had left us a lot of laundry to do. Time was our apprentices would take a hand with that. They are all grown too fine for the tub, that's what it is. So now I'm a washerwoman I suppose.'

'He's not our apprentice Jane. He's my father's responsibility and the terms are what they are.'

'He's been your apprentice ever since he arrived in the village else would he be in the workshops and not gadding about the country, all over. London, Hull. London! Tha's indulged him always. And he's always had his own way on everything. He's a son to you Matthew! And thou hast made the mistakes that fathers make.' Jane Bateson rattled the poker in the grate, aggravated by Matthew's complacence.

'Maybe,' said Matthew reflecting. 'Maybe I have indulged his wishes to be merchanting above what is needed here. But he's a good lad too all the same. Not, - not as, well, as amenable as Dan maybe. More with his own ideas I think. But that's good in a way. He'll go places. His brother has done very well. And that is why we've been taking on and prospering. Phillip's gone to visit with his father and that shows duty in him. And if it should be – should be that he settles for manufacture, then his father will invest and he can do as well as he likes. But he may not settle and that's that. Now I'm for bed. Art thou going to come up or dost tha need to harangue the fire irons before retiring?'

Jane gave the fire another good stir and moved the kettle to the flame.'Which is all very well. But where does it leave our Mary? It was expected tha knows? But it is not to be? Is she not good enough for him now I wonder? And then, there is Dan with every thing that's needed to succeed in the trade.'

'Fox among the chickens tha said. Which is it? Fox or Trustee?'

'I'm worried. That's all. It's a mother's care.'

'I know. But we must trust them all. Mary the most – because she will make her choice and that is how it should be – and it might be that there are others that will come and be the one.'

'Maybe.' Jane sighed. 'It should have been so simple.'

'Come to bed. What will be, will be.'

'I'll just be up in a minute. I've a mind on me to argue with the kettle and complain to the tea chest. Would tha like some bringing up love?'

'Aye.'

It was a fine evening and the last of the sun was hidden from Mary and Dan and they walked up to the town by the warehouses and factories and tall buildings. They had not talked of the cloth trade as yet but instead, Mary had told Dan at his request, all about the Ball. She had described Mrs. Walker and her carelessness and then related all that she had seen and had felt and Dan had listened with interest and with understanding and at length she confided to him that she was not comfortable within herself. The first sally into society had left her perplexed and confused and changing. Questions had lingered unconscious that now rose to be considered. She knew the hardships of ordinary people but until now beside Dan, she had not thought much about how her own comfort was dependent on the struggles of the labourers.

'We think in the Society Dan, we think to save souls, you see? But the more I see and hear, the more I am distressed by need. And in the mills? You said this evening how terrible it is to be doing the same thing hour upon hour and that's just what they do in those mills. And then the people become ill from the dust and the soot and ah, I can't say what I begin to think. Where will it end? What should I do?' Dan listened to this carefully, looking at his feet going forward.

'I should not be talking of these things to you!' Dan nodded and smiled.

'I've me own mind Miss Bateson but I like to hear what others think.'

'What do you think though? You've not said much.'

' That the world is as we make it and it changes all the time. So there are some, like thy father and others of his quality, that make it better and there are some that feed upon others and make it worse. Thou art here in this place and thy eyes are open to things that are wrong and are helping to make things better with acts of kindness.' Mary blushed.

'Yes alright. It's not enough though is it? My giving a few hours of my time to others. I am not better than the people I meet in doing charitable acts, just more fortunate.'

'Aye.' They walked over the bridge and in the dusk the town was still noisy with the hums and thuds of the workshops and mills along the Aire, and the lights of Marshall's Mill behind them like fallen stars. Somewhere from the back courts a baby wailed, a dog yapped and was cursed into silence. For a while they went together in with their own thoughts. Mary regretted that she had confided so much of her inner qualms to this young man and began to fret that she had troubled him with her problems. After all, he was not of her class, not her equal. It was not fair to burden him with what might seem odd misgivings…..

'I'm sorry -' she blurted out.

'Why?' he replied.

'Just – I don't know. You have your own worries and responsibilities. And mine are not important. Something like that. You must not tell anyone how I have spoken.'

'No I won't. What are friends for Miss? For listening that's what. Now I'm thinking to meself that what tha could be about, is getting a better view of what goes in the workplaces and here it is – I think if thou was to move on and stay with thy other auntie, the one in Armley? There's that mill Mr. Lupton has and a counting house there? And help there. Then tha'll get to see how it is without thou art the owner's daughter and all a front for to keep thee happy.'

'They might not like that.'

'Why not?. Who might not like that?.'

'It's not quite ladylike I think. To actually work in the offices even would be quite frowned on.'

'What does Mrs. Nancy do then? And thy mother. I see them everyday and they know just what's what with the books and the accounts and the orders. I think thy father would agree to such a plan, put before him with reasons. Because in the end Miss, tha might be needing to keep thy wits about thee and know what to do in the trade.' Mary was walking in silence, frowning and screwing up her eyes in the struggle with her thoughts. She squinted up at Dan.

'Why are you laughing?'

'I can see thee thinking. What blocks ye?'

'But I will miss my teaching I think. It's too hard to know what to do.'

'Aye. Tha can keep up with the teaching for some of the times can tha not? Stay over with Mrs. Lister for those nights and still be working for Luptons. There's nothing Miss, that can stop thee from doing what tha needs to do. I think they may arrange some small sharing of thee – for thou art doing for them rare service? And for only thy board too! '

'You're right Dan. My family, my aunts - will both have me with them and must learn to share and gladly. I wish I could think straight like you do. Thank you for walking with me. And for thinking with me too. You've got a long walk back I'm afraid.'

Dan took off his hat as a respectful farewell. 'Nay Miss. I'll be running I think. It's a pleasure to talk with thee and hear thy thoughts, and a joy to run free too. All good blessings I have. Good night Miss Bateson.'

Matthew was intrigued when Mary came to talk to him about her ideas of finding out more about life in the mills.

'Well now! I suppose this is right and all. But not here then, but with thy Aunt Sarah's aid? That is very independent of thee Mary and I respect thy thinking. And it is actually almost a God send because my sister was telling me only last week, that John Lupton's book keeping is chaotic and that she is worried that he does not keep his accounts in good order. So there is actually an opening and the opportunity that you wish for. And certainly it won't do thee any harm to know the ins and outs of accounting.'

'I'm not at all sure that I will be good at it though father. What if it get worse not better!'

'John has several clerks there. They know what they are doing. It's himself that needs putting in order. He's never quite liked to be industrious – but keep that to thyself. So it will be to manage him, more than the figures.'

'Well that's better then. I have a lot of experience of managing my uncles! But - I know so little about accounts.'

'Nay. Tha's been with thy grandfather many the evening, helping his accuracy.'

'I suppose I have. Mother will object?'

'I should not think so for one moment. There is one problem though.'

'What's that father?'

'We'll have all the young clothiers beating a path to our door. Nothing is so much to be admired in a wife as a good book keeper in the trade!'

'Oh you,' said Mary. 'Don't tease me. I'll tell you what, if there's a queue then you just send them all away. I've much to learn and I'll not want to be troubled with the young layabouts.'

'Quite right my dear.'

Later, as they lay in bed, Matthew and his wife discussed this new turning and interest for their eldest child.

'She's very independent isn't she. I never thought she would have much spirit, our Mary. She's always been such a - such a very good girl.'

'She's a head on her shoulders that one. Mark my words, she'll know all about it if she puts her mind to it. And it won't go amiss Mrs. Bateson. Time was all the wives knew what went on in the trade. Now I find they are all got to be fine ladies.'

'Oh really!'

'Yes. But Mary wants to work alongside other people like in the old days. She's different I think. I am very proud of her for this'

'Tha just want her nearer home. I know what thou art thinking Matthew. Thou wilt be away down at Lupton's Mill and gossiping with Mary.'

'Might as well eh? Go to sleep now wife.'

Chapter Fourteen

Crossgates House

Mary's small trunk had arrived at Crossgates house in Armley which stood at the top of the hill which was then, and is still, unimaginatively known as Hill Top. The site was convenient because from here there was a good view of Farnley and Leeds but the never ending smoke of the steam engines and brick kilns did not in ordinary circumstances, trouble the occupants.

It was a good house for the family of a gentleman boasting four rooms to a floor and many other conveniences besides. Aunt Sarah was a little harassed when Mary arrived that Monday morning, since the milk had curdled and the maid servant had burnt her hand on the range. And the baby was crying as well.

'Oh thank the Lord, you are come. Dear Mary. How am I to cope with all this? I don't know what's to become of us at all.' Mary took off her bonnet and advised her aunt to sit down.

'Just you sit there Aunt Sarah. I'll hold the baby and then you can take a moment to see what is to be done first.' Sarah Lupton sank gratefully into a padded armchair in her drawing room, managing to mutter some thanks and then sitting with her head in her hands as she noticed that the room was strewn with playthings and that the cat had relieved itself in a corner. Mary saw this too and felt her heart sink. She had not thought that her aunt would struggle to manage the house and she had not come intending to be a superior house servant or children's nurse.

But it transpired that things were not quite to bad as she feared and that the maid was not entirely incapacitated. For the maid was an older woman with a kind heart and strong arms and the injury was minor. Within a few days, Mary felt comfortable and welcome and her uncle had taken her with him on two occasions to work with him around his offices.

'I don't know how I managed without you my dear.'

'Perhaps you did not Uncle John! It has taken me two days to put those ledgers into some semblance of order and those papers – they are my next job. It's a very good thing that my grandfather does not come to visit with you in your offices. He would give you such a blank face.'

'Oh no. Not the blank face. I've had many of those, never you fear. Now I must go round the mill and see that everyone is enjoying themselves this morning. I'll be back in, well, perhaps an hour or two. Put today's correspondence to one side for me and I will look at it on my return.'

'Not to one side Uncle. Lupton. It will go into these boxes and in the proper order. If you did that yourself in the mornings, then we would not have spent so much time sorting it all into piles to put away.'

'Yes miss. And by the by, my father is to dine with us tonight and my brother Thomas. So as to prepare you. My father will be rude to you. Don't say I did not warn you.'

'No, not tonight. I will be in Leeds tonight. At the night school. You have forgotten again.'

'Drat. Yes I forget. And that man from the Upper Mills, he's taking you and that? It's a bit of a thing I believe and to be wondered at.'

'Yes Dan Grady is that man and you know who he is perfectly well. I believe you play cricket and know him well as me.' She sighed, 'he's one of my father's workforce. Very respectful. Don't call him that man from the Upper Mills.No need for concern uncle.' Mary bent over the papers before her did not look up as her uncle John Lupton fussed about and left her to sort out his books. If ever a man needed to employ a Chief Clerk it was John Lupton but he thought that he would prefer to do his own books and so be able to employ more productive workers at his mill. He preferred the office to the fulling stocks or the rattling scribbbling machinery and he kept the office window shut to stop the stench of the yard from offending him. There were indeed three clerks but they had long since given up on the office and were more interested in tallying the lading bills and gossiping in the yard. It was all in a very bad way.

Mary got up as John Lupton left and opened the window wide. The odour was so much of her life that she hardly noticed it now and there was a good breeze coming up the valley which would freshen the stuffy room. Her next task would be to fetch back the absent clerks and remind them of their duties.

She had now been some weeks living with her aunt and uncle in Armley and it had been hard at first. John Lupton and his wife Sarah Bateson were inclined to quarrel and often had harsh words. It had upset her. But little by little she had become used to this conflict and what she noticed was that they always made up with each other and that usually, Aunt Sarah got her way over matters big and small. John Lupton's mill was well run but not with full credit to his own activity it would appear. But he had good managers and good workers and it being solely his own power and premises, the mill was very profitable and the workers were properly paid. She made it her business to know such things. She was now no longer so innocent in such important details. What she did not understand of the books and the operations in the mill yard, she discussed with Dan as they walked into Leeds twice a week. He was good at explaining things to her, in simple words, things that her father had never told her and that she had in her youth, never questioned.

'So why are dyers paid more than finishers?'

'That's a hard one Miss Bateson. I think that wages are set by the Cloth Hall and that we abide by them. As for one man's work being worth more than another's, well I don't know that I rightly understand that. But the weavers get their rate for what they can produce. And the dyers too. But then the finishers. It's not the same. They get to take some for each piece they finish, a bit of the final price like. So they get's more in the long run.'

'So why are you not a finisher then Dan?'

'Sometimes I am. But the best money for me right now is in the dyeing and that's what Maister James has his head in. Proper immersed in too! So I do alright. But I've done all the jobs Miss. Don't you tell on me now. And if there's aught to do outstanding, then I fill in the gaps. Universally useful, that's me.'

'Will they not make you manager then Dan. If you can understand the whole process.'

'All in good time lass. I'm happy with what I get and with lodgings and all, I've enough to get some books and to put a bit by each month. No man happier than me.' Mary, off guard, missed the casual address.

'I know you are Dan. It's your special gift I think. To be happy no matter what.'

'Yes miss. Thank you. Mind that puddle. Oh, too late.'

Chapter Fifteen

The irascible old man of Armley

'What this then?' Old Tom Lupton banged his stick upon Sarah's new mahogany table and Sarah tutted at him. 'Where's that Bateson girl? Is she here, or is she off being a saint for the sinners of Leeds? I don't know. Family she is and never does she give a moment to a poor invalid such as I am become.'

'Here I am Uncle Tom. What do you need?'

'Just some brandy me dear. Go down the cellars and bring me up some decent stuff. Don't give me that in the decanter.' Mary sat beside fearsome Old Tom Lupton and smiled up at him. 'Off you go lass, before they tell me no.'

'I'm to tell you no as well. You'll get me into trouble if I give you any brandy, no matter what the vintage. I tell you what though sir. If you want a cup of tea, I can find you the best, the sweetest and the hottest cup in the whole of Armley.'

Old Tom sighed and surrendered. 'You're a pretty lass but a hard hearted one. Just like the rest of them.'

'But I can make very nice tea,' suggested Mary.

'Just tell that servant they have. She makes nice tea. And you stay by me and tell me anything they don't want me to know.'

'What is you're not allowed to know?'

'Anything important. And discreet. Are yon Bateson's solvent, that sort of thing.'

'Last I heard things were balanced uncle. But if there's anything amiss, I'll come down to the Heights, and you can be the first to know about it.'

'Now that's kind I'm sure. So when are you going to marry then child? Tell me that first so I can blast the scoundrel.'

'Not for many a year. But if I think to marry, I will come tell you first of anyone.'

'Above your father?'

'Oh yes,' lied Mary, to the delight of the old rogue. Sarah Lupton coming into her drawing room and overhearing this nonsense berated her father in law. 'Don't you be seducing our young people into your bad ways. I sometimes wonder at you father. I really do.' Tom Lupton reached out to attempt to catch his daughter in law a slap upon her nether regions. 'Don't you dare do that.' protested Sarah. Old Tom roared with laughter.

'John Lupton, your father is being a nuisance in my house.'

'Dear wife, he's a nuisance wherever he goes. It's not personal.'

'If you should get like him when you age, then I shall put you into lodgings and limit your allowance.'

'Just be careful my love. He's made his Will.' Old Tom roared then 'And I can change it at whim too!'

Chapter Sixteen

Mary calls at Beech Grove

Sarah suggested to her niece Mary, that she might call at Beech Grove to admire the new baby that Mary and Benjamin Beverley had made.

'Must I? I do not know that I should. I have not been fond of Benjamin and my aunt has not been often to visit with me. '

'Yet the child is our kin and should be admired. My sister is besotted with her infants. And I am fatigued. I have been once already to the house, but I do know that she will want more interest in her offspring than this. Do take a walk down there this afternoon and share my duty. It will not rain much longer. There's a brightening in the sky over Pudsey way.'

Mary sighed and put aside her book. 'Very well. I will visit with my aunt Mary. But the credit shall be mine aunt Sarah. I won't go as your ambassador.'

'Whatever,' muttered Sarah, laying her head down upon the couch.

Mary sent for her outdoor things but the weather did not relent and so it was a hard walk down the lane to Beech Grove. She had become rather moist upon her journey and was not grateful to her aunt for the mission.

'Good day, I am come to see Mrs. Beverley, Miss Bateson,' she announced to the maid who opened the door. 'Yes miss,' said the maid who knew perfectly well who had come. 'Step inside miss, do. It's a bad day I know.'

'Well it is wet certainly. Where is your mistress?'

'I'll take you up miss. Give me your things and I will see if we can get them dry. This way.'

Mary visited with her aunt Mary Beverley for some half hour, admiring the baby as she had been urged and noting that her aunt was pale and weak. Footsteps were heard upon the stairs.

'Oh Miss Bateson! How good of you to call!'

'Oh, hello Samuel. How did you know I was here?'

'I am at the workshops today. So when I heard you had come to see my new sister, I came straight across to, to, welcome you.'

'That's kind in you Sam. I love your sister. She is so sweet.'

'Yes, yes.'

'But I am just about to leave.' Mary Beverley, in more perceptive condition than usual, intervened. 'Oh, oh dear. I have not given you any refreshment. Samuel darling, go down and send up some tea for Miss Bateson.'

Samuel went to summon tea. Mary Beverley thought hard and decided to retire.

'I am so tired Mary. Please excuse me if I leave you. Samuel will see to you, I'm sure.'

Samuel returned with the promise of tea assured and with bright eyed enthusiasm, tripped in the doorway.

'Are you alright Samuel?'

'Yes. Yes, I'm sorry. I don't own these feet!'

'Don't worry Samuel. Feet are difficult to manage sometimes and yours are a particular burden. Your sister is adorable and I am glad I have had the chance to meet her so young and so pretty.'

'Miss Bateson?' began Samuel, his earnest face more serious that ever.

'Yes Samuel?' But Samuel Beverley had mastered his feet for the moment and come near to Mary with an imploring expression that alarmed her. She folded her arms.

'Miss Bateson. Mary, may I call you Mary?'

'Yes Samuel, you may call me Mary because in fact, you usually do.'

'Might I be so bold , might I - .'

'No Samuel. Don't'

'But - .'

'But nothing Samuel,' interrupted Mary. ' I have come to call and see your baby sister. And to wish your mother well. There is nothing else that needs to be considered today. You had better accept that this is so.'

'But -' began Samuel lamely, 'tea is being brought,' he finished in acute distress.

'Tea I like,' said Mary sternly but not without compassion. 'And nothing else.'

'Oh Mary!' sighed Samuel.

'Samuel, here's the tray. How much sugar will you take? Oh do sit down.' Sam obeyed her with a serious and sad face. 'Listen to me Sam, we're very young you know. And much as I like you, and I do, very much, but tis as a friend that I like you and nothing else.' Sam hung his head. 'But don't stay away because I have been spoken so frankly. Come up to Greenside on Sunday – I hope to be there on Sunday nights quite regular for the choir and to be sociable. And, and just, be yourself, you know. As if we were still children together? We'll get the other young people together of an evening and have keep company. Winter will soon be here and the evenings will be dark, but we can make our own amusements and entertainments. It will be good for you. Yes?'

Samuel nodded glumly. Then looking up again he smiled wanly. 'I've little time for amusements Mary. The finishing shop takes all my hours and my father has me before him if anything is amiss.' He hesitated then and fell silent for some minutes. Mary sipped her tea. 'I had to let a man go this week and it hangs heavy on me. He puts all the responsibility upon me and I sometimes don't think I can manage it all, the men, and the cloth and then I think of Scott and his family with no wage coming in and it was partly my fault that the cloth was scorched. And my mother is so busy and I try to help her, but with all the little ones in the family...'

'I know Sam.'

'I sometimes think my father thinks we worthless. I think I have let him down and he's right too. It's because I'm worried and everything has to be perfect. I'm so clumsy too. And the men don't like me and don't listen to me and now Scott's out through my fault, and they mutter. I can hear them. Or they laugh. Sometimes I just feel sick, here, my my belly.'

Mary sipped again and thought for a while, how it must be for such a young man whose father was known to be demanding and short tempered. And her aunt, Sam's step mother, thought of nothing but the problems of her younger children. She saw how lonely Sam was and that he had been thrown into the family business without the benefit of kind guidance such as her father and uncles might give to Phillip – also to Dan she supposed, and that his was a difficult position. He was too young to be given so much to carry.

'Sam – I'm going to mention to my father, and Uncle James, something of this. What you need is a good man to work alongside of you.'

'Oh no! My father would even less of me if he were to hear anything from the Batesons that I'm not up to taking my place in the business. I could not bear it. It would be the death of me.'

'It won't come like that Sam. Father will think of a way and he, well, he knows how to manage Mr. Beverley. We know what your father is like Sam, when he gets something fixed in his mind. Now Dan, Dan Grady has told me that he has a man from Batley that' been taken on down in Wortley. Some story of difficulties but this man is a very capable over looker.'

'The one that fell out with his employer. Over the machines?'

'Yes exactly. But he was in the right Sam. Dan explained it to me. It was not that the owner brought in machinery as such . It was that he did not talk to his workers about it and he took on strangers and laid off men and women who had been loyal to him and looked to him for their livelihoods. Their wages were all cut to pay for his investment in that which has acted to threaten the bread upon their tables. And I think that such a man as can speak his mind and hold to his own principles, such a man could understand what complaints come from the working people in Leeds. And you just need a bit of help at this moment in time. A friend to stand beside you. It seems one of those fortunate co incidences that can happen in this world.'

'Oh Miss Bateson. I'm sorry to burden you with my woes. I feel a fool and you'll not think well of me at all, nor yours, that I'm failing before I've begun.' Sam took out a hander kerchief and blew his nose.

'No talk of failing. People are different. You've just got yourself into a difficult place now but things can get better.'

'Would you ask your father? Ask him if I could have Dan Grady back. Just for a period, maybe a few months?'

'I'll see what they say. Yes Dan would be perfect but I think he's a role in the mill that it would be hard to fill. But the other now, he's looking for a position and would be new to your workforce. Wait and see, Sam.'

Mary went straight away to Wortley, trudging along the now muddy roads to seek counsel from her father and finding him with her Uncle James in the millwright's workshop down by the Beck.

'Who is this bedraggled bundle come to see us? Why dear child, thou art soaked! Come in now and take off that wet cloak. What is it that is so urgent that thou must drown for it.' Mary threw the wet wool on a hook and kissed her father on the cheek.

'Oh father. Help is needed. I have been to see the baby at Aunt Mary's and had an encounter with Samuel. It's a hard problem. Samuel is very low and I am worried about him. He talks as if everything is wrong! What can we do?

James sat on the table swinging his legs and looking out of the window apparently without hearing her. He took out his watch from his waistcoat pocket and began to play with it. 'Stop that James,' said Matthew Bateson, ' and tell us what you're thinking.'

'Our Dan says there's two or three of them up at Beverley's in town that are going to meetings and handing out leaflets. Bryan, Collier and Dunn. He told me that, oh, about 6 weeks since. Nancy said I shouldn't mention it to Beverley, that's all.'

'Did you not think to mention it to me?'

'No. I just thought about it a lot. It's not good for Samuel is it?'

'Well no. And here is Mary with the other side of the same problem perhaps.'

'But we know it you see. I didn't think about young Samuel.'

'Oh I see. You know it right enough but not "we". You could have told me though James?'

'I didn't think. I thought you would know.'

'I'm not a mind reader James.'

'Nor me. Samuel Beverley needs help and that we should not mention that to Benjamin?'

'That's just what Mary will be saying we should not do. It's what Nancy said to you.'

'Oh.'

'But we can't have them here. Trouble makers. Not with the new frame going in.'

Matthew sat silent for a while. Indeed, they could not employ finishers who might object to the Bateson's new cropping frame. He chewed his lip and then came to a decision.

'Leave it with me dear child. I think we can have a word with Mr. Gott and come to some arrangements across different workshops. He can have an urgent need to request help from Beverley and Benjamin likes to be in with Gott. And if we prime Samuel about it, then he can suggest names that are idle and would be agreeable to help out. We will move this problem to Mr. Gott who has many strong managers and is determined to have his own way. Then Samuel will find things a lot easier'

'Dan says there is man just taken on here, with management experience that could do a lot more than he has been given?'

'Oh yes. I forgot. We can offer him to Samuel directly. I will go into across tomorrow and put things in motion. 'Good thinking Mary!' Mary kissed her father on his head. She shook her own. 'No, it was Dan that put the idea into mine.'

'So now you know all about our secrets girl. Don't talk to Lupton about it. He's inclined to gossip.'

'No of course not. But thank you both. Poor Sam, he does need a steady man to stand beside him. He has such a nervous disposition.'

'Are you going to marry him?' asked James Bateson with renewed interest in the conversation.

'No Uncle James. I'm not. But he's my childhood friend and he is dear because of that.'

'He has such a lot of spots,' remarked James, mainly to himself, 'but he's going to be a wealthy man. It's a pity really. Just think how great would be a Bateson and Beverley House! But never mind. I was telling your father about this new formula I have for red dye -.'

'Ah,' said Matthew bleakly. 'Aye. Leave quickly Mary. Get on with it then James.'

Chapter Seventeen

Mrs. Elizabeth Lister at home

The maid lit the candles on the round table as the ladies sat beside the glowing coals in the hearth in wing armchairs. There were tea things laid out, with toasted muffins and plum preserve and Nancy was enjoying this little afternoon of idleness with Elizabeth Lister in Leeds. She had been around the shops making some small purchases with Elizabeth, but now they were comfortable and warm and had much to talk about.

'So little Sarah takes her first steps! Goodness, time passes so quickly. It hardly seems a moment since you brought your Thomas here in your arms, and yet here you are today, the mother of four bonnie bairns!'

'Yes. And if James does not stop mithering about we need another son, then he might have to sleep above the stables with the apprentice lads.'

'Do. Do put him outside. Tell him I said so.'

'But he'll shimmy up the drainpipe and climb in through the window.' Elizabeth laughed. 'Yes he would too. I hope he is still not on that dare with the young weaver.'

'Which dare and which weaver?'

'Up the factory chimneys Nancy. Don't you know about that!'

'What! Not again. Well that's an end of that then. I've already had to step in once on such activities. Wait till I get home! That chimney of ours is irresistible apparently!'

'Er. Um. No. I think they do all the new ones? So Will told me?'

'What! Dear Lord! Well thank you Elizabeth. Why did you not tell me before this?'

'Ah, I thought you knew about it. Will did not say it was a secret, so I thought you must know. I fear I have informed on him. Don't be too harsh with him. Give him a blanket to take to the his new quarters with him.'

'And you mean Dan Grady then?'

'I don't know the name of the miscreant. Will said it was the orphan lad? So Dan Grady is it?. Yes of course I should have realised'

'Yes it's Dan. But you know him because he guards our Mary when she is walking about and must be outside your house twice a week at least. And I will be having a word with him too. But he's young and strong and quite an athlete. While James is not and he's getting too old for such antics. And the father of four, even if the most of them are mere girls.'

I had forgotten that he was an orphan. Oh yes, he is the boy that Molly nursed? Now I see. Dear me, I had not realised. Yes, he's grown to be a fine strong man. I miss our Mary sorely. I had not realised how much she did to entertain and occupy my children. While my Samuel is at school, they can be quite a handful. Sarah is very lucky to have Mary for a while. They are good evenings in this house when she needs to stay over.'

'Yes our Mary - and it would seem she has an independent mind after all. Which I am happy about. For too long she was so obedient and submissive. To tell the truth, Sarah has more need than you do Elizabeth. She spends a full half of her time, berating John for one thing and another. I understand that Mary found that quite hard at first.'

'Well she will become used to it I suppose. And John has let her come down and take part in the activities of the mill? How do you like that? A young lady with her background and she is working just like the ordinary folk?'

'I think her background, as you call it, and it is yours too, don't you forget, demands that she knows something of what happens in the business and more so the mills, because we all know that this will be the way that things go. In our day it was the weaving sheds. But times change. It's no use pretending that the womenfolk can spin and keep an eye on the household while they do it. Not any more. If she marries in the trade it will stand her in good stead, as it does me. And if not, then she will have an understanding of the world that many young ladies lack.'

'I did not think she would make such a clear decision in favour of the cloth trade though. I was surprised when she told me.'

'It's not so much the cloth trade though, is it Elizabeth? She wants to know more about the lives of the people that work in the mills and the workshops.'

'I don't understand. She has lived side by side with all the workers in the Bateson business and must of course, be so very much more intimate than others of her class of what this entails. I'm sure she can make a piece too. Just as you and I can.'

'Yes she can. And yes she has lived with the wool about her ears all her life until she came to you in Leeds. But that's it for Mary. She thinks she has not understood from Wortley, how it is for all those common folk that she's been talking to at the night schools. The mill workers. There's a deal of difference between watching the journeymen in the weaving shed and knowing what the labourers suffer in theses mills. Reverend Wood spent quite a whole hour with her just lately, and he says she is to be commended for her interest in such matters.'

'This is quite radical talk Nancy!'

'Not at all. James Wood is hardly a luddite. But the economics of the trade cannot always be detached from the rights of men and the responsibilities of employers. As a mill owner's daughter, she is very right to find out how money is made and where her bread comes from.'

'I had not thought of like that. Of course things were simpler when we were children. Yes I see. Well good for her then. And if Wood approves then it must be the right thing. And then what about that very good looking young man that walks her back and forth into Leeds for her service at the night school? That climbs up chimneys with James! I see him twice a week and yet he will not come even into the hallway but stays in the kitchen, making my cook laugh.'

'That's Dan Grady. We have had this conversation.'

'Yes and what about him?'

'What about him? He's a very intelligent and good natured worker and as far as it goes, he is James' right hand man. Apart from this chimney story, I find he often helps to keep James from trouble.'

'How do you mean?' Nancy rolled her eyes.

'Dan's very useful. I fully intend that he will be our manager in years to come, if he stays with us, and does not get a better offer. James is not always good at managing other people and is best occupied with the machinery and the mill and the dying. But Dan can organise and motivate people. He'll do well.'

'You think very highly of him?'

'He's been a god send. Until I hear he's been encouraging James to climb chimneys!'

'But should he be walking about with our niece? How might that end my dear?'

'There's no need for anxieties there. Mary is quite young in her interests. She'll not be courting for many a day. And even if, even if it were to be that she forms an attachment beneath her, I can't see that is would be an insurmountable difficulty. Not with Dan's prospects - as long as he keeps his feet on the ground that is. He's a lovely boy.'

'I hope you're right. But I had hoped for so much for Mary. She is so pretty and sweet and could have found many admirers if she had just stayed with me and been seen about the town.'

'Well, she's seen about the town now, as you just said!'

'That's not what I mean. And in the company of a weaver!'

'Butcher, baker, candlestick maker. Gentry with gambling debts and young cavalry officers with nothing to do but look out for a simple lass with a fortune. She's a brain in her head so let her use it for herself.'

'You romantic you!'

'Thank you.'

'That Phillip Abbey is something of a favourite here. I wish we could see more of him. He's very much the gentleman and the obvious choice.'

'Yes, Phillip has much to recommend him in his manner. And we hear that his brother is making quite a lot of money in London. Which is fortunate. It is one of our greater contracts now Elizabeth. Very good and very timely.'

'Why?'

'Because Matthew and James have been able to keep all the finishers they can get hold of, even though we've got the cropping frame up and running. That's the increased production that Wells and Abbey have had the benefit of.'

'He's a gentleman, good looking and well connected then. I think that says it all.'

'We'll just have to wait and see. We should not interfere.'

'Oh yes we should!'

'And then there's always Samuel Beverley.'

'Oh the poor lamb. He's such worried face on him. The world on his shoulders.'

'Yes, but things should get better there I think. There's been a few complications with his workforce but it's been resolved. Benjamin Beverley doesn't always know what's going on but he should be grateful.'

'Oh he won't be.'

'Yes exactly. Will must not know and you must forget about it. The least said about that little matter, the better'

Chapter Eighteen

If they like it, then we can agree the terms

In the back parlour at Greenside there were other discussions going on around marriages and money. Mrs Bateson of Farnley had decided that she would propose an arrangement to his cousin on behalf of her daughter Isabella. It would be to her benefit, but also maintain the bonds of family obligation firmly to her successful cousins in Wortley. The Maister John Bateson was studying the wainscot and considering the matter fully.

'So two hundred guineas you say? It's not a king's ransom.

'I said two hundred pounds John. That's on the table for now and the dower to be a part of the lands around me that Thomas left. It's not to be sniffed at I assure you. And your Joseph has had his ups and downs….. and that's why there's not a queue at his door I wouldn't wonder.' John Bateson allowed a brief frown at this remark.

'He and Jack are now most secure as you well know. And were they not, then cousin, you would not be here suggesting such an alliance. What does Miss Isabella think?'

'She'll think as she's supposed to think John Bateson. My daughter has been raised to respect her elders and betters.'

John Bateson sniffed and then stilled his face so that his cousin would not see the offence this remark had caused him.

'Well I tell you what then Hannah, I'll put it to my boy and you put it to your girl. And then it's up to them. If they like it, they so will I. And we can talk about the financial side of it at a later time. It might be that more comes to us with her hand.'

'No. You heard my offer. It it does not suit the young man then I won't speak to my daughter.'

'I'll send him to her anyway. She might want to change your mind. If it suits them.'

As Mrs. Bateson walked back up the causeway to Farnley she thought as her husband Thomas had said often before his death, that for a Christian in the Fellowship John Bateson could be a crafty old bugger. Still and all, she would speak to her daughter and she at that time had little doubt but that she would be at least interested. Joseph was a nice looking young man. And the business difficulties were resolved. There were ten looms that she knew of and who knows more at hire in the busy village. She could not do better. Still, she'd not bargain up her price, the idea of it!

Isabella made no reply when her mother brought her into the parlour at the back of the farmhouse. Her eyes were cast down and she played with the fringes of her grey shawl.

'Well, lass, it's pretty much agreed. Not that the old man of Wortley was giving much away to me. But I suspect the offer was good enough. What do you think of it then, speak up girl!'

Still her daughter did not answer and her mother lost patience at this. 'Go and talk to your sister then if you won't talk to me. But make your mind up. Otherwise or no. And then tell me if I am to write to the chap and invite him for tea.' At this Miss Isabella nodded slightly and when her mother had gone sought out her sister in the kitchen and they discussed this interesting news with much animation. And a note was written and sent the very next day.

'What's that then Joe? Love letter, ah?' asked Jack with unusual volubility.

'It is not! But I am invited to take tea up at Uncle Tom's house in Farnley. Just me though. No mention of you there.'

'When?'

'Saturday afternoon.'

'Good cloth worker's time that. Down the Cloth Hall in the morning - you sort it after.'

'Should I go up to father and see what's being said, do you think?'

'Aye. No.'

'They have a good bit of land up there and still the mill and all? She has a portion too I heard. Maybe I should find out before I take tea with the family?'

'Oh aye.'

Joseph was very careful to make himself presentable for his engagement. He went to far as to have his trousers and coat pressed and brushed and had their manservant starch his linens. He felt confident as he left the house that he and John shared, and set out across the bridge and along the path towards Farnley. He had not gone too far though, when he began to wonder if the young lady would like what she saw. He remembered that he had been loved once and that gave him hope and his step quickened, but then his mind brought further doubts. His step faltered and he stood by a hole in the path and wondered how Grace would think if he should give his heart to a new love. And then he felt sad and found it necessary to brush away a tear. He steeled himself to continue but now he stepped slowly as the land inclined up towards the neighbouring village. Then there was Hannah to consider. Little Hannah that had been taken in by his father and step mother. Would she like to have a nice young mother? Was Isabella Bateson even nice. How long was it since they had seen each other. He had some vague memory of a little girl with freckles who had poked out her tongue when they had played among the woods at Farnley. He stopped again. But children grow. Perhaps she would be pretty and he would have no hesitation. And perhaps it would be nice to have his own house again, away from his brother's boorish conversation and interest in races and shooting. And Hannah would come home and it would be as it was. But the he stopped suddenly as a low branch hung down before him from the elder that grew alongside the grey stone wall suddenly barred his way. But Hannah was so little and well, often had sticky hands and would cry loudly for no apparent reason. Perhaps a man was better with his children in another house? Maybe there were comforts that he had that his brothers James and Matthew lacked? To go to the inn for a mug of ale at the end of the working day and to be able to do as he pleased when not actually at work. He cursed his father for interfering and his Aunt Bateson too. But now even though he had lingered, he found that he was near the village of Farnley and must go on with his assignation. They would expect him and the table would be laid ready. What if he never arrived but turned tail and got safe away home? His name would be whispered around the village and people would laugh at him behind his back. All this and more of a similar kind troubled him as he sidled up the garden path to the old low stone farmhouse where his destiny awaited him. Before he could raise his sluggish hand to knock upon the door, it was flung open and there was his aunt beaming and reaching for his arm and he felt himself being dragged inside the low and dark house. He had not courted Grace, she had made all the moves that were needed. Joseph in abject panic realised that he had no idea at all, how to woe a young lady.

'What's kept you Mr. Bateson? We've had the tea made ever so long and it's got cold in the pot. Come into the parlour please and meet Isabella. To keep a young lady waiting like this. I never heard the like before!' Joseph found himself thrust inside a low dark room where a little grey figure sat with her back against the small light from the window and her face in shadow. Joseph's heart had been variously challenged on the journey here, but now it sank and he gulped. But the excited old mother had quite abandoned him with this speechless form that now rose from her stool and came nearer to him. He managed to take off his hat and looked behind him for any assistance but his aunt had gone and was clattering in the back kitchen. He peered through the gloom and could make out a white cap and dark gown but little more. They remained there some seconds before each other and he could think of nothing to say that would break the silence. The rattle of the tea things could be heard distantly and the room felt very cold to Joseph and yet he found this his hands had begun to tremble.

'Miss -' he began haltingly with a voice that sounded strangely high to his own ears.

'Miss?' interrupted Isabella standing carefully and stepping nearer but with downcast eyes.

'Miss Bateson. I, I'm pleased to see you. I hope I find you well?'

'Well enough cousin. Thank you. And yourself?'

'I'm – I'm well. Thank you.'

'Will you sit?' Joseph sat in the tall carved chair that had been indicated, knowing he sat in his dead uncle's place. Isabella went back to her stool, and bringing it nearer to the cold hearth, she sat herself down with a bump that made Joseph startle. And she waited. Joseph put his hat on the floor and began to wring his hands. He pulled his shirt sleeves down and crossed and uncrossed his legs. At last he thought of something to say.

'It's been mild today, I think.'

'So so,' replied Isabella.

'I hope I find you well?'

We've done that. What else do you have to say for yourself?' She raised her face and he saw to his astonishment, two lively laughing eyes and half smile on cherry lips that were full and rather pretty.

'Don't you want to be here Joseph? Don't you Miss Bateson me neither. It's Isabella to you as has always been. We've know each other since we were little'uns, and I remember you, if you don't remember me. You were always the one with a runny nose. That's what I remember most.'

'You've been away a long time,' said Joseph in his defence. 'And I came of my own choice to get to know you again. To renew our acquaintance.'

'No you came here because my mother a was talking to your father. But that's better,' she said with her head to one side, 'so we'll start again. What's a-going on in your head that makes you so timid? Have you heard aught ill of me and mine?'

'No of course not. It is just, well, I think I have been so hard at work, that I have forgotten my manners and how to talk to young ladies. You see when I was widowed, I had a hard time of it. Took it very hard.'

'Is that it? Well I like that you're hard working. That stands well for you I think. As for your loss, that was a tragic thing to happen to her and so young as she was. Grace, wasn't it?'

'Yes, my Grace.'

'You loved her, didn't you. That's what I've heard and it is a shame that you lost her. But you have a little girl, mother says?'

'Yes, my daughter is called Hannah. She's a darling baby and so beautiful and clever. Do you like children?'

'I do Joseph. I've been nurse with the Farrer's for five years and there were three little ones come in that time. Bish, bash and bosh.' Joseph's mouth fell open. 'And to tell the truth, Mrs. Farrer don't want to lose me and if this don't suit, well, I'll be back there straight away where I'm treasured. Cos little ones don't like to be put here and there and have a lot of people come and go like that. If you think it will suit - then fair enough, but don't think for one moment that I'm going to be put out by you, whichever way it falls in.' She said all this with great firmness, even authority and Joseph was a himself not a little put out by her blunt speech. But Isabella sat upright composed and calm and although she was slight and slender, she was rather commanding and she waited to see what he could manage to say.

'I don't know if it suits.' he said. 'How could I know that? I would, I mean, we, we should see each other and get to know each other. Suiting people is a difficult thing and not to be rushed.'

'Amen. Sense at last. You sit there, and I'll go get me ma and the tea things. Try and make a good impression, there's a good man.' She slapped his shoulder as she walked passed him and Joseph turned to watch her leave the room. She turned back. 'Would you like fruit cake, or scones?' Joseph found it hard to come to a decision. 'Or both?' she added helpfully and went on her way with a decided grin on her young face.

Some few days after, Joseph took the major step that was needed and he invited Isabella to tea with himself and Jack. He had already warned her that Jack was not a great conversationalist. But Jack was on his best behaviour, hardly mentioned shooting ducks or how fast he could run, and was immediately very taken with Isabella Bateson and her forthright character. He insisted on taking her round the workshops and even provided a tour of the Bateson mill. There was a lot of sly nudging and chatter among the work people that Joseph saw and resented as he trailed behind them. He hurried his pace and came upon Isabella and Jack as they the inspected the fulling stocks by the Beck.

'Come back to the house now,' said Joseph taking Isabella by the arm quite forcefully. 'The tea will be ready and I know Miss Bateson does not like tea to be wasted.' Holding Isabella firmly by the hand he led the way back up the little path to the Leptons and Jack followed behind very respectfully.

Over the tea, Jack asked her considerately, if she minded the smell at all, and would she be able to live in the village?

'I'm of the trade, Jack Bateson. I'm used to the smells of the wool workings you know. And I know all about it.' Joseph shook his head at Jack but Jack was in the mood for conversation.

'It's not bad today. But tomorrow there's a load of new fleece to come in and be washed.'

'Sh, Jack,' said Joseph alarmed. 'Don't harp on about work all the time. Isabella said she's used to it and she don't mind it.' Isabella put her hand on his arm and smiled kindly at him. 'But I understand more than that Joe.' Turning to Jack she said,

'You see it takes one barrow load of pig's dung, to eighty gallons of stale urine, let stand for a week, when the dung is to be squeezed out by hand. So it's going to stink tomorrow. I'm pretty sure of that.'

Jack gazed at Isabella in profound admiration. And so did Joseph. The marriage was arranged for the Twenty first day of December and John Bateson secured just two hundred pounds for the arrangement which never the less represented a considerable investment in a still growing concern.

Chapter Nineteen

Urgent Request for assistance

'What this I hear? Petitions from the great man himself?' Matthew joined James and Nancy who had come up to Greenside at the urgent request of the Maister, John Bateson. It was January and there was a strong gale blowing from the west, bending the twisted thorn trees and breaking the branches from the feeble elder bushes. Matthew sat down at the head of the table and looked about him. His father was sat to the left of him, with a letter in his hand and a slight smile upon his face.

'Just hear this.' John Bateson read aloud…

*"My dear friends and fellow manufacturers,
I regret to inform the manufacturers of the district that serious disruptions have been made to trade in my premises. The matter will be dealt with as swiftly as might be possible. However, as many of you work in close partnership with my operations, it might be that it is in everyone's best interests if we can work together to mitigate some of the disastrous consequences of the militant agitators…."*

John Bateson smiled around at his family.

'Militant agitators? Does he say that! He's talking about his own journeymen you know and breaking the rules of the Cloth Hall!' said James vehemently.

'Yes James. We all know that. Please keep your obvious conclusions to yourself. Now listen to the rest of the letter.'

*"I am therefore requesting assistance with the dressing of my cloth from the many co partners that work so closely with my House. I trust I may have your assistance immediately and look forward to your replies within the next two working days.
Your etc.
Benjamin Gott."*

'Well well well.' said Matthew, rubbing his chin thoughtfully. 'What are our thoughts on this matter then.'

Nancy grimaced.'It's strike breaking Matthew. You know that as well as I. And we should not do it, only, you know.'

'I think I understand you, dear Nancy. You think we are compromised because there is a cropping frame in our mill?'

'Just so Matthew. If we send men to Gott's to break his strike and they talk to Gott's "agitators" then it might spread and we'll be in the same position for mechanising.'

Matthew said, 'No, I don't think so. We do not have disaffected labour. Cropping frame or no, there's full employment and full wages at the moment. And we don't break the rules on apprenticeships. I think we can let a few of our finishers get over to the Park Mill. Maybe Dan and a couple of other picked men. That way Gott is indebted to us and if others do the like, than he can get some of his cloth to his customers.'

'But not all his cloth?'

'There has to be some penalty for his obdurate insistence in annoying his workers. He makes his work force unhappy. What kind of mill owner does that?'

'But I understand he had to do all this because of modern invention. I was at a dinner last month, when I definitely heard him say as much,' said James.'Standing suddenly he declaimed, 'We must look to our futures friends!' James made a good imitation of Benjamin Gott's speech.

'So what did you think then. Apart from his good style? What is your reasoning on the matter?'

'I'm still thinking,' said James deflated.

Matthew said softly: 'He puts profit before his people's welfare. He's taken on labour that puts the livelihood of the trained cloth workers at risk.'

'Yes that is what I was thinking. Once the making of cloth is fully mechanised, there'll be no guilds and no apprenticeships. Gott is leading the way forward on it and testing the waters. He's been bitten this time, but next time, he'll take on youth from around the place that have no training. And pay them as he pleases. Because there won't be the same skills needed for the work that they do.'

'Right. So James, you have a word with Dan Grady and send him off to Leeds tomorrow first light to report at Park Mills. I'll write to Mr. Gott and tell how we are coming to his rescue. We'll tell our workers that we have to sort out the affairs of the great merchant and manufacturer and we'll send down a couple of barrels of ale to toast Mr. Gott's good health. That should do it.'

'And you will have your own spy with his ear to the ground at Park Mills? Is that it? John Bateson studied Matthew coolly.

'Yes father. But I would not dishonour our Dan with such a label as spy. I would call him a peace maker for that is his talent. But if we do find out more about what goes on in the town right now. I can see the advantages of that.'

James was still thinking. 'Is it our fault then?'

'What could be our fault?'

'For letting him have the discontented men from Beverley's workshops?' John Bateson frowned at James. 'What are you talking about now? What is this about?' and he looked from one to other of the group. Matthew reassured them, 'No. Mr. Gott knew the men that went to him were trouble makers. I know they are still there. But this is the Guild workers that are unhappy. It's nothing to do with us.'

John Bateson said coldly, 'Well thank you for keeping me informed of your arrangements then.'

'It was mill business sir. Nothing for you to be concerned about,' James said, intending to be helpful.

His father merely looked at him.

Chapter Twenty

a washer woman

It was a cold and blustery March morning. Mary struggled with an end of the wet linen as the maid from the village reached to haul her share of the sheet onto the rope line that was stretched from the hawthorn tree to the house. Draped in a wet white apron and with her hair escaping from her cap to be whipped by the wind, Mary could have been taken for any servant girl in the village. If she had not had two wooden clothes pets in her mouth, she would have laughed out loud as the wind tore at the heavy sheet and the two girls battled to secure it. At least there would be good drying - if they could ever get it onto the line and secured. The clothiers in the village knew this too, and all the tenter frames along the valley had their cloth stretched taut on the metal hooks, in the public and private tenter grounds all across the fields.

And so it was that Phillip did not recognise Mary as he rode into the garth at Greenside.

'Where's Peter', he yelled at the two girls against the force of the wind. He brought his horse to a halt and slid from the saddle looking around him for assistance. Mary could not answer because of the pegs in her mouth and this the maid quickly realised. Jeannie yelled,'he's away up the field sir. Thou mun hold thine own nag for now, sir.' Phillip scowled. Mary seeing this did not suit the apprentice, managed to heave her share of the heavy cloth onto the line and between them, she and the maid put out the pegs to hold it, battered by the flapping cloth as they did this. She went to restless Phillip and took the horse from him. 'Hello,' she said with an appeasing smile. 'Leave this horse with me and go on into the house. I'll see to it until Peter comes down.'

'Oh! Mary! I did not know you. What are you doing here, and outside washing the clothes?' He looked confused.

'I've been back home for a few weeks now. My step mother is very ill and there is so much to be done here. Grandfather is within and Molly will see to you. I'll come in when we're done with the laundry. Do you go inside and make yourself comfortable.' Phillip left Mary to see to his horse, but took down his bag, and holding his hat with one hand, he sauntered away. Mary turned back to her task and she called to the maid to bring the next basket from the kitchen while she herself led the hired mount into the stables and set about removing the saddle and settling the beast. She knew it to be a hired horse and that it must take precedence over the mere laundry. It occurred to her that Phillip must be under some time pressure to have undertaken such expense. She hardly thought that his masters would approve of such unnecessary convenience unless time was pressing. She stroked the mare's ears and neck and wondered if perhaps Phillip was unwell and that is why he had ridden instead of walking over from Leeds.

Phillip did in fact have some need to return to Wortley but not such that he should have arrived in such style. But Matthew and James did not notice this so much as they might have done since neither of them looked into the stables that day. If they had done so then questions might have been asked. Phillip had come to personally bring orders of some importance and to confirm that these could be met within a restricted time frame. He had in fact ridden most of the way and was able to justify this because it was mitigated by the loan of a mount from Hull to York from his increasing circle of affluent friends.

Phillip had taken great pride in that his journey from Hull was made with the independence of a rider, - as a merchant should. He has doffed his hat at those he met along the way and passed the regular coaching diligences with a smug countenance and a wave of his hand.

Mary had much to do and little time to talk to Phillip. Her sister Anne had been sent to assist in the kitchen and Mary was quick to take advantage of the opportunity to delegate chores to her younger sister. 'You're not the mistress of Greenside,' said Anne in protest. 'Not yet. Don't take advantage so.'

'Just make sure the peas don't burn.' said Mary, busying herself with the dishes. She turned away and Anne made faces behind her back, causing Molly to chortle. 'Don't you be laughing at me Molly. I've been hard at my lessons all day. I'm worn out. I shall complain to mother.'

'Do,' said Mary curtly and flustered by the situation.

'And just look at you hands dear Mary. Look at her hands Molly! They are so red. Those are not the hands of a lady!'

Molly turned on Anne. 'Just mind thyself there, Miss Anne, some on us get them hands with what we do and there's not shame in hard work. The Lord has a special place in Paradise for them's as does the 'ard work.'

'Well I hope I don't get them,' protested Anne. 'I'll just take the other rooms in Paradise if you don't mind. And when I leave school, I'm off to Aunt Elizabeth's and I'll not be coming home.'

'What a thing to say!' said Mary, quite shocked. 'And for that matter, when you've left school, you'll do what needs to be done. Such impudence.'

'Impudence can be very useful.'

Molly pushed Anne to one side to reach for a jug. 'Tha means tha won't care to help out here then, Miss Anne. Just tha be careful, or them shortbreads'll be hidden next time tha comes a sniffing round for sweet things.'

'You don't mean that Molly. I'm your favourite. Me and Dan.'

'Whose the favourite?' said a voice from the doorway. Phillip was stood leaning there and laughing.

'I am.' asserted Anne. 'Not you, not Mary. Me.'

'That's nice Anne. Where are the biscuits then?'

He came into the kitchen and sat himself down at the old scrubbed table. His meeting with John Bateson and Matthew was concluded and he could think of nothing better to do with himself than come down and see what the daughters of the house were about.

'You can't set there Phillip! Not with that suit on you. You'll get flour on it. Is that your riding outfit?' Phillip leant back and looked down at himself proudly. 'Yes. It does not do to dress badly. I find it makes quite a difference in the orders that the House is given. It's a good business strategy. Dress well and people believe in you.'

'Really?' said Anne, momentarily impressed. Then she looked again at Phillip as he sat resplendent in his good and fashionable coat at their simple kitchen table. He did indeed look very handsome. Mary glanced up from her work and met his eyes. She smiled. Molly plonked down a tankard of weak ale before him and a good slice of cheese as well. She sniffed and went back to the stirring of the soup. These youngsters with their airs and graces. Strutting around her kitchen looking like their betters. She'd be having a word with Mrs. Bateson then, soon as she was up and on the mend, about her apprentice getting so high and mighty. And eating all the cheese.

'But look at Mary's hands Phillip. Mary, show Phillip your hands.' Mary ignored this and continued to peel potatoes.

'Oh dear,' said Phillip. 'You do look like your belong in the kitchen Mary. Should you not take better care of yourself?'

Anne laughed and Mary frowned. She said nothing for a moment. 'I should, you are right Phillip. But then there is work to be done and we should all work together when it is needed.'

'Amen,' said Phillip, with his mouth full of cheese, and wondering if the prayers before supper would be longer because Mary would be in attendance.

Chapter Twenty One

Hostilities Renewed

In the happy month of May, when the hawthorn blossom brightens the hedgerows and all is fresh and green, the village had news brought by a messenger from Leeds whose haste and feeling of self importance was of equal measure. James Walker had come home as soon as he heard the news in the town. He came first to Greenside and alarmed all within by riding into the garth and bringing his horse to a sudden harsh stop.. Hearing the urgent hooves and cries, those at home came out at once to see who had come with such haste and with a flutter of the heart for such news as is brought with disturbance

'What is it? Ah Walker. What do you want now?' said John Bateson, leaning on his stick and standing in his doorway with a grim face. Walker came up boldly to the old clothier. But he took off his hat and John Bateson nodded slightly at this respect. 'It's War, Maister. We are at War again. It's certain. Let me come in and I'll tell you all I've heard.'

John Bateson sighed and looked up at the soft clouds in the blue sky. 'We'll not ring the Chapel Bell just yet,' he said half to himself. Then rousing himself he called Peter to him and sent him down to the mills and workshops to give a more gentle bulletin to the community. Only then would the bell be rung. And to be truthful, John Bateson half desired one other confirmation of such bad tidings. Walker was never one that he had put much trust in. But such was only a delaying tactic while the old man adjusted to the tidings. It had been expected. But the official proclamation of hostilities would spell a period of uncertainty for the wool trade and for the export trade in particular. He expected his sons would come home as soon as they heard and so Molly was sent to make ready a dinner for the clothiers' comfort and consolation. Even now he thought he could hear in the distance, the bells of Leeds ringing. Then he remembered James Walker who was stood scowling at him and waiting to be invited into Greenside. 'Come in then, you rogue. Never was ill tiding brought by such a proper person.'

'Now then sir. Don't shoot the messenger, as they say. I'll come in until the others arrive. Ale would be good.' As he came across the threshold into the cool flagstoned passage he remarked 'it's a pity Jack did not keep the warehouses on Water Lane. Sir. We'll be needing to store wool I think, at the very least.' John Bateson followed the mill owner inside with his face completely neutral. Walker was walking on dangerous ground.

In London the Admiralty was in turmoil. So many ships had been cast aside and had been de commissioned when the Treaty of Amiens had come into force. There was no appetite whatsoever in the Kingdom for the mighty drain on the economy which was the truth of the possesion of many warships. These had not been needed just at that point in time. Now in all urgency were those ships needed to be put to sea, to blockade the ports of France where it was known by the government that Napoleon had already commissioned a maritime force of previously unheard of size and potency. It was also known that the French were now planning an invasion of England which would destroy the last vestiges of resistance to the establishment of their Empire and their plan of the domination of Europe and the World. Now would the East India Company need armed escorts to continue their trade with the east and the colonies. Now would it be vital to keep the

French penned into their own ports along the Atlantic seaboard and within the Mediterranean.

For Abbey and Wells, that thriving agency of the cloth trade in Millbank Row, Lambeth, there was much to do. A sense of urgency pervaded their offices and the wharves that they frequented. As yet their project to lease the York Stone Wharf had not come to fruition but in other ways, the business and the profits were very successful. John Wells had developed his relationship with the wool staplers of London and the warehouses in Hull that the Batesons and their associates used were well stocked with fleece bought at a better discounted rate than could have been got in Leeds or Hull. It might be that in the current climate of panic and alarm, that this would need to be adjusted upwards - to ensure that they were rated as priority clients. But such was business. It was balancing the books that mattered.

It had become habit that occasionally Phillip would come down to London to check the figures of the company which gave also gave Abbey and Wells close communication and a realistic idea of how things stood in the north. It was a beneficial arrangement.

Phillip did not relish the days spent in the office of Abbey and Wells but he made good use of his evenings. He and Parr were a good match at the gaming tables and Parr knew the best houses in the capital where there could be found gentlemen of means who were drunk or reckless. And so Phillip maintained his now increasing income with his usual good fortune at the card games and with an improving knowledge of how money could be borrowed.

Henry Abbey and John Wells had substantial debts to various merchants banks, but no business could continue without good backers. What is investment if not a profitable loan? Profits kept them solvent and everything was very comfortable and promising. Which is as much as to say, that they owed a great deal of money.

In June, Henry and his man had come to Leeds via Hull travelling in the ordinary style by stage coach, because they had with them one of Henry's favourite dogs. The red and white springer bitch was in pup and answered to the name of Floss. She was a beautiful dog with glossy coat and intelligent brown eyes. Also, she was a proven gun dog of reputation, always quick and obedient. She had become of infinite value to Henry as he made his contacts with the men of the world who had money. He had brought the dog from a game keeper in Yorkshire and had already had the benefit of a fine litter - he was generous in presenting to potential backers and investors such a unique gift. Nothing pleases the country squire or the idle lord, so much as a good gun dog!

Henry had left Floss with his man and gone out about the town to make some social calls. Floss had been let wander about inside the Inn because she was faithful and did not stray. So it was with consternation that Henry returned and could not find Floss anywhere. He shook his man roughly, distressed for the loss of the pet and when Phillip came to him that evening he found his brother Henry calling to Floss along the banks of the river, by the warehouses and workshops., forlorn and weary

'Ho there! Henry! What's up man?' Henry replied heavily, 'It's Floss. She's gone....'

Phillip put his arm round his brother's shoulders.

'But I must go back tomorrow, up to London. What will I do if she can't be found?' I must find her tonight or leave her!'

'I'll put out a reward for her. Put in that she may be returned to me at Wortley. I will let them know there, that if the dog is brought to them, they must keep it for me until my next visit. Then I can get it back to you when you next come down to Hull.'

'Yes alright. But she will pup and will they see to her?'

'Oh yes, of course. They are such people as would tend to a cat that had kittens. Very soft hearted. Even the old man. He can cut up rough sometimes but he never does anything any harm. But give me the five guineas, would you? I'll get over to Greenside and leave it with one of them.'

'Can I trust you to do that even?'

'Yes of course. I love the dog nearly as much as you do and if you would take my advice to leave it here when it whelps – that is if it is found, - then Jack Bateson will get good money for the pups, as good as you'll get in London. Let us hope she has wandered and not been taken.' Henry's head bent and he nodded sadly.

Chapter Twenty Two

" Wanted. Middle-aged married man to superintend the poor in the Workhouse Wortley. If he has been accustomed to Parish Business, the more agreeable. He will have to keep the Town's Accounts A handsome salary will be given . William Walker or James Bateson the Overseers."

Summer sun beat down upon the common grazing of Armley and the pasture was yellow seared. Hay had been harvested dry and the thatched ricks were dotted about the fields and small farms.

The family gathered inside the Armley Chapel welcomed the shade and cool of the old stone building. James Bateson studied the tracery of the east window and read the dedications around the walls. His mind was elsewhere. That prophecy that haunted him had come back in his sleep last night. Each time his beloved wife quickened with child he prayed for another son. It had now got to the point where his sisters or those that attended on the birth, came to him to tell of the child with hesitancy. Yet another daughter. He knew it was nonsense. But still in his tired mind the thought dragged and meandered and sometimes real fears came upon him, that his life would be short if he had no son. And if anything then happened to Thomas? What would then become of his wife and his many daughters, without a father to protect them. Yet, what sort of thinking was this for a man of his status? A mill owner, an Overseer of the Parish. A man of science? So James Bateson studied the old monuments and made no sense of them or of himself.

Nancy held their new daughter in her arms, cradling her gently, protectively. Her daughters Hannah, Maria and Sarah gathered round her and went from their aunt and uncles to their grandfather, restless because of the heat of the day but not noisy. Nancy and James' son Thomas now seven years old was keeping very still though, conscious of his increased responsibilities as the elder brother of so many sisters. The baby was named Ann and James came back to his senses to realise that the little ceremony had been concluded and that the others were leaving. His saw his father watching him coldly and he withered inside.

Four daughters. He stood a moment watching his little family as they wandered back into the glare of the relentless sunlight. Shafts of light fell from the windows making alternate bars of light and dark along the stone flagged pavement. He shivered. Was this part of a curse that had been made upon him when he had been young and foolish. He paused a moment to repent his sins before God, before following the small crowd outside. He did his duty by Nancy but still the sons did not come. Only Thomas. Without realising it he studied the boy frowning. Thomas saw his father's look and stare and his face fell. He stood up straight in case he was found wanting in decorum and went to grab hold of his grandfather's hand, looking back over his shoulder at his father, whose face changed back to its common pleasant expression. Thomas smiled and James grinned back.

'Will I walk back with you to Greenside,' asked Samuel Beverley stumbling over to Mary's side. He knew that he could. But he knew it was civil to ask and this had been enough to bring out the frown to his face. He had come with his parents and the rest of the family from Beech Grove, in his case, relishing the opportunity to make some awkward excuses and again join the Batesons at home. He cast a glance over his shoulder at his father. Benjamin Beverley, suave and assured, who was talking to the parson and unusually for him in matters of church, had an agreeab expression on his dark face.

'Oh, yes, of course,' said Mary, taking his arm to reassure him that he was welcome. 'Will your mother not come down too?'

'I think she goes to call on Mrs. Lambert. But my father may come I think.' He said this wretchedly.

' I see. Never mind Sam. My grandfather will deal with him. Come on then, we can make up a small party, us young people. See, here is Anne and Robert Wood too.'

'Oh! Is he here again?'

Mary giggled then and Samuel scowled. Anne glanced behind her and caught Mary's eye. Robert Wood with excellent hearing. diplomatically caught up with John Bateson and enquired about a recent trip that the Maister had taken to Scarborough. Anne stood a moment to let Mary and Samuel catch up with her so that she could tease him. Mary shook her head slightly but Anne just smiled innocently. She wondered how long it would take her to make Samuel blush.

'We're so glad to have you here today, Samuel. You know I do like this coat you have on. But you must be warm I think. You look very warm. Are you warm?' Anne asked this with solicitation but her attention was enough to make Samuel blush to the roots of his hair and he became conscious of his sweating hands too. He tripped and nearly pulled Mary over and then began to apologise profusely for his clumsiness. James, coming up behind the group of young people and seeing Samuel stumble, released from the gloom of the chapel and feeling the joy of the warmth of the sun and his family all gathered round him, gave Samuel a thump on the back that sent him flying again and then began advising the unfortunate young man to make use of a walking stick if he could not stay upright without such assistance. Samuel managed to steady himself and looked at James' departing back blankly.

'Oh!' said Mary, 'oh dear, oh dear. Here Samuel, let me take your arm again. He's a lout sometimes, my Uncle James. But he meant no harm. He just doesn't think so much as he should.'

'You be careful,' advised Anne. 'If you take Mary's arm and you stumble, she'll tear her best frock.' She took hold of his free arm and squeezed it, suddenly feeling some pity for her victim and repenting of her cruelty. But then unable to resist temptation she said; 'We'll hold you up until we get to the bottom of the lane.' Samuel smiled in gratitude. 'And then there's a railing by our Chapel, and you can hold onto that.' Samuel could think of no reply to this. Mary said quickly, 'Don't mind Anne. But think what I must suffer with that she is such a tormentor. We have Reverend Wood here you know, well not today, but he has been and is now in Huddersfield. Robert is to stay a few more days but must go back home before the month is out.'

'Well that is nice for you Mary. And Miss Anne. For you all I mean. Do you, do you take him into Leeds at all? Or just walk about the village?' he trailed off.

'We have some fun with Robert. He's not dull for all his father is so renowned. Anne took him fishing in the Beck yesterday and they both came home, I hear, as wet and muddy as children. Not that I mean that Reverend Wood is dull at all. That is did not mean to imply such a thing.'

'Yes we were wet. There's nothing wrong with being a bit wet,' commented Anne to herself. Mary gave her a warning look. Anne continued; 'And when Mary comes down of an evening, when she's not out saving souls that is, we get up a musical party as you know and usually miss. Oh, and we had an evening up at the Heights with the Luptons all together.'

'That's nice,' said Samuel, gratefully. 'I wish I had time to be idle.'

'Idle?' warned Anne, narrowing her eyes.

'No, I didn't mean that, I mean that you enjoy yourselves. Time to be, well, I -"

'You should come down on Monday Samuel. I will be coming too that evening because it is my agreed day off. We have permission from Mr. Armitage to be go up to the woods and we are taking a picnic. Are you free on Monday evening Samuel?'

'Thank you Mary. But I'm not. I promised I would go to a Lecture at the Institute. But it was kind in you to ask.'
Having reached the railings Anne let go of Samuel's arm and ran ahead to catch up with Robert Wood.

'Don't take too much notice of my sister,' advised Mary with a smile. 'You must become used to it and take it as interest She likes you really, or she would not trouble herself with you.'

'Does she? I hope she does, but the way she taunts me! I'm sure it is worse than ever it was in the past. Does she like me?' struggled Samuel. Mary shot him an enquiring look. This was a new thought. She nodded and reasurred,'We all do Samuel. You're part of the family.' Samuel smiled at this and then wiped his brow with the back of his shirt cuffs. It really was a very hot day.

As they came into the garth at Greenside there were chairs and benches set out in what was optimistically known as the garden. The farm yard merged into sometime pasture, but there were roses blooming along the far wall and a view of the Beck valley below. The family had gratefully sat in what shade they could find. Nancy was holding court with her new baby, allowing the child to be admired by all comers. John Bateson's wife was behind a plank table serving out ale and cordials to the thirsty. By the barn, Dan Grady was leant upon the stone wall in just his shirt with his sleeves rolled up, chatting to Jack Bateson and James. He waved to Samuel who left Mary with an awkward nod and went across the yard to join Dan whose conversation was never pointed. Dan took one look at Samuel and excusing himself from his masters took the young man by the arm and led him into the out kitchen to beg ale from Molly.

'Take your coat off sir,' advised Dan firmly and getting hold of the collar. Samuel protested but Molly had already got behind him to assist and Samuel could not resist both ministrations. 'That's better. You must be cooked sir. It's not a day for wool, to be sure. They've all got their coats off. Do what they do and you won't go far wrong. Here, get this in you. By, and I am glad not to be traipsing about the place in this heat.'

'Tha's to listen to Dan sir. Ee's in the right of it. Tha's the only one come down the road with thy coat still on. What were tha thinking of?' Molly chided Samuel as she went about her domain and the servant girls looked over at Samuel and Dan and smiled. Dan pulled a stool to the old rough table for the exhausted clothier.

'Thank you. But you are in the wrong there. John Bateson did not take off his coat.' said Samuel, taking the mug of cool ale and surrendering himself onto the stool.

'But the Maister is old and don't get warm, lad. Hark to my Dan. Don't ee always give thee good advice, Mr. Samuel? He do, don't he? Lord be praised and he's the one to watch, my Dan.'

'He is, he does, I mean. I thought I would fall. Oh Dan.' Samuel sighed weakly and Dan pulled up another stool close to the boy and winked at him.

Meanwhile the daughters of Matthew Bateson had retired to their room briefly. Anne teased Mary. She declared that Samuel was so smitten that he could not keep on his feet. He's falling for you, said she, 'literally. You must pity him, poor little Sam. And if the family think upon it, that's where you'll be. Part and parcel of the great House of Beverley. With Benjamin as your father in law.' Mary grimaced. She tidied her hair in the little looking glass they kept by the wash stand.

'I don't think so Anne.' She turned about and looked at her sister. 'Let us be clear about this. We've known Samuel since we were children together and I do know he is fond of me. There was a time indeed, but that is passed I do believe. He understands me very well. So I don't think it's like that.'

'Like what? What sort of thing are you comparing it too. This former fondness?'

'You know minx, you know what I mean. Don't be so abstruse. But what if, what if he comes so often now, as he did when I was here at home and he had formed misapprehensions. What do you think that means?'

Anne threw herself backwards onto their bed and covered her face with her hands.

'Oh no no no. Oh dear me no! I look to a future bright with lovers, flowers and romance. If Samuel Beverley thinks of me, then all that is at an end.' She gestured dramatically about her. 'The world will be at an end.'

'Get up dear. We must help wait at table. The village will be passing through the house and we can't lay about idling.'

'Oh yes. Idling. There's me forgetting and become idle. Up I get then and down we go. Ale and cake and good luck to baby Ann. What a lovely name the baby has!' As they left their room young Robert Wood came down the passage and joined them.

'Tell Anne to be kind Robert. She does not heed me.'

'Kind to who? Be kind to me Anne.'

'I will be kind to you boy, if at all possible, because I know you can give as good as you get. But I do struggle with some others.'

Robert Wood grinned mischievously. 'You mean our poor Sam. Why did he not take off his coat? He nearly expired coming down the hill. Is he trying to impress someone with his acts of sacrifice?'

'He won't offend grandfather. I don't know why. Uncle James always takes his coat off if he can. But poor Sam! It's difficult to resist tormenting him.'

Mary turned and faced them on the stairs. 'Robert Wood, now you may be the minister's son and give this girl some much needed advice.'

'I would,' said Robert, 'but sometimes it's just too much of a responsibility.' At which Anne laughed triumphantly and pushed past protesting Mary. Mary shook her head as her sister skipped away to enjoy the busy, sunny day.

'Where's your Uncle James? Can you see him?' asked Robert Wood cautiously.

'I can't see him just now. He might be in the out kitchen with Molly. Or playing with the children in the field. Why? Are you wanting him?'

'No. But we had a very long conversation yesterday about the proper chemical mixtures of dyes; followed by a discourse on the economics of opening the poor house again.'

'Ah,' said Mary. I'll keep an eye out for you and if I see him back in the garden I'll signal.'

'Would you? So kind. I can see there are many here that will be most interesting to talk to. There's Mistress Gaunt. She's got three cats you know and I should like to know if they are keeping well.' Mary raised her eyebrows at this and went away into the kitchen to fetch her apron. There was much to do. Something sped across the hall and landed by her feet. It was a small paper projectile. The sound of pattering feet brought her cousin Thomas into view and he grabbed the paper and disappeared into the great parlour. Mary followed curious. Within the great parlour, her Uncle James was sat on the stone floor, with a group of children about him, talking quietly and folding paper. He held something above his head and sent it gliding through the air to the delight of the children, who leapt up and raced to be first to the toy.

'Uncle James, is that your father's paper you are making free with?' James was startled and looked over his shoulder. He grinned. 'It's alright my dear, my father won't mind. We'll make it right again after we're done and put it back. He will not know.'

'He'll be much put out Uncle James. If you have not asked.'

'Oh,' said James thoughtfully. 'Yes. He'll not be so happy I suppose. He might mind after all. But he will get used to the idea. By tomorrow.' This was a pragmatic view of the situation. Children gathered round James again begging for more creations and James returned to his play among the little ones. Mary shook her head. She mentioned it to Nancy when she saw her in passing, and Nancy thought that she should remember to bring James home before John Bateson became aware of the misuse of the expensive paper.

The community melted away once the ale barrels had dried and the family were left to themselves at Greenside for supper. The young people had gone into the great parlour and Anne had suggested that they should make music for her grandfather. She fetched him down his fiddle and made sure it was in tune for him. He sighed and frowned, but he was pleased to be included in the matter. Here were some of his favourite grand children and it made his old heart glad that they included him sometimes in their activities.

For Mary the household duties had been onerous. Her step grandmother was still not as strong as she had been and Molly was always glad of a pair of hands that were willing and capable. She had born the burden of labour this day. So in the out kitchen as the day waned, there could be heard the distant sounds of laughter and singing and Anne's very accomplished pianoforte skills could be heard throughout the old house. But Mary stayed at her duties and assisted with the domestic tasks. Dan was there too, still in his shirt, and he worked quietly alongside Molly, doing the heavier work as she directed him. But it was getting late, she must think about the walk up to Armley. Dan too, had been thinking of that.

'Shall I have a word with Mr. Samuel, Miss? He'll be walking up in that direction and I know he won't mind if he goes up to the top of the moor with you.'

'Perhaps. But maybe you could come with me. We're nearly done with the pots and Molly will spare you for half an hour.'

'You're leaving him here then? What for?' smiled Dan.]Molly listened intrigued.

'Yes perhaps I will leave him here as late as he likes. I think he will be enjoying himself and it's good for him to have young company and forget his woes. But he's been better in spirits of late I believe and this will do him good.'

Molly said, 'Off tha goes then children. I can manage now. If it had not been for thy help though, it would have been midnight by the time this kitchen was clear. Go on Dan, take Miss Mary home and then come by and I'll have a little bite of supper ready for when tha gets back.' She remarked to herself as she put the dishes upon the dresser. 'Just like her grandma, that one. Always thinking of others first and doing what's right. Them others, tsk, they think they can play all night.'

The moon was rising and the evening was still warm, but pleasant now, not stifling, and such nights were not many in Yorkshire. But Dan had put on his coat and was decently dressed to safeguard John Bateson's granddaughter over the mile up to Crossgates. There was a path up the steep bank that led to the old Manor House and although there were the bell mines and pits to avoid, it was a quicker way home than up the Wortley Lane.

They were as old friends now, he and Mary and they walked some way in companionable silence, enjoying the warmth and listening to the owl hoot from Tingle's barn. As the light of the Manor House came in sight, Mary stopped and looked back down the hill at the village below. Dotted down the hillside the cottages nestled together with the occasional light showing from windows or doorways. The workshops had their watchmen's lights that shone more brightly than the homesteads. Above them, the Manor House was in darkness save for one small lamp by the ancient porch.

'Look at it Dan. Take it in this one night. Who knows where our paths will lead us. You and me I mean.'

'Well I hope your path won't take you away from us all miss. I can't see as I'm going any place just now, neither.'

'No. And I don't have plans to wander. It is just I don't know what lies ahead. I would like to see a little bit more of the country though. Wouldn't you?'

'Aye. I've a yen to go to Halifax, one day.' Mary gave him a playful nudge. 'I'll tell you what my Aunt Sarah says about Halifax Dan. She says it is much as Wortley but when it rains here, it snows in Halifax. She's says the roads are terrible and the food worse. And as for the cloth they make there, well!'

Dan laughed. ' I had best stay put then.' But Mary pushed on, thinking out loud.

'Where do you see yourself Dan, in ten years from now?' He said nothing. They began to walk up the hill again now having recovered their breath. Dan walked behind Mary for the footpath was narrow here, skirting a small copse of gorse and young birch. He still did not answer. It was for Mary to wonder if her life would change, because of course, for her, there would be a marriage and that might take her away altogether. Dan shivered.

'What do you think Dan? What does Uncle James say to you now you are managing in the dye works? He always says, "That one will go far!"' she mimicked her uncle's manner. Dan had to laugh. 'Yes miss. Now let me see. I may go far as you say but still remain faithful. One day I may have my own house. I would like that. But that's not a worry to me. That's for the Lord to decide.'

'You'll stay in Wortley forever then, if you can?'

'Just at this moment, I'm following right behind you and we will both be in Armley before the night is done.'

Mary laughed and waited for him to come beside her as the path widened behind the brick factory. But still he kept a respectful distance from her and kept his own counsel. They walked on a while in silence, coming to the lane that led out to Tong village further up the twisting Beck valley. Then Dan spoke out.

'Miss Mary. If I can get a bit laid by, enough to rent my own house and a loom or two, then that will make me happy. But above and beyond that, if there's some things that needs to be done, with the other kinds of problems that we talk about, then I hope to be of service to others. I been talking to Reverend Wood about such things. About making sure that us working men and women get the proper wages and so on. He's giving me encouragement. But that is between you and me, as good friends. I know you will not think less of me. But if you don't mind, I don't want your uncle or your father to know about that now. That's for the future if I can get better established and financially secure.'

'On Dan!' said Mary, and she was unable to prevent herself from taking his arm and squeezing it. 'That is good to hear. You are a good man. And you are wrong you know. Because if you did speak to my father he would able to understand and help. He's not like some of them and you know that.' She let go his arm and headed up to Hill Top and Dan stayed a moment, glad for Mary's reaction but in other ways, very sorry for it too.

Once Mary was safely home at Cross Gates House, Dan walked thoughtfully home. He has shared his private ambitions, such as they were, and Mary had approved him. Nothing more. He still felt the touch of her hand upon his arm. He shook his head.

Mary kissed her aunt good night and thanked her for waiting up for her. She retired and laid awake in the cool dark, thinking about what Dan had told her and she was troubled. Not about that perhaps? But something was amiss. She thought of Dan's familiar shy smile, his ready laughter and his constant humility and told herself that he had come on very well and that had she not been his guide and helper, then this would not have happened. She was proud of the man he was becoming. She lay awake a long time, thinking about Dan and perhaps allowing herself a little pride in how he grew in mind and principle which might she hoped be in no little way due to her time. So much for thinking. Deeper than this was a turmoil that kept her tossing and turning through the night. By morning, she had made a prudent resolution, given herself a good talking to and made one decision in her innocence that would rule her future.

In the garth late at night when they summer sky was bright with stars across the distant hills Robert Wood spoke to his father. He told him that he so liked all the girls and his father agreed with him.

'Thou'll be thinking then Robert? Maybe there's a special one for thee here?' he enquired only half expecting an answer.

'I'll be honest with thee sir. I would have all four but I fear I must be so harried and worn with all their humours and energy. So in fact I will none - because there lies my protection and good health.'

'Wisely said,' replied his father quickly. 'Not to mention that thou art to go Bristol to train and have not a shilling to thy name!'

'Nor ever will if I follow the path before me.'

'We have been fed and have somewhere to lay our heads. But look Robert, look at the stars! The Lord provides. Go say thy prayers. I have a sermon to prepare for tomorrow.'

But the Clothiers had also been thinking about Mary and her future. Benjamin Beverley had taken Matthew aside before the Baptism and among the tombstones had put forward what he considered to be a good proposition.

'She's ripening then, thy Mary? Not long before she'll want to wed I'll warrant.'

'Not all Ben,' said Matthew guarded and with a spark in his eye. 'She's a mind of her own that one, and a mission and all for the time being.'

'Now then. Don't be letting her go about wasting her life with good works like thy sister Sarah.'

'Come come. Is not Sarah well settled now with Lupton's lad? Did tha ever think she'd do other?' Benjamin was forced to laugh.

'Gave us a moment or two of worry I think? But it is going well now I do believe. Mary says so anyway.'

'So what do you want then Ben?'

'I'd have her in the family but our Samuel says she's too mature for him. He's to look otherwise he says, but no more that that. He's an awkward cuss. And like thee, I'd not force a match on the children. But I have an idea which tha might see the sense of, that's if that apprentice of thine is not already expecting the family blessing? There's a merchant in Manchester with a great lad that is looking….' Matthew turned now to follow the family into the Armley Chapel. 'Oh no no,' he said smiling. 'She's but eighteen years and for all she's grown so tall and so fair, she's but a sweet child yet with many things to think about, and marriage is not on her mind. Let be, my friend. Let them be young when they may. For there's time enough to rue as thou doest well know. And we have no commitment with any course. These things are for the young people among themselves. We do but guide I believe?'

By candlelight before they laid them down to sleep Matthew's wife Jane, suddenly remembering, enquired of Matthew what Benjamin had needed to say to him in private. Matthew yawned and pulled back the blankets, sitting on the side of their old carved bed.

'Just some business dealing my dear. Nothing untoward at all.'

'Really? And what else?'

'Very well. He was making some suggestions for the disposition of our daughter.'

'Was he really! Well he can go and suck his thumb then. I hope tha did tell him to mind his own business?'

'Of course I did. My very words if I recall rightly. Go sort out thy own children, was exactly what what was said.'

'He wants to use our Mary for some advantage to himself. He's an old rogue and a -'

'Yes we know all that. No need to bring up the past. But I did tell him that Mary is not interested in such arrangements.'

'I have always hoped that she and Phillip? But now –

'I know. Leave it be my love.'

'

Chapter Twenty Three

On the breaking of hearts

Summer was as dry and harsh in London as it had been in Leeds. Phillip had come back in August, which was a good time for auditing accounts and stock, because many of the more interesting and influential inhabitants of the capital were presently in the countryside and were looking forward to the sport of the coming autumn. In the offices of Abbey and Wells, in the rear of one of the tall houses on Millbank Row in Lambeth, Phillip was hot and more than a little irritated.

The room was small and dingy and for some odd reason Parr seemed to fill it with his dark presence.

'Why though?' demanded Phillip. 'Why does this not balance? Don't talk to me as if I am a child Parr. I will go down to the shop and the warehouse and take stock of merchandise and then, dammit, I will have to begin again tomorrow. London is hell in the heat and the stench of the place is appalling. If we close the window we are toasted, and if it is open we are like to smother in fumes from the Thames.'

'Don't take up a post in India then young man.' Parr smiled, nodding. 'I heard at my club that this is nothing compared to what the agents suffer in foreign climes. Take Buenos Aires for instance.'

'We're not talking about foreign climes though are we? We are trying to find out why this company owes more than it earns. It's quite important.'

'You're very innocent Phillip. In Yorkshire, they keep it all so close for fear of Rothwell Gaol. But in London it is the case that all the merchants companies have large investments – investments they are termed – and then the business can grow.

This is what pays for your damned Yorkshire cloth. But the profits don't come back for years, if at all. We are all at the mercy of the capricious oceans, the thieving Frenchies and the incompetence of the Navy. Just leave those figures alone. You are only here to see to this year's reckonings and they are as good as any one elses.'

'They had better be,' threatened Phillip darkly. 'For I have many personal debts and I know my brother has too, without Abbey and Wells owing so much to the bankers and money lenders.'

'Come sir, understand things better than this. What the company needs is more investment of the right kind. Just be calm will you? I can help you sort out your own monies. I have a contact that can with ease take care of anything you might owe and lend you more to boot! Why don't we leave this and go down by the river where the air is a little cooler? We can walk back to Vauxhall where you can rest and tonight, well, we can go about town and find a few fools for a game or two. A good dinner at my club and a rare port. What say you?

'Oh fuck you Parr. If you can get me five hundred pounds that might see me clear.;

'Five hundred? Oh. Well. Never mind. That is more than I thought you would be short of. I'll see what I can do for the best. We'll play tonight though. We might even win more than that, you and I? In the right places?'

'Maybe,' admitted Phillip. 'Alright, I'll give a try. But I am going now on my own back to Vauxhall. I wish a small rest from your good self.'

'Quite.' said Parr, picking at his nails. 'Off you go then. We can meet at my club at ten o'clock and I will have some sport arranged. Count on me, dear friend.'

Phillip pushed his arms into his coat and in doing so cursed the woollen cloth of Yorkshire because he would be too warm as he went upon the streets. Outside he stayed in the shade of the tall houses and set out to walk back to his brother's house at Vauxhall. At the end of the row, a carriage had stopped and as Phillip approached a gloved hand waved from it. Phillip walked faster, curious now. When he came up with the door, it opened and he pulled himself up onto the step. Sat just beside the window was Lady Catherine.

'You may come in and be seated for a moment I think.'

'How kind. Is it not very hot in here?'

'Yes I believe it is. Hot and dangerous. Come sir. Would you refuse a lady a moment of your time?' Phillip cautiously, entered and sat opposite and Catherine smiled charmingly.

'What service might I offer you, my lady?' he asked softly and on his guard. She laughed. 'I just thought to see if you are well, Mr. Abbey.' She fanned herself and then hid her face behind the opened feathers. 'It is dull in London at this time I find.'

'Oh sadness. But for myself I have a great deal to do you know? Being in trade and all that. How is it that you have no better place to disport yourself then? I am sure there must be many who would want your company who are in better situations.'

'Oh, very harsh sir! I will not take offence. But I am very comfortable, I do assure you. And yourself?' Phillip hesitated and reflected.

'But bored? There are many fine walks I believe. Would you care to visit the gardens with me, my lady? Tonight at say, seven o'clock' This was met with mirth. 'Oh my dear boy. How you do tease! Of course the answer must be no. I am greatly entertained and I believe your interview is at an end.'

Phillip exited the coach humiliated. He stood fuming on the stone pavement and the coach pulled away. How dare she taunt him so. His anger lasted only a moment. He watched the coach turn the corner and he laughed to himself. Maybe next time. Maybe he should be more forceful as Parr would recommend. Perhaps she did not like good manners. If there was a next time, he would at least steal a kiss before she mocked him. Why else had she stopped but that she liked him?

He went on his way his optimism restored. There was little point in worrying about Henry's finances. His own were perilous enough without he was embroiled in sophisticated dealings. A bath would be good and some food. And then he and Parr together would make a fortune from a couple of numbskulls. There was much to delight in in London and no point in being provincial in attitude. But, should he go to the gardens at seven o'clock? He studied this dilemma in greater depth than the disordered accounts of Abbey and Wells. He came to the conclusion, as he crossed the river Thames, that he would not. She would beg him in the end. He would not dally for her.

Chapter Twenty Four

Hearts are Broken

It was a very reviving journey back to Hull. The best thing for a trying stay in London was always and ever a good, fast sail up the coast to the home port, with a fresh wind and the free seas about you. Phillip settled back into his business duties and then was pleased to find that he had an invitation to join in a hunting party somewhere in the county. He did not dwell on the origins of the invitation. But he reminded himself that he was of some interest to a certain lady and was optimistic at least, if not certain, of further flirtation. For he believed now, that the lady was interested but somehow constrained and he thought he understood now, something more of the terms of this game of unavailability. She wanted but must resist yet could not help herself. He wanted and would take what was offered. He believed himself to be as yet unencumbered with genuine attachment despite his hostage thoughts………

He had had a letter at this time from Matthew Bateson suggesting that he would come to Hull and bring his daughter Mary to see for herself how the cloth trade was embedded in the imports and exports there. Phillip considered this for a moment and then cheerfully wrote back, that the garrison had an outbreak of typhoid and the town had seen many cases of small pox and that though he would be sorry not to see the family in Hull, still it would be best to wait for a more convenient and secure time, the summer having been so hot, etc. And then he made sure of the equipment that he would need to join his betters in sport and regretted that he did not have one of Floss's pups with him, - but she had never been found.

It was indeed as he had surmised that Lady Catherine, her brother and some of their friends were nearby. But contrary to his hopes, Lady Catherine for the first day of sport took no notice of him, did not acknowledge him or send a message. He was not hopeless though and told himself he was entertained by this. It was on the following day that he was given a paper, discreetly, by the maid at his inn. It occurred to him to ignore it. He was content to be among his betters with his gun and to promote his own interests and to make useful contacts among those who had influence. He resolved that he would not attend upon so provocative an invitation. But then, when the hour approached, he found he had no better means to amuse himself. Accordingly he made his way without haste or certain expectation to the summer house by the river. He had slipped away from his other companions after a good dinner and a generous consumption of wine and the evening sun was warm on his back and all was well with the world. He might indeed be lucky.

The light was failing as he strolled the river bank. The summer house was in darkness before him. He waited a moment before it then entered. A familiar cool voice came to him from the shadows.

'Well here you are sir! I fancy you are tardy in your attendance upon me? It is not wise to keep a lady waiting.'

'You have been waiting with urgent anticipation my dear? And in this cool place, you will have been recovering from the warmth of the day. Or are you cold?' Phillip smiled and waited. He could just see in the gloom that she was arranging herself, touching her hair and posing to effect, letting her wrap fall to reveal her sharp shoulders.

'Hardly. Do come in and take a seat.' Phillip wasted no time now. He entered and was about her in a moment, his arms holding her close and his mouth against hers. She pulled away genuinely shocked and protesting.

'Oh, Mr. Abbey! Please -' But Phillip had grasped her again and pressed his lips to hers, laughing, and she surrendered. He had been well schooled, so he believed. They were laid upon the earthen floor of the summer house.

At length, sitting up and adjusting her clothing she was silent. Phillip followed suit and gently took her hands in his. Then he knew. Then it was that is happened. He knew he loved her.

'Dear Catherine. What would you say, if I were to pledge to you my heart?'

'I would say thank you. I collect such things and have quite a few to display. We are all hunters I think. So that's good sir.' She turned to look in his eyes. 'Well. Love is good, I think. If that is what you mean? I am given to understand you have quite a habit of making pledges.' He watched her and did not speak for a while.

'I have never yet pledged my heart. Believe this and have your answer.' She looked away and began to arrange her gown and tidy her hair, refusing to meet his eyes. He continued, quite zealous at this moment:

'We are two hunters. But life too short for this chase. Come away with me. We can be together always. You are beautiful and I am lucky and clever. My heart is yours as you knew I think, only too well. I know that others press you to marry for wealth. But I can do so much - I know I can. We must not part.' She pushed him away and stood.

'Lovely. Beautifully said. If a little naive. If you can find twenty thousand pounds, then I shall give my heart to you immediately.'

'That is absurd! You know I don't have so much.'

'Yes, isn't it? And you don't? But there you are. That is how the world is. Do get up now and adjust yourself. This has been a moment of folly for both of us. Forget it ever happened. We are not children to carve our names on trees in a heart! If you wish to be a man of the world, you must not make a fuss about these things. Forget it, like the gentleman you think you are.'

'But -'

'But nothing. This had been a little amorous adventure, nothing more. Pass me my shawl, will you?'

Phillip, disorientated, took up the woollen shawl and put it round her shoulders. He turned her to him and he looked at her keenly, his hands upon her shoulders, wondering at her rejection of his entreaties, and frustrated and a little relieved at the same time. Wretched even, wanting suddenly to have her more than ever before, and feeling again, something of a fool. But she made courageous sacrifice to hold his eyes boldly and at last gave him a quick kiss on his cheek. She put up one slim hand and patted his face. 'Poor lamb. Never mind my boy, there will be others. You are the better placed for these things. Your looks will not fade as mine will. Time will heal my dear.' Phillip laughed lightly and let her go, knowing defeat when it came with such callous words. Perhaps it was for the best. He was not yet established and he would come again, in the future and then she would not refuse him. Yes, time was on his side in this as in all things.

Lady Catherine, properly attired, outwardly composed and smiling, left him in the summer house and walked purposefully up the path to the great house. Tears ran down her cheeks.

'Well here you are Kate! And just where have you been? We have been wanting your company these last two hours. I hope it was diverting.' Her brother, laid on a couch in the salon watched her sit gracefully on a satin cushioned chair.

'Yes thank you. I have been gainfully occupied, you will be pleased to hear. And what have you been up to?'

'I've been doing well at cards with one Mr. Jones. He can't give me my just rewards at the moment. But I have this.' Her brother took from his pocket a paper and flourished it before her. 'Oh,' she said yawning. 'What is that then. Can we use it pay our bills?'

'It's a debt. That clever little merchant – that ambitious clerk I mean – it's one of his masters' little understandings. It's not much but we can get something for it I am led to believe.' Lady Catherine, her face in shadows watched her brother with narrowed eyes. He gloated.

'Don't please,' she said harshly and standing came near him, her eyes bright with anger. She snatched it from his hand and turning on her heel, went intending to find Mr. Jones' man to return the bond and make at least some sense of her frustrations. Her brother's laughter rang out behind her.

'Read it then. Look at it!' She stopped, her hand on the door and opened the paper struggled to read it in her distress. Her brother languidly walked to her side and snatched back the letter. 'Ha ha. So now we know what you're about.' He put his arm round her waist. 'Never mind my dearest. We shall away to Lincolnshire. It seems your work in London bore fruit. His Lordship has seen your true worth and – what does it say here? Oh yes, he most ardently admires you and would make you his bride. Had not slept an hour since he parted from you. Cannot stomach his dinner. Etc. Etc. Excellent. Well done Katy.'

Phillip did not see Lady Catherine the next morning though he looked for her in something of a muddled emotional state. Finding that she and her brother had been called away urgently to the bedside of a dying and wealthy aunt, gave him some food for thought, not least because the footman that first told of this, had rolled his eyes. He shrugged then and went about the slaughter of various wild fowl with keen interest and a clear conscience. She had not wanted to go away with him, that was clear. He could not have pressed her harder, he told himself. There would be other meetings, other opportunities and he would win her one day.

It was many weeks later that he read in the newspapers the announcement of the marriage between Lady Catherine and Lord Hornsbury. Anger flooded his mind momentarily. But then he smiled, remembering a night of passion in the Autumn chill airs. So that was how it was to be. A brief attachment, he told himself, is quite satisfactory. The pain in his chest was eased by a half bottle of French brandy and the attractions of certain other amusements would help at times, to drive her from his mind.

Chapter Twenty Five

Steam Hall

'You are not going to the mill! What's wrong with you, are you sickening with something? Come let me feel your forehead. What's this then James?'

'I feel quite well. I see I am become too much of a man of routine.'

'It's the first defence of the father of many small children. I can well understand how you find refuge in your machines when the house is plagued with your offspring'

'I will not go be going far. Don't be fearful my dear, it is just a fancy I have.' Nancy tutted. James continued oblivious,' I'm just going down to Holbeck. Murray has designed a house with piped heating. He's going to link it up with a steam engine. No more cold nights for him and his family. Just think, how wonderful that would be! Why don't you come with me?'

'Oh stuff and nonsense! Engines and heating. Don't the world get by with coals? And I don't believe you. I have heard as you will have too, that there is a new chimney on Water Lane. If you so much as look at it, you're in big trouble. Where's Dan Grady then? If he's going with you, I will know what you are up to.'

'He'll not be with me, I swear it. Those days are gone. Sadly. But Murray will give me dinner of course. Dan can stand in for me at the mill. Mock if you like at the inventions of modern science. But Murray will be a snug as a bug while we are shivering by a coal fire. Look at you, huddled by this hearth with your shawl on. Mark me Nancy. This is the future. Piped hot water to heat the home!'

'I think I heard something about this being the method of the Romans in heating their villas? It's not modern then, is it? It will be a clanking monster of a thing; the people won't be able to hear themselves speak and it will never catch on.'

James had been on the site of the new hall for some time, talking to the builders and to Matthew Murray about the details of the plumbing and admiring the pipe work when the stable boy came running and out of breath from the weaving house with an urgent message from his wife. It would seem that his sister Mary Beverley was suddenly very ill and he must go at once to his home so that he was at least was in the village should matters deteriorate and his father need to be taken to Beech Grove. James considered this and wondered if in fact he should go to stand with the family at Beech Grove and let Nancy deal with his father. But it might be an unnecessary alarm. For was not his sister Mary a strong woman and all her little children as witness to this? But then, Benjamin Beverley was a passionate and demonstrative man and he had already once, been driven to distraction by the death of his first wife, James' eldest sister Hannah. So all in all it was better that Nancy attended to her sister in law and would be there to manage Benjamin should it be needed…....

Murray advised he go at once, alarmed because a sickness was sweeping the town that he had heard was sudden and deadly. So a small feeling of anxiety began to rise and fighting it, James found his horse Stocking ready saddled, mounted and rode with haste back to Wortley. There was a light fall of snow as he rode towards Mill Green, but he left the road there and came across the back ways and fields to his home. The sky had grown heavy and he could feel that snow would come soon. Such soft winter nights brought sad memories to James

Bateson of the night this first son had been born and then been lost. By the time he slid from the saddle at the weaving house, he thought he knew in his soul, that his sister Mary was dead. When the messenger came up from Beech Grove his forebodings were confirmed and he made his way to Greenside to break the news of this blow to his father. John Bateson was watching from a window, a book in his hand disregarded. When he heard footsteps in the lane, primed for news, he came to his own front door, haggard, with; 'Am I to go then? It's nearly night!' and put his hand out to push James away. James took his father's arm gently and took him to sit in his chair by the fire in the small parlour. Then, still in his cloak, he sat heavily into another chair and wiped away the fast tears from his own face with his hands and his father, grim, just watched the fire and let his fool of a son weep.

'I'm sorry,' said James at last. 'I'm sorry to be so sad. It's the snow I think, that upsets me. I came to be your support and I am no help at all.' And then he saw that his father's cheeks were wet with tears and he rose and threw his arms about him.

Later, James now composed, took his father on foot to Beech Grove and those they passed took off their hats as a token of respect.

Leaving his father and wife in Armley to manage the disaster there, James came home wondering what Benjamin would do and how he would handle this loss. But Samuel was nearly grown and that must make a difference? Among such thoughts the dark road passed and he waited at the Weaving House, with brandy, until his wife should return. When he heard the fly rattle on the cobbled lane, he took a dry cloak out to bring her in out of the bitter night, but held her close first, with his head on hers.

Samuel was the was most afflicted by the death of his step mother. The funeral was grim, in the biting January weather and the Batesons and Beverleys were united in grief as in business. It fell to Mary to comfort Samuel. Her sister Anne too, was kind for once to the distraught young man. They waited with him in the graveyard among the heavy tombs and looming stones. Snow had come and gone and left soiled ice behind the monuments. Samuel had wept openly and was now ashamed. He hid his swollen face from Anne and turned to Mary who put her arm around him.

'She was a loving mother to you Sam. She was always so - so tolerant. You would not be the kind lad you are now but for her. She would not want you to weep so much. Be brave now. I will come tomorrow and we can walk a little. Remember Sam, that your father will lean on you now as never before. He will take it hard we think.'

'I must wait here until I am composed. The world will see I have been weeping.'

'That does not matter Sam,' said Anne moving closed to peer round at him. 'It's a hard man that does not weep at the death of his mother. Or anyone loved one I think. People won't think less of you for it.' Samuel straightened a little. Anne smiled at him.

'Yes,' said Mary. 'Your father will struggle. And perhaps will be difficult too and more irritable than usual. But I will be up at Crossgates if you need to talk. If you need a manager for a week or two then my father has said that he will let Dan come down for a few days to the workshops and mind things. And Anne will be kind to you. Won't you Anne?' Anne raised her eyebrows at her sister, but said, 'We will go now Samuel. Go and get some sleep and I will come to take you for a walk tomorrow, in the afternoon.'

'You were very kind to Samuel Anne. Can it be that he will find solace I wonder, with you?' Anne made a choking noise.

'I am sixteen Mary. And except for that he is destroyed by grief I would not give Samuel one moment of my time. But you do know, don't you, about Aunt Mary and Benjamin Beverley?'

'No, why? What has that to do with anything now? It's Samuel we are talking of.' Anne laughed.

'Oh Anne. But I think he does care for you. You can be the one that helps him now and comfort him at this difficult time. Think how much he needs some loving care!'

'He can have some loving care. Tomorrow I will march him up to Farnley Woods and tell him sensible things. After that, he's for you to mother again.'

'Don't be so hard Anne'

'Hard I am. Tough as an old boot. Go back up to Aunt Sarah's Mary and leave me be. I regret my kind offer. You did not fall for Samuel when he was at your feet? Why do you think I could care for him? Away home to your social conscience and your examinations of the working man.'

Phillip Abbey, informed of the bereavement of one of his employers was distracted from his own affairs and to do him some justice, planned to come back to Leeds to discover how things lay with the Beverley House. Affairs and business delayed this duty. Having come on from Leeds, he was at Greenside when Anne returned, red cheeked in the bitter air. He swept her a bow and she felt more blood rise to her face.

'Well here you are again,' she said 'And did you not think to bring your mourning clothes with you?'

'Why Miss Anne! I am not in mourning. It is for you to wear your black dress. It does nothing for you, by the way. Not with those red cheeks.' Anne Bateson, second daughter of Matthew Bateson, Clothier of Wortley finished taking off her cloak and tossed her head dismissively, stalking from the room. She glanced back at Phillip from the stairs and he smiled at her. John Bateson who had walked very slowly home from the burial of his second daughter, the one with nonsense in her head who had born so many children to lusty Benjamin, found his apprentice sombre and sympathetic and was ready for some gentle commiseration. 'Come Phillip. Come and we will take a little brandy together. It is not my usual way at this time of the day, but my bones are cold. I feel my age boy. I feel my age.' Phillip followed the Maister into his office at the back of the old house and sat in silence while they waited for Molly to bring the brandy.

'I hope you know that Benjamin's mind may wander for a while. You had best call at his house tomorrow and see Samuel for anything outstanding.'

'I will sir. Whatever I can do to help will be done. Samuel and I are in close contact at all times. I believe that everything is well in hand.'

'You're a good lad Phillip. Ah me, I am growing weak with grief and worry. Two daughters gone before their father. What a woe is that? How does the Lord try me!'

'Yes sir. Perhaps you should rest a while too? This will have an effect on your health I should not wonder? It's a great deal for a man to carry.'

'Yes indeed. You may be right.'

When John Bateson had drowsed off after his third glass of medicinal brandy, Phillip gratefully left and went to see how Molly was doing in the kitchen with the progress of his supper.

It was late now and the mill shifts had changed over, and Dan had come down the lane, concerned, to help with the heavy tasks in the kitchen. Phillip was greeted with warmth and much shaking of hands. 'Now then sir. It's good tha has come back. Sure and the Maister will glad to see thee, and Mr. Matthew too.' Phillip, leisurely, leant and stole some meat from a platter and then spoke while chewing. 'And you too I think. You're glad to see me aren't you Dan?'

'Of course sir! And if tha's here till the next Sunday, there's a race over the hills that'll interest ye!' Phillip did brighten then.

'Tha'll be able to lay out in wagers then Mr. Abbey, no doubt. Get over away from there now. Move. I'll be bringing the meat from the pot and I needs room. And tha'll spoil thy nice suit if I splashes.'

Dan looked at Molly thoughtfully and then; 'Come outside sir. We're in the way here I think. I'll come back in a minute for you Molly and help bring in the dishes.' To the kitchen maid he said, 'Becky, wilt thou take in the tray and lay the table?'

Outside Phillip enquired. 'What's up with old Moll then? She's not usually so bad tempered.'

'Well, yes she is, to be sure. But see here, she's lost her little Mary. She's been with the family when Mrs. Beverley was a bairn. And she's grieving. Lost once to Mr. Beverley tha knows? And once to death. And that's a final loss that can't be mended. So be kind to her sir and try to see how she's afflicted. She's in there weeping and making the dinner. It's hard sir.'

'Oh,' said Phillip. 'I had not thought about that.'

Chapter Twenty Six

Jane Bateson

Phillip of course, had his own losses to deal with. Back now in Hull and living in some comfort he continued to organise the Bateson and Beverley exports, those that could be made in times of War, to buy in wool whenever it was to be had, and the purchase of cloth by Abbey and Wells in London continued. But there was a sad loss at the card tables which put him personally, to a great deal of trouble.

He did not often think about Lady Catherine now. Maybe if he passed the coffee house he would think of her and a pang of pain would come and need to be forgotten with a fast walk along the quays until his mind was again diverted.

It was some eighteen months later that he returned again to Leeds, there being much to keep him in Hull or indeed, in London on two occasions. But Mary wrote, as she did from time to time, and told him that Benjamin Beverley was to marry again and that Samuel was mightily put out about it all. It was an amusing, intelligent and enlightening letter and it stirred Phillip to make the long trip from Hull to Leeds. His intention was strengthened when he was told that Lydia Smyth was to marry in Leeds in November. Having missed Benjamin Beverley's marriage to Elizabeth Guy, Phillip arrive shortly before the more important marriage of Miss Lydia.

Mary was home at Greenside ,sitting with her mother and sister in their parlour and telling stories about the night schools, her successes there and her failures with Uncle John Lupton whose papers were always amiss. 'He puts his boots upon his desk mother and then he opens the newspaper!' and Mary acted this out for them. Her mother had been laughing until the tears ran down her face and Anne had listened smiling as she stitched. Nanny now fourteen going on forty had been keeping a record of all she heard. Then they heard the sound of hooves distant in the lane and drawing nearer and into their own yard.

'My word,' said Jane Bateson, 'who comes at this hour of the night? It will only be ill news. The French are in Scarborough. I suppose they won't be here for a couple of days yet. Go see who is come Anne.' Obediently Anne put down her sewing and went to the door. Her eyes brightened. Phillip, having had words with the stable man was approaching, a smile on his face and his arms outstretched. 'Why Miss Anne! How you are grown. Come into the light while I see you. Well here I am. It's been a long journey let me tell you.'

Anne, suddenly shy, led him into the parlour where Mary, Nanny and her mother stood to greet their Agent, with a kiss on his cheek in two instances, and a shake of his hand in another. 'Phillip! You should have told us you were coming. I hope you have had a good journey so late in the year?'

'I have, thank you Miss Mary. I have hired a horse though and it is in your stable for tonight.'

Mrs. Bateson told him that was as it should be.

'Why are you late?' enquired Nanny.' You were supposed to come back for Mr. Beverley's wedding. They had a dance and we needed you.' Phillip smiled a little and shook his head. 'Sh,' said Mary. 'Phillip had to see to our business else he would have come. Don't be impertinent.' Nanny sat and slumped back in her chair, amused and watching with interest.

'I am disturbing your work ladies with my arrival. I regret I did not inform you, but as Miss Bateson says, I was detained by business. If you will excuse me I shall go and make my excuses to the Maister and hope that Molly can make my lodgings ready. I look forward to seeing you all in the morning.' With that, Phillip took himself away and through the great parlour to the other side of the house to wake Molly sleeping by the kitchen fire and demand she make up his bed and warm it too with hot bricks.

'See that mother? Phillip has come for Lydia Smyth's wedding. I bet he is invited! He did not come for Mr. Beverley's.' Nanny perceptive told her thoughts. Mary said astonished but placating, 'Hush Nanny. That does not matter. It cannot be neglect of duty. He has come now and can give his respects to Benjamin Beverley.'

'How can it be Mary dearest, that you espouse the rights of the working man and yet think that our agent best placed to toady with the gentry?'

'That is enough Nanny,' said their mother. 'Quite enough.'

'Oh,' said Anne, lazily, 'she's right of course. Phillip is quite the beau now. Did you not see his new hat? He has his sights on advancement in the world, so of course, he's come to see the new Mrs. Osborne. Perhaps he should see to getting us some coals. I can imagine him a coal merchant. Dusty though, coal.'

'That's not fair Anne!' replied Mary quickly. 'Of course, his role means he must dress the part.' Nanny, prescient; 'Dan has a new suit of clothes. I saw him yesterday and he's got a brown coat now with no patches at all and Jeanie and Lucy Scott were giggling at him when he came up the lane from Leeds. He winked at them too.'

'What has that to do with anything Nanny? That is not what we were talking about,' said Mary energetically. 'And Dan must dress better now because he's to be given more responsibility - .'

'He was got up for you Mary! To walk about with you. You walk out with him and that's what everyone is saying in the village. And I'll tell you something, I'll never speak to you again if you go on like this. He's nothing at all and he should - .' Mary felt the blood rush to her face. 'Don't you dare, you horrible child! Don't say things like that about him. And me.'

'Well now,' said Anne, 'you were telling us about the working man just a moment ago and how much you do to improve their lot in this world of woe. But now you are all for our apprentice and his ambitions when he came to us already a gentleman but has his eyes on further advancement? Where do your loyalties lie then Mary.' Mary was hot now and she said in irritation, 'I will defend neither of them then. It seems both my sisters wish to think badly of both our young men. In which case I can discuss this no longer.'

'Oh,' said Anne, entranced by his sisters chagrin, eyes laughing and brain working fast. 'But Mary, when you were helping the carpenter that had no shoes, did you not think that a perhaps boots or new suit of clothes would be of better assistance to him, than to be shown his alphabet? For then would he be able to impress in the world and advance. With new breeches I mean of course, not a nursery primer for his pocket.'

'Don't be so silly Anne,' replied Mary stiffly.

'But we have the cloth do we not? And if we made all the poor a good suit of clothes, then they would be both warm and able to impress? Is that not right mother?' Jane, plying her needle her eyes on her stitching did not look up. She said, 'But Anne dear we do provide cloth for the poor each year and you know it. Mary is talking about something else. She is telling you that in the world of men, those who succeed are judged not on the truth of their hearts but on the price of their attire. That money begets money. That appearance matters in the world of the merchants and dealers and that Phillip must conform to that if we like or not. The word for this is fashion; and for us, this is something we understand to be both superficial and deceptive She is telling you Anne, and you should listen, that we judge people here by the truth of their hearts. Is that not right Mary?'

'Yes mother. That is right. Thank you.'

Nanny completely enthralled, 'So mother - is Phillip to be applauded or condemned for fashion? What about Dan? Are they both dissemblers?'

'Neither my dear troublesome one. They are just doing what they have to do to act for our interests, and those we protect and defend, here, in this place, so that we can make sure men have work and women can put food on the table. You must speak I think, to Mr. North. If those who are not guided by the Lord hold sway, then all is lost.'

'We hold sway?' enquired Nannie pertly. Her mother said nothing but looked up from her work and regarded her third daughter until Nannie, defeated, looked away. Anne unable to restrain herself; 'So might I have a new gown mother? It is for the good of all I believe?'

Jane, evenly; 'Yes Anne, when you need a new gown, then you may have one.' Anne looked at Mary to see if she was amused by this quick answer but Mary was no longer attending to the conversation but lost in her own thoughts.

'Go to bed girls,' said their mother. 'You are all talking nonsense. You had better say extra prayers.'

But Jane Bateson spoke to Matthew that night. She told him that she thought Phillip was above himself.

'Why does tha say that?'

'Just call it intuition dear,' she replied.

'Well he was perfectly respectful to me, this evening.'

'He was to be making cloth I thought and ever had looked to this. Here in Leeds. But he won't come back from Hull now. Never. He's after setting up like his brother in London I'll warrant he is. What would happen husband, if thy father were to die, and thee and James? Who would take on our manufacture then?'

'Why Phillip of course. Or Benjamin Beverley. Until James' lad comes into his own. What a depressing talk to have late at night!'

'He'll not settle here. What about Dan Grady? He's the best apprentice we ever had and no airs and graces about him.'

'What about him lass? He'll keep on managing where he's needed and he and Phillip are good friends. It's nothing to fret about.'

'He should take our Mary then, and make his way in the world.'

'We've had this talk may the times wife. I would not put our Mary in the position of having to disappoint us and that is what she may well do. And she would feel that very hard. Let it go Jane. Let it run how it will.'

And Matthew slept but Jane lay awake. She knew Mary should marry with Phillip. But for whose sake that was necessary she was not entirely sure. She would see the girls settled before she died. She laid this need before the Lord her God with intense prayers often. Why should she worry, when there were many who would be ready to marry sweet Mary? Good Clothier's sons who were strong in their commitment to the Methodist faith too, and other eligible partners too. But Matthew had not understood her because he thought always with partiality for this one child. She had not meant Phillip.

Chapter Twenty Seven

Long Marston

The farmhouse that was the home of the Abbey family in Long Marston was lacking in the modern style of the fine houses of Hull which Phillip graced with his notable looks and easy manners. There were barns and stables in plenty and a kitchen of hams and ale. But there was no high plaster frieze nor polished panelling but rude flagstones and low rough plastered wall. Henry Abbey, widowed just after Phillip's birth was a wealthy farmer, with investments in the Tockwith brewing trade and a love of rural life and sport. He studied his youngest son across the laden table and heard the petition for yet more money, this time for a certain investment in a new direction.

'You want to move stone around? That sounds onerous and difficult work.'

'Yes sir. But with the right transport, which is by water, it's a very good investment. London is building still and the appetite there for Yorkshire stone is insatiable. I have contacts for this in Leeds. In London they'll pay over the odds for it. Then there is the import – from Italy and the Antipodes. South America….. They load it as ballast and there we have the marbles and granites that the sculptors need for their monuments and statues. Just ask Reverend Fisher. His family will tell you the value of such a commodity. Henry and I have made a detailed survey of all this. We have costs and projected profits and are certain of much -'

'Always Phillip. Always see my way to give you money! I told you before now, that there is no more money from me. You had your share two years ago for the money lenders in Hull. Or so you told me. It runs through your fingers does it not? So find some other fool to fund your fantasies.'

'But father, sir,' pleaded Phillip in desperation. 'But father, this is the best opportunity I have ever put before you. I am not asking for - for more allowance. It is not a fantasy. This is a well thought out and certain commercial venture. You will prosper by it! Nothing more secure. I am not asking for a loan or an advance but for financial investment in a very safe business prospect

'But nothing. If it's such a good plan there will be queue of investors. Go put it to one of your fancy friends in Hull or Leeds. I'll none of it. And you forget sir, that your apprenticeship, - that one hundred pounds I paid out for your training and way into the world, that was to be in the cloth trade, which is solid and ever lasting. So don't talk to me about stone. I won't hear it. Pass the port.' Phillip, his eyes bright, passed the decanter to his obstinate father. If this did not work then he would indeed have to think about starting a company to make cloth. But that would be his last resort. He studied his glass of purple wine. No, he'd rather go out to South America. Or India. Perhaps he should do that. Leave England and his debts behind and go abroad, mend his heart even and live as a gentleman should, as some agent for trade in the East India Company perhaps. His father interrupted his thoughts.

'But you are missing the obvious action boy. If you need money in the bank, go find a wealthy widow.' Henry Abbey leant forward, his old head gleaming in the candle light. 'Or better still. The father thought that you'd get one of the girls. That was what we spoke of back in '99. How does it happen that they don't want you now then? Tell me that.' Phillip shrugged casually which enraged the old and honest father. Eyes narrowed the father snarled. 'M. and J. Bateson and company are immensely successful. You played a part in that didn't you. So go and ask for one of the girls. Take your pick. I take it they are all still on the market?' Phillip shocked at his father's stony words did give it a moment's thought. 'It's not like that sir. They are nice, but that is all. Only the eldest is of an age to marry and she would not look at me.'

'Why not. You're a good looking man and a gentleman as well. She could not do better.'

'I don't mean that. I mean - . she is a very pretty girl and has a sweet nature. But she's a country girl and a pious maid. Unsophisticated and diligent.' His father interrupted him with spluttered laughter.

'I see it now! She sounds perfect. Go back and marry her and when you've got your own business running and can prove some substance in the bank, then I'll put money into this other plan. Until then, keep your mind on wool. If you do this I will lend you some capital on a good rate of interest and you'll be signing for it like any other borrower. That's all. I shall retire and hope you give this your best thought. Don't drink all the port. Good night!'

Chapter Twenty Six

Decisions.......

Phillip left the next morning with no fond farewells to his father or his oldest brother John and riding through the ploughed fields and green pastures of Yorkshire he returned saddle sore, weary and financially embarrassed to his comfortable rooms in Hull. He had a great deal to consider but his mind was not easy about any course of action that would see him tied to the stink of the wool cloth trade in Leeds. More than that. Not if his needs would in any way injure such a sweet girl as Mary Bateson. Some days later he had a long standing arrangement to meet Samuel Beverley in the market halls and they went together to an inn where Phillip knew they would be royally fed.

'It's a great spread this Phillip,' said Samuel, taking a heap of roast fowl onto his plate. Phillip watched smiling as Samuel made short work of the pile.

'We can come here whenever you are in Hull. I take it that your father is happy for you to wander?'

'Oh father. Yes, he's reconciled to the fact that I'm an idiot and has agreed I should travel,' said Samuel reaching for more sauce. 'And Mrs. Beverley is with child.'

'Well done Mr. Beverley,' said Phillip laughing.

'And what about you then Samuel? You could marry. Or does your father pay you a wage that won't allow that?' Samuel chewed and thought about that. 'I don't get a wage Phillip. I get my expenses and an allowance. How about you?'

'Can I afford a wife do you mean? No I can't unless it's and arrangement so who knows? But I get commission – that's the best way for me at the moment and it's good money but somehow it seems to be spent!'

'Thought you were good with money Phillip. That's what I'm told.'

'I am with other people's. It's mine that I have trouble keeping But that's not for you to worry about. So have you anyone in mind. Anyone I know. A Sowry or a Walker perhaps?' Samuel, full with good food and mellow with wine, wondered if he should confide in Phillip. 'Yes,' he said, blushing. And then gabbling told Phillip that he was in love with Miss Anne, Miss Anne Bateson, but that she did not care for him and he did not dare speak to her.

'But, since we are such good friends I must ask does she have another in mind then or is she merely obdurate for the sake of obdurate?'

'No I don't think so. I've spoken to Miss Bateson, Mary, often about it, because she is the kindest of friends. I did think once, but it was only my fancy, that Miss Anne is partial to you?' Samuel said this with his eyes fixed on Phillip's face and his heart on his sleeve.

'That's unlikely,' said Phillip, lounging. 'She just lashes me with her tongue. 'I hope our Mary is well?' he continued, probing.

'Oh yes. We were at Maister Jim's only last week for a good dinner, all of us; me, Dan and Mary and Anne.

'Oh!' said Phillip. 'I see.'

Now was an anxious time for Phillip. He had one demand that he could not meet and would need to borrow again and with more penalties for the privilege. Parr would laugh and arrange it saying that this was how men lived. But Phillip did not like to owe so much. If he was ever to be his own man, he must find a way to set up in business, as Henry had done and urgently too. He went to take some exercise in the busy streets of Hull, looking at the shops and traders and reviewing his options and found himself outside the coffee house in the centre of the town which brought him to a halt and a sharp jolt of reality. He trudged on, the wind whipping his clothes and went down onto the mud flats that bordered the river at low tide. His state seemed hopeless. Should he go and ask for Anne? Would they give her to him before her elder sister? That would not be proper. And now Samuel had set his mind on that one. He laughed the out loud, to think that Anne would ever have hidden feelings for him. But Mary! No, she was a paragon, not to be considered for such as he had become. But perhaps there was a chance, if Anne could like him and he not know it, then maybe Mary too, hid feelings of a stronger kind than sisterly affection. And would it be so bad if she did not? Was not that how the world was turned? There was no animosity between them and there was no reason at all in all the world why he could not become a respectable manufacturer and merchant. He clapped his hat back on his head , found his feet had sunk in the soft mud but pulled them clear and scrunched across a bank of gravel. He hauled himself up the weed clung wood steps that would bring him back into to the solid respectable streets. Yes, this was the course of action he would take. He would go to Wortley and try his fortunes there. While there was still time.

Chapter Twenty Nine

Salvation

It was spring when Phillip returned to Wortley. He had heard through the letters that came and went between Hull and Wortley, that James and Nancy had been blessed with another daughter and so Phillip timed his visit nicely to coincide with the family's modest celebrations and with other intentions drifting through his mind, brought a gift for the baby.

'That's very kind Phillip, thank you,' said Nancy unwrapping a small silver spoon. 'Would you care to hold Elizabeth? She's already been sick on me. You should be safe for a moment or two.' Phillip carefully took the shawl wrapped red faced bundle into his arms and gently examined the blue eyed face.

'It's funny isn't it? How they are so, well innocently incapable. And they look at you with almost a knowing look in their eyes.' Nancy stood beside him, smiling, touched by his tenderness, and he handed back her daughter.

'You'll be finding out more about them I hope without too many years passing. Babies I mean.' And Nancy laughed at him as he expostulated. But this was just necessary display at this moment. His attention was distracted though. Mary and Dan were by the window, watching Nancy's other children in the yard outside, chasing each other about, and gambolling in the sunshine. Dan commented on something to Mary, leaning towards her and Mary laughed brightly. This was not the moment and Phillip's fingers betrayed him, tapping irritably on his knee.

It was evening then, when Phillip found Mary alone in the parlour at Greenside House. 'It's been a good day, hasn't it

Phillip? For the christening I mean. I might go down in a little and take another peek at the baby. I like them like this, when they can't answer back.' Phillip smiled politely and stood before her blocking the evening sun as it came through the stone mullioned windows. 'We could go together,' he said simply. 'And take a walk. I am only here for another day and it is too good an evening to miss seeing the primroses by the Beck.'

'Yes alright,' replied Mary carelessly, standing and adjusting her skirts. 'We can go over the Beck and up to Farnley and it will do us both good. It's so bursting with green everywhere. You are right, it is too good a spring evening to waste and Anne is gone out visiting. I will just get my bonnet. I won't be a moment.' Phillip waited for her, listening to a blackbird trill and wondered at himself. But his mind was made up now.

Again the right time did not come. Mary chattered brightly about her work and the Lupton Mill and sometimes about Dan Grady. She walked at a good pace and Phillip at times struggled to keep up with her. The walk was completed without any approaches being made and Phillip cursed himself for the foolish good manners and the consideration he could no longer afford and went into the town to find some company and consolation at the Three Legs Inn.

Much later, too late, he returned and found that Mary had sat up for him. She had been worried that he might be in drink and with her misguided kindness was intent on protecting him from her father's reproof. Matthew with some unfortunate perception had agreed to this and had gone to his bed with careless trust. Mary had fallen asleep in her chair when she heard the sound of hooves and harness outside. She slipped on her shawl and went to see if Phillip needed help. The night was departing and the first glimmer of dawn lit the horizon.

'Sorry,' said Phillip, now sobering rapidly. 'This will not do, will it?' He smiled sheepishly.

'You had better go get some sleep,' Mary said sternly. Phillip laughed. 'I had hadn't I? I have a place inside the Hull Coach this afternoon. Mary brushed past him to help with the saddle and he firmly caught her arm. 'Mary, I need your, need your help,' he said softly. Should he tell her the truth and trust to her mercy and forgiveness? Would she understand his dilemma and accept his hand with the threat of his insolvency a dangerous risk to the Bateson House? She, turning to him, saw his eyes glint in the dim light and shook her head, 'What can I do for you Phillip?'

'It's hard to explain.'

'Well you had better try,' she said practically. Now he had come this far, Phillip thought he had better continue although his head hurt and his throat was dry. 'It's just that. Well. I have to tell you this. I must.' And then his courage failed him. 'I love you Mary.' She looked out at the yard and stared at the stone walls.

'I love you. I always have. Say that you could care for me? Every time I leave my heart is torn and if you are not mine I cannot live.'

'Nonsense,' said Mary quickly questioning the fidelity of the statement. Phillip moving swiftly, took her in his arms and pressed his lips to hers remembering that women should be handled without nonsense, "like wayward horses". She should have struggled but did not and her mind went blank. With little difficulty, as the horse untended munched at the hay box, Phillip laid her down and with expert skill put his arms about her and began to caress her. She lay mute and unfeeling as he touched her face and arms and then pulled her into his embrace. He put his hand on her cheek and felt a tear and brushed it tenderly away.

'Say you will marry me Mary. No matter who else asks for you.' Mary recovered a little and gasping struggled to sit. 'I – I don't know. No. I need time to think. Don't.' He had sat too and his arm was about her waist. 'Let me go and next time you come back to Leeds we can talk about it. This is all too sudden for me and I need time. I need time to consider it,' said the object of his salvation, desperately seeking to escape with mere words.

'No,' said Phillip resolute and with demands more pressing than this awaiting a reckoning. 'No it must be now. Let me speak to your father today! Promise yourself to me.' Now the iron was in the fire, now the act was done, Phillip was suddenly certain that this was the right way not just for him, but for Mary. Of course it was! Otherwise, who else might come sniffing round her and that would not do at all. He was her rescue. And if he did not press her now, and win her, then he would find himself in the future, the agent of a weaver! Of that he had become quite sure. 'Besides,' he said with sudden revelation and conviction. 'Besides which you must marry me. It would not be right after what we have been about, that you should reject me. We have embraced on the floor of the stable and that is a good as a betrothal.' Mary confused, stood up and Phillip got to his feet beside her. While she delayed, stood, frozen with shock, he stole another passionate kiss and then let her go. She stood utterly immobile on the frigid stones of the garth.

He turned to see to his horse, working swiftly to remove the saddle and looking across from time to time at the girl without any thought of mercy and said casually, and without intention, callously, 'and perhaps it might be that this is the best thing for your father and your family? Perhaps there are other more complicated reasons that you would not understand, around obligations, agreements and financial pressures?' He relented then and cursed his honesty and turned back to the horse, hiding his face. Across the yard Mary perceived in abject alarm, a figure in the coming light, old and bent and headed straight towards them

'Good morning to thee both,' said Peter. 'Let me see to thy horse sir. By, tha's up early both of thee!' Mary, picking up her skirts fled across the yard and into the house and in panic crept up the old staircase to the safety of her bedchamber where Anne still slept unaware of Mary's late night duty and encounter. She quietly took off her boots and laid herself automatically beside her sleeping sister with eyes that would not shut and a mind that could not focus and thoughts that were jumbled. Again she saw Phillip's bright eyes and his smile and felt his arms press her and cradle her. Caressing her. Had she permitted him too much? She did not think so. But then Peter had seen them both there in the dark and what else could have been the nature of such a liaison. She put her hands to her hot face. What had she done? But then he had asked for her help. She was not stupid. She knew from servant chatter and rumour in the town that not everyone believed Phillip Abbey to be innocent from sin. Gambling, she had heard. And drink, he was a one for drink too! But then, how would it be if she did not marry him and he carried on with his downward path and how would her father be bitterly disappointed and betrayed! She fixed on this thought with horror. Perhaps, perhaps Phillip was a soul that was worth saving and perhaps it was her duty to change his ways. These were not easy thoughts for one so young and so dutiful, and then, she thought in alarm, there could be a threat to the security of the business - and the trust of her father was placed with such certainty in Phillip. But how could she say such things to her father? That she was planning to marry a man she thought might not be honourable so that she could manage him and bring him to the light and save them financially! Her father would laugh at that. Perhaps it was not true and her father would think badly of her if she made accusations that could not be substantiated. But her father would only agree to such a match if, if she could assure him that she loved Phillip and wanted to marry him and how could she say something like that that was so untrue. If only she had someone she could talk to, that could guide her and advise her? Aunt Elizabeth. Yes, she could find her aunt and tell her all that had happened. She would know what to do.

Phillip however had left his riding boots in the kitchen for Molly's convenience and gone upstairs most confident that he had succeeded and was anticipating both an interesting conversation with Matthew, and future solvency and indeed the possibility of great wealth. How much would Matthew give her? A thousand pounds? More? He would find Mary later and speak again to make sure. He thought he could sway her now. She had hesitated. She was lost. His luck had turned. And after all he told himself repeatedly, it was certainly for the best that matters should be thus settled. Poor Mary was mixing with all sorts of men of all sorts of rank in life and that could lead to so many difficulties for an innocent young lady. It had always been the plan. No doubt at all about that. And he slept very well.

It was mid morning when Mary with dark rimmed eyes came downstairs at last and her mother had been concerned but had been called away to visit a sick widow in the village. There was no sight or sound of Phillip within the house. So Mary avoiding everyone and hating herself for this, took her bonnet and went as fast as she could down through the fields feeling relief flood her as she breathed in the spring air and saw the open sky. She took the path through the fields hoping for once to avoid anyone else abroad and was dismayed to see Dan coming up from the bottom lane where Walker's Mill threw out a spire of smoke and waving to her in the distance. She could not avoid him.

'Miss Mary, how are you this lovely morning?'

'Oh Dan. I'm well, thank you for asking and yourself?'

'Well, I'm grand,' he replied noting the shadows under eyes that would not meet his. 'Where are you bound? If you're away to town I'll be over late on today and can walk with you home Miss. But it will be after supper I fear.'

'No. No, it's alright. I'm coming back quite soon I think. It's just, an errand. That is all. I'll not be late. But thank you. Thank you Dan.'

'Can I help Miss?' hazarded Dan, hesitant and in fear of indiscretion on his part. Mary stood, her heart thudding and strove for words. 'No. Thank you. I must go.' Dan nodded and Mary, again severely agitated walked with stiff pride and urgent speed as fast as she could without actually running and arrived without permitting further interruption in her muddled thoughts and extreme emotions at her aunt's house in Park Row.

'Why Mary! Whatever is wrong? You look exhausted. Come in child and sit down. I have never seen you so flustered.' Elizabeth Lister put her arms about Mary and then brought her into the drawing room, all attention and concern.

When tea was brought and Mary had composed herself her aunt waited without pressing her niece to hear what had brought her in such a condition this morning. Mary looked at her lap, made several attempts to begin, and at length found some words to say.

'It's Phillip Aunt Elizabeth.' She looked up hopefully at her aunt, longing for an expression of dismay or at least a frown.

'Our Phillip? Phillip Abbey? Oh my dear,' her aunt took her hands, 'my dear, you don't mean that – is it what I think it is?' Elizabeth Lister's face glowed with delight. 'That is wonderful news!' Mary, horrified but covering it too well looked her aunt in the eye and knew she was lost. A silence grew and her aunt, perceptive, considered what this might mean.

'Mary dearest. If there is a problem? Perhaps there is some urgency that you wish for me to act on your behalf? I can speak to your parents for you, if you like?' Mary, not fully in control of her mind yet sought hard for meaning in her aunts words. 'No. No not that,' and blushed with memory of the stables in the early morning light. 'No it's not that at all. You see, to be clear, I don't know if I do the right thing?'

'Well of course Mary. We all do wonder at some point. It is a big decision, a great change and must be given lots of thought. But Phillip is a nice boy, and so handsome, such a gentleman. He will suit you I am sure, very well. And you know too, that you have known each other for so many years and grown up together too and that stands for a lot, in my opinion anyway. It's not like some one you hardly know and some young women do find themselves in that situation sadly? But a girl such as you will be thinking in great depth about what all this will mean for you, and not jumping in without caution in the midst of a passing fancy. That much of you I am sure.' And as her aunt went on, Mary realised that no help for her would come from this quarter. Her aunt just would not understand.

'And do you know?' went on Elizabeth, 'I met Mr. Abbey's sister only a few weeks ago? Yes Mrs. Fisher. She is a most charming woman and her husband is an extraordinary minister – in the main church of course, but still quite an evangelical and with some very interesting ideas. You will find yourself with a most respectable and notable sister and brother in law! So there is no need for anxiety Mary. I take it your parents are happy?'

'They don't know yet,' said Mary flatly. 'At least I think they don't. Perhaps today though.' She looked blankly at her aunt and struggled to make her mouth smile. 'I think they will be delighted.'

'That's better darling. Of course they will. I am so pleased for all of you. This is just what I hoped for and it's wonderful news.'

Mary stood. 'Well I must be going,' she said feeling odd and light headed. 'Thank you for the tea and the guidance. My love to the children and to William too.'

Elizabeth watched her niece walk away from her windows and wondered at Mary. She really was such a sensitive and unusual young woman. She sighed. It would work out well, she felt sure of that. Mary found the walk home difficult and her remaining energy sapped with each step along the busy town streets and then the long lanes to Holbeck and home.

Anne had gone out with a message for Mr. Oddy, her mother was again out visiting and Mary went, bleary eyed, knowing that her father was alone and writing but would bear interruption on such a matter. She knocked and came dully into the room. 'Why, Mary, tha's looking tired? Did tha not sleep well lass? Was Phillip so late then?'

'No father I didn't sleep well. Phillip indeed came back very late sir - and then we were talking, talking in the stable as you may hear from Peter.' Matthew looked at his daughter in astonishment and she blushed and looked away. 'It's not what you think -' and then she stopped. Was that true or not? Matthew turned his chair and signed her to the only other in his study. He waited then to give her time to say what needed to be said, wondering at this, that the plans laid some years back were perhaps, after all the doubts, to come to fruit. Nothing could be better in his mind than that his favourite Phillip Abbey would marry his Mary. But she sat down and did not speak. Thoughts rushed through her mind but she could not bring herself to speak them. At last her father tried to help. 'Doest tha want to tell me something Mary? If it is what I think it is, then thou must not be afeared to say it.' Mary still did not speak, she opened her mouth and shut it. 'Does Phillip want to marry with thee child?' he said gently.

'He does father,' she said weakly. 'He has told me he loves me.'

'Well then dearest. And what did tha say to him then? Speak up Mary. Not but that I am the best father in the land, but I don't read minds. How doest thou feel about Phillip?' Mary unable to say those thoughts that had troubled her through the long day said nothing. It was better to say nothing than to lie or to give her father unsubstantial fears that after all, might just be imagined. Instead she nodded and tears ran down her pale cheeks.

'Aunt Elizabeth has recommended him. This is all I can say just now.' Her father at a loss reflected on this but had to continue with the matter somehow.

'He may speak to me then. Go thou and find him. He has stayed here although I understand though he should have been on the coach today. Send him to me dear.' Mary, head down and stumbling a little left her father and went in search of Phillip who had taken shelter in the kitchen in spite of Molly's grumblings and warnings. He was sat with a newspaper and quite at home in the kitchen fireside chair.

'Phillip,' said Mary, trying to smile and catching Molly's fierce eye upon her. 'My father would speak with you. He is in his study and waiting.' Phillip stood, dashingly handsome in his best coat and kissed her hand. Molly looked aghast at Mary and Phillip smiled and went through the house to find his master.

'Why Miss Mary! What's the matter. Tha looks like a sheet been in the mangle! What's going on?'

'Nothing Molly. No mangling. Phillip will ask my father for my hand in marriage and, and I will give it to him. That is all. Now is the roast basted? Give me the potatoes and I'll peel them.'

'Tha won't!' said Molly blazing suddenly. 'Peel the potatoes! Go to sit in the parlour Miss and I'll bring thee some tea. Peel potatoes. Indeed!' Molly went muttering and complaining to see about the tea and Mary, with a forced smile left to find her sister Anne returned and already in possession of the parlour, sat gazing from the window, pensive, pale and diminished; and was too late to avoid her attention. 'What's going on?' said Anne softly.

'You must give me your loving wishes Anne. I am going to marry Phillip.'

'Don't,' said Anne carefully. 'You should not, I think.'

'Why Anne, why would you say that?' Mary was swiftly beside her sister on the window seat and they looked into each others eyes. 'It is - , do you? I mean, if it should be – do you care for him.'

'It would not matter if I did,' said Anne with stark honesty. 'We should neither of us marry him.'

'Why? Why say that?' Anne took her sister's hand in hers. Still quiet and without energy Anne replied, 'Because, whatever else he may be, he's a gambling drinker and he'll bring us into disrepute. You know it really Mary.'

'It's just gossip Anne. Father - ? . Well if he is then maybe we should save him. He's young and had bad company but if he's wed then he must mend his ways.'

Anne, clever, bright, perceptive Anne, gazed in silence from the stone window. A clock ticked out in the hall.

'Yes Mary. And if we were both of us being honest here, which I am, then of the two of us, only you will have the character – the position and experience and – and something I cannot name, in which to rule him. If you do this, marry Phillip, then you save me from something far, far worse. That is all I can say.' Anne got up then and hurried from the room, leaving Mary struggling with Anne's clear understanding and waiting to face Phillip when he returned.

In the kitchen Molly saw with alarm that Dan was come into the yard with some orders in his hand and she rushed out to pull him into the kitchen before he should meet with a successful and conceited fool. 'Oh me dear lad. Oh me dear.'

'What is it Moll? What's amiss?'

'It's Miss Mary. Thy Mary - ' She need say no more. Dan stared past her at the living rooms beyond and a shadow crossed his face for one brief moment. Then rapidly adjusting he smiled. 'Come now ma, thou dost not begrudge them their happiness. Not our Mary and our Phillip?'

'No Dan. No! I'm as good as thy ma and I know what's behind that smile. God save us, to see this day.'

'Leave it Molly. Please. I'll cope if we don't talk about it. I'll go down and ask Maister Jim if I can take a run.'

'Oh Dan,' said Molly weeping openly.

'I'll be reet, ma. I'll run I think. Out upon the hills yonder and when I return I'll be ready to do what's to be done. Maister James will understand.'

'No he won't lad. He won't at all.'

'He will Moll. For he knows as much as thee and I and he knows too, my heart.'

'It's a bloody shame then, that he can't talk to his brother about such things then..' Dan went and put his arms around Molly, and with an adaptable but faithful heart on fire, left her to her outraged despair.

Chapter Thirty

the memory of the just is blessed

Years pass and the world changes. Seasons come and go and love also can come and go; flourish or diminish - or be utterly lost in anger and bitterness and recrimination. While wool continued to be worked by hand looms in the rattling cottages of Wortley Mary and Phillip Abbey began their life together but it is to be wondered if they would find happiness.

Phillip Abbey, reluctant Clothier of Wortley saw three children born to his wife Mary Bateson. A son and two daughters.

For what Mary in had innocently imagined would change, did not. Perhaps there was a superficial attempt at respectable industry and domesticity but it could not and did not last.

Matthew would have understood quickly that the marriage was a disaster. He would see his beloved daughter harden and a profound remorse would colour his remaining years. He blamed himself.

John Bateson the Maister in his last years regretted that he had ever taken an apprentice. Molly forgave him and her mistress too, for she saw how they realised that the promising young man was false and had taken the flower of their family to make only grief.

There were good times when the babies were born and Anne Bateson, clever Anne, was as loving her bewildered sister to the children that came, to Henry Bateson, Mary and then Sarah; and stayed by Mary's side with selflessness and without complaint to comfort and support her courageous sister who had sacrificed her life on a Forlorn Hope of Redemption.

It was Wells and Abbey that failed first. James Bateson and Francis Sowry were the creditors and with feelings of guilt and inadequacy James went to London to the attorney's offices and tried to save what could be rescued from the catastrophe. He knew then as they all did, that his niece's husband was a rogue. He remembered too, in his odd way of random thinking, that Phillip had asked him once, many years ago, about the brothels in Leeds. James had thought it odd then but he had his own past and so was not inclined to judge.

In January 1811 Phillip was arrested and found himself in Rothwell Gaol. There followed in short order the sale of all his household goods, property and all the looms, gearings and slays of his workshops, plus 70 rolls of fine wool cloth, ready finished and lying in his warehouse. Mary with three small children and baby Sarah not even a year old on her hip withdrew quietly into a kind of protected seclusion and found comfort in her children and their lives and always her son Henry Bateson Abbey remained at her side. And Phillip?

This story is loosely based on the bare facts to be gleaned from births, deaths and marriages and very slightest of hints of character.

Factual Information

Matthew made provision for Mary's children in his Will and no provision for Mary herself. This is telling. Her children were to be maintained and educated at his expense and would inherit when they came of age, if indeed they survived. It could be assumed then, that Phillip Abbey had died before Matthew's Will was made.

However, intrigued by the quotations on Matthew's and his daughter Mary's tombs we might be led to think that there was some event in the past that could not be forgiven or forgotten even in death. And these were righteous Christian people who would forgive their enemies.

Phillip's death was difficult to find.
It was necessary at this point to research the Abbey family and eventually records were discovered -

To Be Let
The Old Established Stone Yard called York Wharf, Princes Street, Lambeth, London, where an extensive trade was carried on by the late Mr. HENRY ABBEY. The local situation of theses Premises makes them particularly desirable for a Person in the North who has a few Hundred Pounds Capital, and can command a supply of good Yorkshire Stone, there being no other Stone Wharf near this, on the South side of the River Thames, although there is an extensive and increasing

neighbourhood. The Wharf possesses a good Crane and sufficient Water-way for Humber Keels, etc.
and
The Person who conducted the Business of the late Henry Abbey offers his services (at a Moderate Salary) to any Gentleman who may be disposed to engage in the Trade.
Furthermore in the Yorkshire Herald it is stated:
The Brother of the Deceased who has long conducted the concern as Clerk will be glad of an Engagement and might be found beneficial to any Person taking the Business.

References to Henry Abbey's brother as Clerk therefore date from August 1817.

The proof that Henry Abbey of York Wharf is the brother of our Phillip lies here in an excerpt from the **London Gazette,**

November 11th1811.
Notice is hereby given, that the partnerships formerly subsisting and carried on between Henry Abbey and John Wells, **Stone Merchants, of Princes Street, Lambeth,** *in the County of Surrey……*
and John Wells and Henry Abbey of Millbank Row, Lambeth were those merchants who failed in 1808, certainly connected to James Bateson and Francis Sowry of Wortley.
Additionally, that the Abbey family married with the Fisher family, long notable for Sculptures in York, is clear. Stone. Good Yorkshire Stone! (And Portland stone and foreign marbles imported as ballast from around the world and brought for the making of London and the funeral monuments of the wealthy citizens.)
So what happened to Phillip?

Tasmania – the 24th of August, 1839. Death - Phillip Abbey, Stone Cutter, Paralysis.
Phillip had travelled to Tasmania without fuss a few years before his death. He embarked from Liverpool on the "Lavinia" and his arrival in Hobart Town was not remarked upon. With thanks to the Tasmania State Archive and Library Service.

Engraved on the tombs in St. John the Evangelist's Graveyard in Wortley, Leeds -

"the memory of the just is blessed" (Mary)

"Keep innocence and take heed unto the thing that is right, for that shall bring peace at the last" (Matthew)

Henry Abbey born 1779 in Long Marston died in 1817 in Lambeth leaving a son, Henry Abbey, who went on to fame and fortune.

Sarah Abbey married Robert Wood. Their daughter Mary Ann Everett Green born 1818 became a noted historian.